FIX IT
Yourself
FOR LESS

THE HOMEOWNER'S LIBRARY

FIX IT *Yourself* FOR LESS

MORT SCHULTZ
and the Editors of Consumer Reports Books

PHOTOGRAPHS BY MORT SCHULTZ

CONSUMER REPORTS BOOKS
A Division of Consumers Union
YONKERS, NEW YORK

Copyright © 1993 by Mort Schultz

Published by Consumers Union of United States, Inc., Yonkers, New York 10703.

Troubleshooting Instruments and Tools (Appendix A, pages 161–65), *Brand-Name Directory* (Appendix C, pages 179–91), *Microwave Cookware* (page 72), *Air Conditioner Cost Calculator* (pages 80–81), and *Insulating a Water Heater* (page 153), copyright © 1992 by Consumers Union of United States, Inc., Yonkers, New York.

Library of Congress Cataloging-in-Publication Data
Schultz, Morton J.
    Fix it yourself for less / Mort Schultz.
      p.   cm.—(The Homeowner's library)
    Includes index.
    ISBN 0-89043-482-4 (pbk.)
    1. Household appliances—Maintenance and repair—Amateurs'
manuals. 2. Do-it-yourself work.   I. Title. II. Series.
    TX298.S37 1992
    843′.6—dc20   92-31551
                                         CIP

Design by Ruth Kolbert

First printing, January 1993

Manufactured in the United States of America

Fix It Yourself for Less is a Consumer Reports Book published by Consumers Union, the nonprofit organization that publishes *Consumer Reports,* the monthly magazine of test reports, product Ratings, and buying guidance. Established in 1936, Consumers Union is chartered under the Not-For-Profit Corporation Law of the State of New York.

    The purposes of Consumers Union, as stated in its charter, are to provide consumers with information and counsel on consumer goods and services, to give information on all matters relating to the expenditure of the family income, and to initiate and to cooperate with individual and group efforts seeking to create and maintain decent living standards.

    Consumers Union derives its income solely from the sale of *Consumer Reports* and other publications. In addition, expenses of occasional public service efforts may be met, in part, by nonrestrictive, noncommercial contributions, grants, and fees. Consumers Union accepts no advertising or product samples and is not beholden in any way to any commercial interest. Its Ratings and reports are solely for the use of the readers of its publications. Neither the Ratings, nor the reports, nor any Consumers Union publication, including this book, may be used in advertising or for any commercial purpose. Consumers Union will take all steps open to it to prevent such uses of its material, its name, or the name of *Consumer Reports.*

*Special thanks
to Robert Volatile
for his review
of the contents of this book.*

Contents

FIX IT *Yourself* FOR LESS

Introduction

When a major household appliance breaks down, some homeowners' first thought is to call in a professional technician to service the unit. Others may even discard a perfectly usable small appliance that needs only minimal repair. This book gives the interested do-it-yourselfer another, less costly, option—fix it yourself.

Here are a few examples of how you can save money:

- The belt that drives the drum of your clothes dryer snaps. A visit from a professional serviceperson will cost you about $85. By following the instructions provided in this book, you will be out-of-pocket only about $5. All you need is a nut driver, a new belt, and about 45 minutes of your time.

- You own a walk-behind lawn mower with a starter cord that is frayed and close to breaking. The professional will charge about $30 to replace the cord. In 30 minutes you can do the repair yourself, for about $4.

- You find a layer of ice covering the floor of the refrigerator compartment of your self-defrosting refrigerator/freezer. This condition usually means that the drain system has clogged. A serviceperson will charge about $50 to fix the blockage; following the simple instructions in this book, the cost to you to do this simple repair is zero! You can't do better than that.

All of the procedures discussed in this book are easy. Any adult can handle them with complete confidence. The only obstacle that some people encounter is *fear-of-disassembly syndrome*. This special kind of stage fright often attacks those who are newcomers to do-it-yourself repairs, but this fear is unfounded. Most large appliances are designed with disassembly in mind—the manufacturer has made sure that the inner workings of most appliances are readily accessible. The only exception to this are small appliances that are intended to be discarded as soon as they develop a problem.

• HOW TO USE THIS BOOK •

Each chapter in this book focuses on repairs to a particular appliance or piece of household equipment, such as refrigerators, ranges, microwave ovens, or various garden and lawn tools. All the repairs in a particular chapter are listed at the beginning, along with tools and materials necessary to do the job. The actual malfunction is described at the start of each repair, including signs and symptoms as the homeowner would see them, followed by step-by-step instructions for resolving the problem.

Occasionally a problem may have several causes and solutions, so you may have to troubleshoot or test the unit before you hit on the right answer. If that is the case, the instructions for each possible repair follow in sequence.

Once in a while, you will encounter some procedures that don't seem to apply to your make and model of appliance. This is because manufacturers vary in the way they design and assemble units. These differences are minor, however, and should not hamper you unnecessarily.

Similarly, at times a repair procedure is accompanied by a photograph that may show a unit at variance with your type of appliance. For example, small gasoline engines are

equipped with two common types of vertical-pull recoil start mechanisms. The text may describe one kind, while the photo shows the other. But again the differences are minor, and the actual repair procedure the same.

The three appendixes at the end of the book are invaluable sources of information for the do-it-yourselfer. Appendix A describes in detail the troubleshooting instruments and tools that make the difference in completing a repair quickly and easily. It's not necessary to own a full complement of tools, esoteric and otherwise, before undertaking these repairs. The simplest and most common tools are sufficient, supplemented by only a few more-exotic items, such as a clutch puller or a deep-socket wrench.

Appendix B gives a complete listing of where you can locate old and new appliance parts, including the addresses and phone numbers of "after-market" parts dealers—a vital source list for the do-it-yourselfer.

An up-to-date brand-name directory is found in Appendix C. This list of manufacturers' names and addresses and telephone "hot lines" can come in handy when you have questions about your particular unit.

• SAFETY RULES AND CAUTIONS •

As stated earlier, all of the repairs described in this book are easy and safe to do, *as long as you carefully observe all the cautions found at the beginning of each chapter and mentioned throughout each repair.* Most of these safety rules pertain to checking and rechecking that all electricity has been disconnected from the appliance in question; other cautions relate to the safe handling of gas appliances and small gasoline engines.

Never take shortcuts where safety is concerned. And never try to save a few minutes by working on an appliance still connected to an electricity source. If any repairs are too complicated or potentially dangerous, we advise you to call in a service technician; in no case should you attempt to do such repairs yourself.

1

REFRIGERATORS/ FREEZERS

Your refrigerator/freezer was probably your most expensive appliance purchase. It is also the most expensive in terms of energy consumed over the course of a year. The most common repairs your refrigerator is likely to require are easy to make, which means there will be little if any disassembling of the unit.

Safety Precautions

The following important safety precautions must be observed before attempting any of the procedures in this chapter:

• *Disconnect the refrigerator/freezer from the electrical supply.* You must make sure that the power is disconnected before you begin work on the appliance. This is particularly important when attempting to deal with refrig-

erator problems, some of which may have resulted in flooding around the base of the unit. Water is an excellent conductor of electricity, and to avoid a serious and potentially fatal shock, you must be sure you are not standing in water around the base of a refrigerator still connected to a live electrical line.

If the outlet into which the refrigerator power cord is plugged is accessible without moving the refrigerator, and there is no water underfoot, remove the plug from the outlet. If the outlet is behind the refrigerator, or if there is water in the area, first switch off the appropriate circuit breaker in the house or apartment's electrical service panel. If your home has fuses rather than circuit breakers, remove the appropriate fuse and put it into your pocket. *Do not simply loosen the fuse.* A loose fuse can become just tight enough to restore electricity. Or someone passing the panel can try to restore current to another outlet on the same line by tightening the loose fuse, not aware that you are working in some other area of the house on an appliance connected to the same line.

Check to see that you have interrupted the current in the appropriate circuit by opening the refrigerator door and noting whether the interior light goes on. (This test is valid only if the bulb was working before you interrupted current to the unit.) To be doubly safe, before you begin to work, move the refrigerator away from the wall and remove its power-cord plug from the outlet. Now you can work with confidence.

• *Arrange to have someone help you move the unit.* Trying to maneuver a heavy refrigerator/freezer by yourself can cause an injury to your back or elsewhere.

• *Read cautionary notes on all tools or devices you may have to use in making repairs or applying a preventive tip.* Manufacturers have learned over time of the risks their products pose if used improperly. You can reduce these risks by reading the advisory labels carefully.

• *Protect yourself against injuries caused by products or tools that inherently pose risks.* For example, if you are going to use dry ice to store food temporarily, wear heavy gloves and a long-sleeved shirt to keep the ice from touching and burning your skin.

• REFRIGERATOR/FREEZER REPAIRS •

Following is a list of the repairs presented in this chapter, and the tools and materials needed to make them.

REPAIR	TOOLS AND MATERIALS
1. Saving on energy	None
2. Fixing water leaks	Two open-end wrenches, carpenter's level, portable room heater
3. Preventing and treating odors	Baking soda, door wedges
4. Operating failures: • Failure to start • Warmer than normal temperature	Electrical surge protector Brush or vacuum cleaner, screwdriver, adjustable wrench, nut driver, masking tape or self-adhering labels
5. Troubleshooting a defrost timer	Screwdriver, TV tuner cleaner, nut driver, masking tape or self-adhering labels
6. Buildup of ice in refrigerator/freezer: • Ice forms on ceiling of refrigerator compartment • Ice forms on floor of freezer compartment • Ice forms on floor of refrigerator compartment	Masking tape or self-adhering labels, ohmmeter, carpenter's level, pliers, ⅛-inch-thick shims, screwdriver, meat baster or ear syringe

REPAIR	TOOLS AND MATERIALS
7. Replacing a door gasket	Nut driver, screwdriver
8. Replacing a noisy evaporator fan motor	Nut driver, screwdriver, masking tape or self-adhering labels, ohmmeter
9. Replacing a faulty light switch	Screwdriver, nut driver, needle-nose pliers, masking tape or self-adhering labels, ohmmeter
10. Repairing an ice maker: • Scatters cubes • Ice cubes unformed or watery • Ice maker overflows	Adjustable wrench, nut driver, toothbrush Pliers, ⅛-inch-thick shims Screwdriver, nut driver, ohmmeter, nontoxic silicone sealer
11. Fixing an in-the-door ice or water dispenser	Screwdriver, nut driver, masking tape or self-adhering labels, ohmmeter

REPAIR · 1

SAVING ON ENERGY

PROBLEM: Your refrigerator/freezer seems to be using an excessive amount of electricity in its daily operation.

Refrigerator/freezers are one of the most electricity-hungry appliances in the home. But there are ways to cut down on the amount of energy they use:

• If your refrigerator is next to the oven or any other heat source, or is in a spot where the sun shines on it most of the day, consider moving it to another location. Once you are used to having the refrigerator in one spot in the kitchen, all other locations may seem inconvenient at first. But moving the refrigerator away from a heat source can reduce your electric bill substantially over the course of a year. Nearby heat also can force your refrigerator to work much harder day by day, thus making breakdowns more frequent and shortening the unit's overall life.

• Wipe all moisture from bottles, cartons, and cans before putting them in the refrigerator. Excess humidity collects in your refrigerator as frost. Because the automatic-defrost feature of your refrigerator is expensive to operate, frost caused by adding moisture to the food compartment will make a defrosting heater work overtime and contribute to the cost of operating the appliance.

• Don't overcrowd the refrigerating compartment. If overstocked, it will require extra electricity to maintain a proper temperature. Along these same lines, don't refrigerate food that doesn't have to be refrigerated. Certain items, such as peanut butter and mayonnaise, need to be refrigerated only after they are opened. If the product is not refrigerated in the supermarket, it does not have to be refrigerated in your home until it is first used.

Putting warm food in the freezer costs you extra energy because the food must be chilled down to the temperature of the freezer. Once chilled, the food won't add to the operating costs of the refrigerator. For this reason, it's recommended that you keep your freezer full at all times, or at least fill up any empty spaces. Crumpled newspaper is one way to do this. Or, if your freezer compartment is generally less than full, keep a few sealed picnic icing bottles in the freezer. They will help stabilize temperature, as well as provide some short-term protection in the event of a power failure. Plastic bottles filled with water can be used for the same purpose, but make sure the plastic in such bottles has enough flexibility to allow the water to expand as it freezes.

• Take out only the number of ice cubes that you actually need. Because ice cubes are nothing more than water, we tend to view them as having little monetary value. But when we take out a full tray of ice cubes, remove one or two for a cold drink, and then leave the rest to melt in the tray, we are wasting not only water but the actual energy it took to turn that water into ice. It may seem a small thing to do, but it helps: shortages of water and energy are often cited as among the major threats to our planet's future.

REPAIR · 2

FIXING WATER LEAKS

PROBLEM: Water pools on the floor around the refrigerator.

Water dripping from under the door often indicates that the refrigerator isn't positioned properly. A refrigerator should have a *slight* tilt toward the rear. When the refrigerator is properly tilted, water will flow in that direction and into the drain system instead of collecting in the main compartment and eventually draining out at the front.

To make sure that your appliance does have the proper angle, open the door less than 90 degrees. Release the door. Does it close by itself? If not, you will have to adjust the front legs of the unit.

Adjusting the legs. Under the front two corners of the refrigerator are "feet" with threaded shafts (actually bolts with large furniture buttons on the bottom). Some refrigerators have these bolts threaded directly into the casing of the refrigerator. Others have the shaft threaded through a locking nut first.

You will need an assistant, who should tip the refrigerator back just far enough to take the full weight off the adjusting bolts. If your refrigerator has the locking-nut arrangement, you will need two open-end wrenches, one to hold the locking unit and the second to free up the adjusting bolt. After you have freed up the adjusting bolt, thread it up or down to adjust the height (once you have properly freed it, and once the weight is off the front legs, you should be able to thread the bolt up or down by hand).

Adjust the leg bolt at the other front corner. To make sure the refrigerator is level right to left, place a carpenter's level across the top of the refrigerator. To check the front-to-back pitch, repeat the door-closing test. When the door closes by itself, you will know you have made the proper adjustment.

Once you are satisfied that the refrigerator is level and is pitched correctly toward the rear, retighten the lock nuts of each front leg bolt.

•

PROBLEM: Puddles appear under a freezer chest or upright freezer.

Puddles of water that keep forming under a freezer chest or upright freezer that is kept in an unheated garage or basement are caused by the heat given off by the freezer motor. As this heat wafts across the cool metal freezer cabinet, condensation forms and drips down onto the floor.

To verify that this is happening, do the following:

1. Wipe up the existing puddle.
2. Place a portable room heater near the freezer. Turn it on. (*Caution:* Do not leave the portable electric heater unattended. Check it frequently to make sure it is not overheating. Do not leave it on overnight or if the house is unoccupied.)
3. After 12 hours, check the floor for water. If there is none, then condensation has been causing the puddles.
4. To cure the problem permanently, move the freezer to a warmer location.

If, by some remote chance, the puddles aren't caused by condensation, then the freezer is experiencing a rise in temperature well above the normal range of operation—5 degrees below zero to about 10 degrees above zero. The frost that normally forms is therefore melting, resulting in puddles inside and beneath the freezer.

The cause of this temperature change is a leak in the system that holds the refrigerant, which is the medium that lowers the temperature. Loss of refrigerant causes higher interior temperatures, resulting in puddles and also in food defrosting in the freezer. Arrange for a professional technician to check this problem as soon as possible.

R E P A I R • 3

PREVENTING AND TREATING ODORS

PROBLEM: A strong odor forms in a disconnected refrigerator.

A refrigerator that has been turned off for a while, especially when the doors have been left closed, may develop an odor that is quite difficult to remove. This odor is a consequence of the rotting of tiny particles of food left in the refrigerator and freezer compartments, along with the buildup of mold. To avoid the problem, follow this procedure whenever your refrigerator is turned off for a prolonged period:

1. Unplug the unit from the wall outlet. Remove all food.
2. After the appliance defrosts, thoroughly wash the compartment with a mixture of two tablespoons of baking soda and one quart of warm water. Remove even the tiniest particles of food that may lie in the creases and crevices of the refrigerator and freezer compartments.
3. Rinse the compartments with cold water and dry with a clean cloth or paper towels.
4. Air circulation is needed to prevent a buildup of mold, so you must leave both doors open and make sure they can't swing closed in your absence. One way to do this is to place an object in front of the doors to prop them open. Another way is to wedge something between the doors and the frame, such as pieces cut from a thick sponge. (See caution in next section.)

H E L P F U L   H I N T
Moving a Refrigerator

Even though the refrigerator/freezer in your home may be on casters, moving the unit away from the wall to clean under and behind it can still damage a vinyl floor. To prevent this, and also to make the heavy appliance easier to move, do the following:

1. Buy a piece of lauan mahogany at a lumber yard. This is ¼-inch plywood, with a top laminate of lauan mahogany—a rather hard, smooth finish that is used as an underlayment for vinyl flooring. Cut two strips for use as runners, each about 4 feet long and about 9 inches wide.

2. When you are ready to move the refrigerator/freezer, spray the top surfaces of the runners with silicone. Then, as an assistant tips the refrigerator/freezer to one side, slide one of the runners under the legs at one side of the appliance. Tip the appliance the other way and place the second runner under the other side. You will now be able to move the appliance easily by sliding it along the runners.

— • —

If you have to haul a refrigerator/freezer from one location to another, follow these steps:

1. Disconnect the power cord from the wall outlet.

2. Remove all food. After that's done, leave the doors open so the freezer will defrost rapidly.

3. If you cannot borrow freezer space from a neighbor, pack the frozen food in receptacles containing dry ice. Place cardboard between the food and the ice. Wear gloves to protect your hands and wear a long-sleeved shirt to protect your arms.

4. Remove shelves and drawers, and place them in cartons for transporting.

5. When the appliance is completely defrosted, dry the insides of the compartments.

6. Tape the power cord securely to the cabinet. Close and tape the doors so they won't swing open.

7. Place the appliance on a dolly (rent one, if necessary) and wheel it out to the vehicle. If you have to go up or down steps, place heavy planks on the steps and roll the dolly over them. Try to keep the refrigerator/freezer upright.

8. To get the appliance into the bed of a pickup truck, place planks from the ground to the bed of the truck and roll the dolly on the planks. Again, try to keep the appliance upright.

9. If the unit has been kept upright during transport, you can plug it in and put it back into use immediately after arriving at the new location. However, if it has been transported on its side or back, oil will have flowed out of the compressor and you will have to wait 24 hours after setting the appliance upright before you can turn it back on. This length of time is necessary to allow the oil to flow back into the compressor. If the appliance is plugged in and used prematurely, the compressor may be damaged.

•

PROBLEM: A lingering odor develops in your refrigerator.

If an obnoxious odor develops in your refrigerator/freezer, do the following:

1. Disconnect the appliance by pulling the power plug from the wall outlet. Remove all food.

2. Keep the doors open for 48 hours. *Caution: If there are young children in the home, skip step 2. The danger of a young child going into a refrigerator compartment and drawing the door closed on himself or herself, or having a playmate do so, is too great a risk to take under any circumstances.*

3. Prepare a mixture of 8 ounces of baking soda to 2 quarts of cold water and wash down the insides of the compartments. Follow this by wiping down the compartments with clean rags that are soaked in cold water. Finally, wipe the compartments dry, close the doors, and restore current.

4. At the end of three hours, open the doors to determine whether the odor is still there. If it is, but is not as offensive as before, the washing procedure is helping. Repeat the process.

5. If the washing procedure has had no effect on the strength of the odor, fill the compartments with rolled-up newspaper and close the doors. Over a period of time, the newspapers will absorb the odor. Leave the doors closed and the current on for five days. At the end of this time, remove the newspaper and repeat steps 3 and 4.

REPAIR · 4

OPERATING FAILURES

PROBLEM: The refrigerator fails to start.

There are several reasons why a refrigerator/freezer won't start. Here's what to do in each case:

Electrical system failure. Open the door of the refrigerator. Is the compartment light on?

If it is, a lack of electrical power is not the cause of the unit's failure to operate.

If the light isn't on, you will have to backtrack to see why power is not being delivered to the refrigerator. First, check to see if someone disconnected the power cord plug from the wall outlet and then failed to reconnect it.

Next, check the electric service panel to see if a circuit breaker has tripped or a fuse has blown. If so, return the circuit breaker to On or replace the fuse.

Wait a period of time to see if the circuit breaker or fuse shuts down the circuit again. If it does, you will have to call an electrician. There may be a short in the system or the particular circuit may be overloaded. In the latter case, the electrician will have to rewire some of your outlets so that the refrigerator has access to another circuit with less demand on it.

Finally, check to make sure that the bulb isn't burned out.

Burned-out starter relay. If the refrigerator does have power, the next possibility is a burned-out starter relay. The starter relay is a switching device that provides the compressor, the electric motor, with a surge of current so it can start up and gradually attain full speed. When the compressor reaches this running speed, the starter relay switch then switches off. If the starter relay switch didn't shut off, a high electrical surge would continue to be delivered to the compressor, damaging it. If the starter relay switch has burned out, no current is reaching the compressor and the compressor can't operate. In that case, you will have to have a service technician come in and test the starter relay, and replace the defective part. This is not a job for a do-it-yourselfer, because a starter relay switch must be tested with the electricity turned on—much too dangerous a job for an untrained individual.

Burned-out overload protector. The overload protector is an internal circuit breaker that protects the compressor in case of electrical overload or overheating. These conditions may indicate a compressor that will soon fail or a compressor struggling to operate under the reduced voltage that occurs during a brownout. If the overload protector's elements burn out, current can't reach the compressor and it won't start up. You will have to have a service technician come in and test the overload protector, and replace the defective part. As with a starter relay switch, testing is done with the electricity on, so you shouldn't tackle this job by yourself.

Note: If you reside in a region where thunderstorms are prevalent, you can help prevent damage to the electrical components by using a surge protector. Plug your refrigerator into the surge protector, and the surge protector into the outlet. Surge protectors are available in hardware and home supply stores, and also in stores that sell electronic and computer equipment.

PROBLEM: The refrigerator operates, but keeps the food at warmer than normal temperatures.

As liquid refrigerant evaporates into a gaseous state, it absorbs heat; in doing so, it drops temperatures in the refrigerator and freezer compartments to levels ideal for food preservation. For the refrigerating cycle to continue, this gas must be returned to a liquid state. In the condenser, the liquid refrigerant is transformed from a gas back into a liquid. If a flow of air does not circulate over the condenser, however, the air in its coils will not be cooled. When this occurs, the condenser cannot surrender a sufficient amount of heat to allow all the gas to return to a liquid state. The efficiency of the refrigerating cycle will suffer. Furthermore, if the condenser coils get hot enough, the cycle could even be interrupted and the temperature inside the refrigerator and freezer compartments will rise, often to the point of food spoilage.

In some refrigerators, the condenser is attached to the back panel and is readily accessible. To find out if this is the case with your unit, pull the appliance away from the wall and look for a large, wiggly coil at the back. This is the condenser, which ideally should be brushed or vacuumed clean every few months. If the condenser on your refrigerator is located on the back panel, don't push the appliance too close to the wall, but leave at least six inches of space.

If the condenser is not attached to the back panel, it is to be found under the refrigerator. A small fan near the condenser blows air across it. Air circulation, therefore, can be restricted by a dirty condenser, an inoperative fan, or some object that has slipped under the refrigerator (like a paper bag) and is now blocking circulation to the condenser.

To make the necessary repairs to the condenser, do the following:

1. Disconnect the refrigerator/freezer power cord from the wall outlet.
2. Pull the appliance away from the wall and look for a rear access panel at the lower part of the back. Remove the screws holding the panel. Remove the panel. If there is no rear access panel, remove the front skirt under the door to reach the condenser and fan (Figure 1.1).
3. Insert the nozzle of a vacuum cleaner through the opening and vacuum the condenser (Figure 1.2).
4. Restore electricity and wait for the compressor to start. When it does, look at the fan blade to see if it is rotating (Figure 1.3).
5. If the fan blade is not rotating, again, *pull the power plug from the wall outlet.* Only then, remove the bolts that hold the fan motor to the cabinet. Draw the motor toward you until the wires attached to it restrict further movement (Figure 1.4). Be careful not to overextend the wires.
6. Using self-adhering labels or strips of masking tape, label the wires so you can tell which one goes to each terminal of the fan motor; then disconnect the wires from the motor. Take the motor out.
7. Unscrew the fan blade from the motor. Unbolt the motor if it is attached to a bracket.
8. Take the motor to an appliance parts store and buy another one. Then attach the fan blade and bracket to the new motor.
9. Connect the fan motor to the wires by using the old motor as a guide. Make sure all wires are connected to the correct terminals.

Figure 1.1 Remove front skirts of most refrigerators by pulling them free.

Figure 1.2 Vacuum dirt from the condenser to make sure that air flows freely over the condenser.

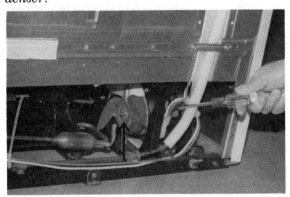

Figure 1.3 Refrigerators that have condensers placed beneath the appliance also have fans to ensure a free flow of air over the condenser. If the fan motor has burned out, the fan blade (arrow) won't rotate.

Figure 1.4 Remove bolts, and take out the damaged fan.

10. Mount the new fan motor to where the old fan motor was positioned. Screw the access panel back into place or reinstall the skirt. Restore electricity.

H E L P F U L   H I N T
Power Outages

If you live in an area that has frequent power outages, you can keep food frozen in a freezer during these periods by doing the following:

• If possible, keep the freezer full at all times. Keep a few artificial-ice containers (the kind used in picnic coolers) in the freezer to take up the extra space. Otherwise, fill plastic bottles with water and put them in the freezer. The water will freeze. When there is a power outage, this extra ice will help maintain cold temperatures for a relatively long time.

• If your region experiences a prolonged outage, buy dry ice to place in the freezer. Roughly about 25 pounds of dry ice will keep food in a 10-cubic-foot freezer adequately frozen for about three days. Place cardboard on top of the food and dry ice on top of the cardboard. Remove and dispose of the ice when electricity is restored.

Caution: Always wear heavy gloves when handling dry ice.

R E P A I R · 5

TROUBLESHOOTING A DEFROST TIMER

PROBLEM: The compressor does not come on, or runs continuously, causing a buildup of frost.

Oddly, these two problems, which seem to be directly opposed, can have the same cause: a faulty defrost timer.

A self-defrosting refrigerator/freezer has a timer that initiates the defrost cycle by turning off the compressor and turning on the defrost heater. If this timer doesn't work, one of two consequences may occur, depending on how the timer is stuck: either the compressor won't go on, or it won't shut off. In the latter case, because self-defrosting cannot take place as long as the compressor is running, a buildup of frost results.

Test the defrost timer by doing the following:

1. Remove the front skirt at the bottom of the refrigerator. This is done by pulling on one end of the skirt and then the other. Removing the skirt may expose the defrost timer, but if it doesn't, the timer may be located with the other controls.

2. Insert the tip of a screwdriver into the slot of the timer and turn the mechanism slowly in a clockwise direction until you hear a click. If the defrost timer is with the other controls, you can reach it by finding the access hole to the slot in the timer (Figure 1.5). Turning the timer with a screwdriver will allow you to determine one of the following:

- If the compressor has not been running, and turning the timer results in the compressor starting and running, the defrost

timer is not working properly and may need replacement.

- If the compressor is running at the start of this test, and turning the timer causes it to stop running, the defrost timer is not working properly and may need replacement.

3. Don't buy a replacement yet. Check first to see if dirt may be causing the defrost timer to stick. Wipe the surface of the timer clean with a rag and inject a small amount of TV tuner cleaner (available at electronics supply stores) into the crevice around the mechanism.

4. If the problem doesn't clear up, you will have to replace the timer. Disconnect electricity, unbolt the timer, and disconnect the wires, first using self-adhering labels or strips of masking tape to label where all the wires go. Take the old timer to an appliance parts dealer and purchase an exact match. Reinstall the new timer, making sure to connect wires as they were before.

It's easy to remove a defective defrost timer and install a new one (Figures 1.6–1.9). Although a popular brand of refrigerator/freezer is used for a model in the accompanying photographs, one that has the defrost timer positioned with other controls, it's just as easy to work on a refrigerator that has a timer located behind the skirt.

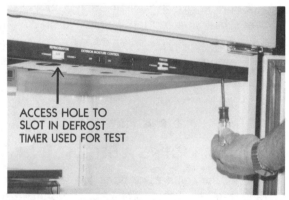

Figure 1.5 *If the defrost timer is not behind the skirt, it's usually located with the other controls. Turn off electricity and use a nut driver to release the control panel trim piece.*

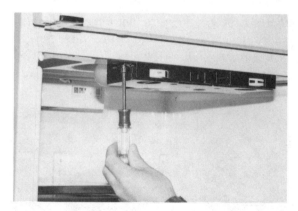

Figure 1.6 *After removing the control panel trim piece, remove the bolts holding the control panel.*

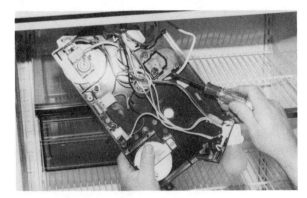

***Figure 1.7** Turn the control panel over and identify the defrost timer.*

***Figure 1.8** Release the screws holding the defrost timer to the control panel.*

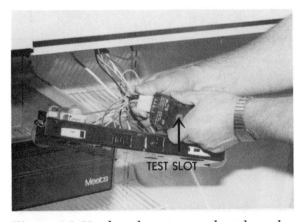

TEST SLOT

***Figure 1.9** Unplug the wires and replace the defective defrost timer with a new timer. Notice the slot in the timer (arrow). This is the part you turn with a screwdriver to test the timer.*

REPAIR · 6

BUILDUP OF ICE IN REFRIGERATOR/ FREEZER

PROBLEM: Ice builds up on the ceiling of the refrigerator compartment.

The defrost system of a self-defrosting refrigerator/freezer includes a heater that melts frost on the evaporator. The water created during this cycle flows from the freezer, where the evaporator is located. It goes into a drain cup in the top or bottom of the refrigerator, and down a tube extending from the cup to a pan under the refrigerator. Several kinds of icing problems can result from defective heaters and/or clogged drain systems.

In the case of a defective heater, do the following:

1. Turn off power, empty the freezer compartment, and remove the panels from that compartment.
2. Using self-adhering labels or strips of masking tape, label the wires so you can tell which one goes to each terminal of the defrost heater. Disconnect wires from the defrost heater and use an ohmmeter to test the heater. (See Appendix A for instructions on how to use an ohmmeter.) If the ohmmeter needle falls on infinity (∞), the defrost heater must be replaced with a new one.

•

PROBLEM: Ice forms on the floor of the freezer compartment.

The refrigerator/freezer may not be positioned correctly, so water produced during the defrost cycle can't drain. Some of it may drip out the door, on to the floor. The rest will stay in the refrigerator and turn to ice. To take care of this problem, do the following:

1. Using a carpenter's level, or the door-closing method described on page 6, check to see that the appliance is correctly pitched, slightly to the rear.
2. If the angle isn't right and the refrigerator

has adjustable legs, turn them out a little to give the appliance a slight pitch toward the rear.

3. If the legs aren't adjustable, place a ⅛-inch-thick shim under each front corner.

•

PROBLEM: Ice forms on the floor of the refrigerator compartment. (In this case, the cause is not an incorrect pitch to the rear.)

A faulty defrost timer is another possible cause of ice buildup on the floor of a refrigerator. First, do the test described in Repair 5, above. If the defrost timer passes the test, the icing is probably the result of a plugged-up drain tube. To make the repair, do the following:

1. Pull the power cord plug from the wall outlet.

2. Empty the refrigerator. Remove the shelves to gain access to the drain cup. There is probably a cover over the drain cup, which will have to be removed to allow you access (Figures 1.10–1.12).

3. Remove the drain cup and wash in warm water (Figure 1.13).

4. A drain tube sits directly behind the drain cup. Water flows from the cup into this tube and down into a drain pan lying under the appliance (Figure 1.14). Fill a meat baster or ear syringe with hot water and flush out this drain tube. Do this several times.

5. Remove the skirt from the lower part of the refrigerator. Then pull out the drain pan. Be careful, for if your flushing has cleared the drain tube, the water will have flowed into the pan. (If there is no water in the pan, the drain tube is not yet cleared. Repeat step 4.)

6. Empty the pan, wash it in warm water, put it back in place, and reinstall the skirt.

7. Place the drain cup back in position, wipe water from the refrigerator, and restore the unit to service.

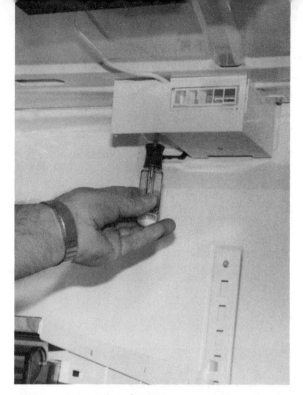

Figure 1.10 The drain cup is under a cover. Look for a screw (hidden from view) to release the cover.

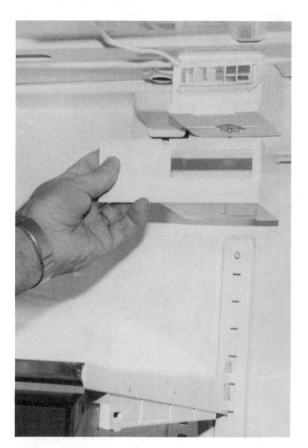

Figure 1.11 Once the screw is removed, the cover can be taken off.

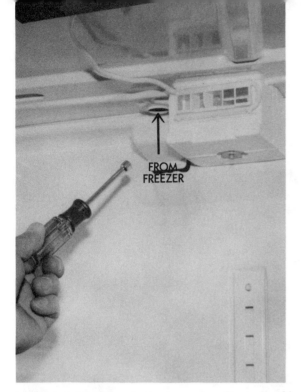

Figure 1.12 *The drain system of most self-defrosting refrigerator/freezers uses a cup to catch the defrost water coming from the freezer.*

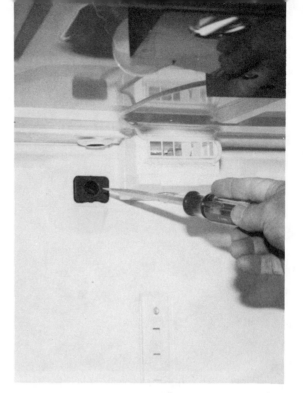

Figure 1.14 *Insert a meat baster or ear syringe filled with hot water into the drain hole to which the screwdriver points. Flush out the drain tube.*

REPAIR · 7

REPLACING A DOOR GASKET

PROBLEM: Condensation accumulates on the inside of the refrigerator door.

When warm air hits the cold surfaces inside the refrigerator, it condenses and causes excess moisture to form in the interior. This condensation is usually caused by a worn door gasket.

To determine whether a gasket is sealing properly, close the door on a dollar bill. Pull on the dollar. Do this all around the door. You should feel resistance at each location. If you don't, the gasket is worn and you need a new one.

Gaskets are secured in one of three ways: with screws and metal or plastic retainer strips (the most common method); with metal or plastic retainer strips alone; or with screws alone.

To replace a gasket and adjust a door that uses screws and metal or plastic retainer strips, do the following:

1. Disconnect the power cord from the wall outlet.

Figure 1.13 *Remove the drain cup and wash it out.*

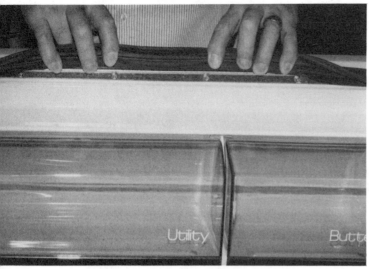

Figure 1.15 *Roll back the gasket to find out how the gasket is held to the door. Here the gasket is held by screws and metal retainer strips.*

2. Open the door. Roll the gasket back to uncover screws and retainers (Figure 1.15).

3. Using a nut driver or screwdriver, loosen the screws. Do not take them completely out (Figure 1.16).

4. Slip the gasket out from behind the retainers. If the gasket resists, the screw in that spot is not loose enough (Figure 1.17).

5. Buy a new gasket from an appliance parts store.

6. Position the new gasket so that its right- and left-side top corners lie over the right- and left-side corners of the top retainer. Then, starting at one of those corners and working toward the other, slide the gasket under the retainer.

7. Secure the top part of the gasket by tightening the center screw of the top retainer, but only enough to hold the gasket in place. Do not tighten the other screws yet. You may have to shift the gasket around to get it into an exact position.

8. With the gasket in place along the top, start at one of the top corners and work down one of the sides to slip the gasket under the retainer. Do the same on the other side and, finally, along the bottom.

9. Shift the gasket around, if necessary, to

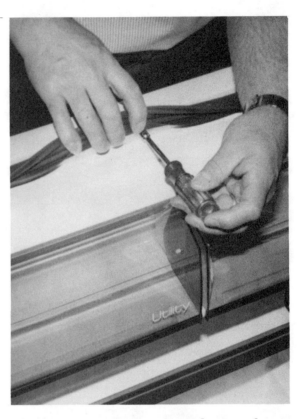

Figure 1.16 *Loosen screws with a nut driver, but do not remove them, especially if they are used in conjunction with retainer strips, as seen here.*

Figure 1.17 *Slide the old gasket out from under the retainer strip. Install a new gasket, starting at one of the corners at the top of the door.*

get it straight. Then tighten the center screw of each retainer, followed by the corner screws, and then the remaining screws. Do not overtighten screws; turn them just enough to securely hold the gasket to the retainers. Overtightening the screws can compress the gasket and cause an air leak into the compartment.

To replace a gasket and adjust a door that uses only metal or plastic retainer strips, do the following:

1. Disconnect the power cord from the wall outlet.
2. Open the door and roll the gasket back. Notice how the gasket is held in the grooves of the retainers. The new gasket has to be installed in this same way.
3. Pull the gasket out of the retainer grooves. Take it to an appliance parts store so you can buy a new gasket to match.
4. Place the top of the new gasket over the top retainer so that the corners match, and the narrow edge of the gasket is in contact with the retainer.
5. Beginning at one of the top corners and working toward the other top corner, press the narrow edge of the gasket into the groove along the top retainer. When this has been done, begin at one of the top corners and do the same thing moving down one of the sides, then from the other top corner down the other side, and finally across the bottom.

To replace a gasket and adjust a door that uses only screws, do the following:

1. Disconnect the power cord from the wall outlet.
2. Open the door and roll back the gasket.
3. Using a nut driver or screwdriver, remove all the screws. Then remove the gasket.
4. Place the top of a new gasket along the top of the door so that the screw holes in the top corners of the door line up with the holes punched in the gasket.
5. Insert a screw through the hole in the gasket into the hole in the top corner of the door. Then secure the gasket across the entire top of the door, down each of the sides, and finally along the bottom. Be sure that you don't overtighten the screws; make them just tight enough to securely hold the gasket to the door.

R E P A I R · 8

REPLACING A NOISY EVAPORATOR FAN MOTOR

PROBLEM: You hear a high-pitched chirp, especially when you open the freezer compartment door.

A high-pitched chirp, most pronounced when the freezer compartment door of a self-defrosting refrigerator is open, indicates that the evaporator fan motor is worn out. To replace the motor, do the following:

1. Turn off electricity by pulling the plug from the wall outlet.
2. Remove food, trays, and racks from the freezer compartment.
3. If there's an ice maker in the freezer compartment that interferes with removal of the evaporator cover (located at the rear wall), remove the screws holding the ice maker (Figure 1.18) and take out the ice maker. Then un-

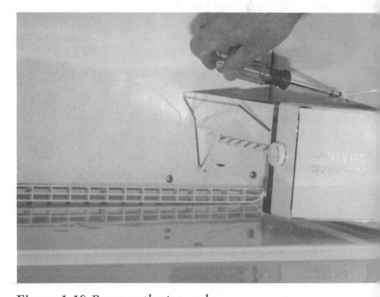

Figure 1.18 Remove the ice maker.

screw the evaporator cover to reveal the fan (Figure 1.19).

4.   The fan may attach to a scroll. Unscrew the scroll. The fan and scroll will come out in one assembly (Figures 1.20 and 1.21).

5.   Undo the screws holding the fan motor to the scroll (Figure 1.22). Put screws and rubber bushings, if they are used, in a safe place. (Bushings act as insulators between the fan assembly bracket and scroll to prevent vibration and noise.)

6.   Wires are attached to the fan motor terminals. Using self-adhering labels or strips of masking tape, label each wire so you are able to identify which one is connected to each terminal when you install a new motor.

7.   Buy a new fan motor. However, don't buy a new fan blade assembly if you can unscrew and use the old blade unit (Figures 1.23 and 1.24).

8.   Connect wires to the terminals of the new motor, attach the motor to the scroll, and insert the assembly into the freezer wall. Reinstall the cover and the ice maker and restore power.

Figure 1.20 Release the screws holding the fan motor and scroll to the back wall.

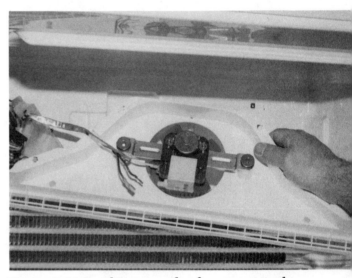

Figure 1.21 In this case, the fan motor and scroll come off together as one unit.

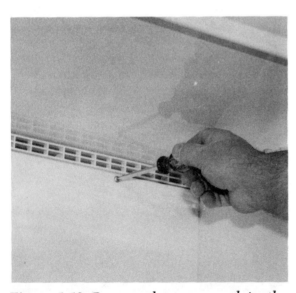

Figure 1.19 Remove the rear panel in the freezer compartment to get at the evaporator fan motor.

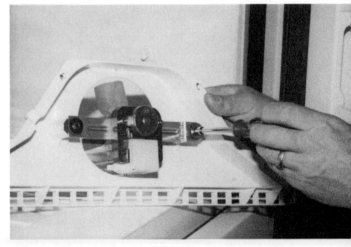

Figure 1.22 Remove the screws holding the fan motor to the scroll.

Figure 1.23 Remove the fan blade assembly from the damaged motor.

Figure 1.24 Attach the old fan blade assembly to the new motor.

REPAIR · 9

REPLACING A FAULTY LIGHT SWITCH

PROBLEM: The interior light doesn't go on when you open the refrigerator door.

If changing the bulb doesn't restore light to the inside of a refrigerator, the light switch is probably at fault. In many refrigerators, the switch protrudes through the side breaker frame panel against which the door closes. In others, the switch is in a panel with other controls.

To replace a switch that is in a panel, refer to the accompanying photographs (Figures 1.25 and 1.26). To replace a switch that pro-

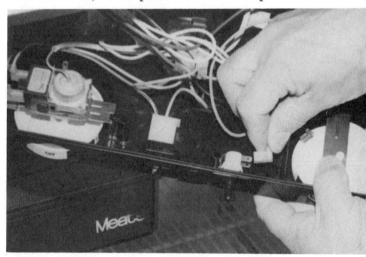

Figure 1.25 This unit has the light switch in a panel with other controls along the top of the refrigerator compartment. Disconnect the electricity, release the panel, and disconnect the wire from the light switch.

Figure 1.26 Detach the light switch from the panel by pressing the tangs on the sides of the switch (arrows).

trudes through the side breaker frame panel, do the following:

1.   Turn off electricity by pulling the power cord plug of the refrigerator from the wall outlet.
2.   Insert a small screwdriver between the flange of the switch plate and breaker frame panel. Pry the switch out of the breaker frame.
3.   With some refrigerators, you have to remove the breaker frame by pulling on the edge of the panel with your fingertips until the frame pops out of the flange.
4.   Using self-adhering labels or strips of masking tape, label which wire attaches to which terminal of the switch so that there won't be any doubt where to reconnect the wires. Then disconnect the wires.
5.   Touching each terminal of the switch with the probe of an ohmmeter, press in the switch button (Figure 1.27). The needle of the ohmmeter should rest on infinity (∞) to indicate an open circuit. Release the button. The needle of the ohmmeter should swing to zero or a couple of ohms at most to indicate continuity. If neither of these readings is obtained, the switch is defective. Buy and install a new switch. (See Appendix A for instructions on how to use an ohmmeter.)

Figure 1.27 Test the light switch with an ohmmeter.

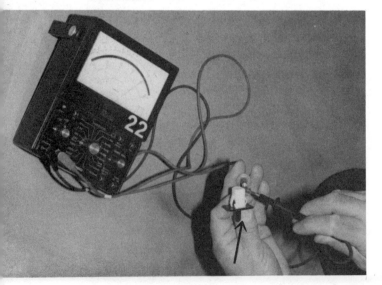

REPAIR · 10

REPAIRING AN ICE MAKER

PROBLEM: Your ice maker scatters ice cubes over the floor of the freezer compartment.

You may encounter a puzzling condition with an automatic ice maker. The arm that ejects the ice cubes from the tray can fling them with such force that they are scattered in the freezer compartment rather than neatly piled in the ice bin. The reason: often the cubes are too small and light. Cubes made by an automatic ice maker should be ¾ inch to 1 inch square. Small cubes occur when there is a diminished supply of water filling the mold, usually caused by a clogged filter in the water inlet. To resolve this problem, do the following:

1.   Pull the plug of the refrigerator power cord from the wall outlet. Pull the unit away from the wall so you can gain access to the water line leading to the ice maker.
2.   Turn off the water.
3.   Disconnect the water line from the water-inlet valve (Figure 1.28).

Figure 1.28 The water-inlet valve for an ice maker is usually located at the rear of the refrigerator. To reach the filter, you have to unscrew the water line (arrow). If the filter isn't accessible, remove and disassemble the valve until you can take out the filter.

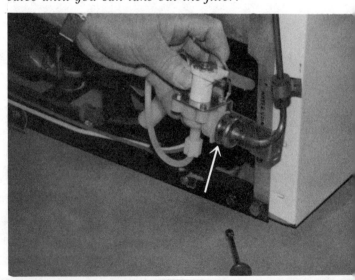

4. Remove the filter and wash it out, using a toothbrush to remove any sediment that has accumulated in the mesh.

5. Reinstall the filter, reconnect the water line, and turn on the water. Check to make sure that you have tightened the line enough so that water isn't leaking from around the fitting.

6. Push the appliance back into place and restore electricity.

•

PROBLEM: The ice cubes come out unformed or watery.

An automatic ice maker will produce cubes having watery or hollow centers for the following reasons:

1. The refrigerator/freezer or ice maker is not positioned properly. Make sure the appliance has a slight pitch to the rear. If the refrigerator/freezer has adjustable legs, turn them to get the correct position. If legs aren't adjustable, place a ⅛-inch shim under each front corner.

2. An obstruction is impeding the amount of water entering the ice maker. Check the filter (see above).

3. The ice-maker thermostat is cycling on and off prematurely. If the other two repairs don't solve the problem, the thermostat is at fault. First determine availability and cost of parts. You may reach the conclusion that it is more practical to buy another ice maker.

•

PROBLEM: Your ice maker overflows.

Water or a layer of ice in the cube tray of an ice maker is a sign that water is overflowing the mold. To determine the cause and make the repair, do the following:

1. The refrigerator/freezer should be tilted slightly toward the rear (see above).

2. Is the water intake adjusted correctly? Wait until the mold deposits a load of cubes into the tray and watch as the mold fills with water. Does the water flow continue and over-

flow the mold? If so, turn the water-level adjusting screw clockwise to reduce the amount of water entering the mold (Figure 1.29).

3. The water-inlet valve may have failed. If turning the water control fails to reduce the amount of water entering the mold, the water-inlet valve is malfunctioning. Turn off the water and disconnect the water-inlet valve from the refrigerator. Test the valve with an ohmmeter (Figure 1.30). If the valve isn't working properly, replace it with a new one.

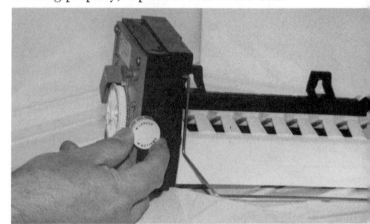

Figure 1.29 Most ice makers have a mechanism that enables you to control the amount of water that flows into the mold. If water overflows the mold, adjust the control to see if that reduces the flow.

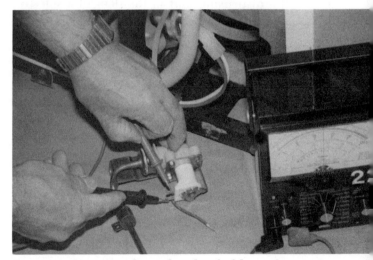

Figure 1.30 Test the valve by holding the probes of an ohmmeter to the valve terminals. A reading of infinity (∞) means that the valve is defective and should be replaced.

4. If you have gotten this far without finding the cause of the overflow, then the ice maker is leaking. Turn off the water, disconnect the unit from its source of electricity, and remove the ice maker from the freezer compartment. Look for signs of ice, which can pinpoint the spot that is leaking. For example, if there is ice on the *rear* of the ice maker at the spot where a fill cup attaches to the mold, take out the screws and remove the fill cup. Then cover the top edge with a bead of nontoxic silicone sealer. Reinstall the fill cup, pressing it against the sealer. Wipe off the excess, reinstall the ice maker, and turn it on.

If the ice is on the *underside* of the ice maker, the ejector arm seal has probably failed. In that case, take the ice maker to a technician for repair. A special tool is needed to remove the damaged seal and install a new one.

REPAIR · 11

FIXING AN IN-THE-DOOR ICE OR WATER DISPENSER

PROBLEM: Your ice or water dispenser fails to provide either.

If a dispensing unit in the door of a side-by-side refrigerator/freezer fails to eject ice or water, the reason may be a defective switch. You can test and replace the switch that controls the ice dispenser and the switch that controls the water dispenser in the same way. Do the following:

1. Turn off electricity to the refrigerator/freezer by pulling the power cord plug from the wall outlet.
2. Take out the screws holding the cover over the dispensing units. Remove the cover.
3. The switches are probably attached to the back of a bracket that spans the width of the dispenser housing. Remove the screws that hold the bracket to the door and turn the bracket over. If the back of the bracket has a cover, take off the cover to reveal the switches.
4. Using self-adhering labels or strips of masking tape, label the wires leading to the switch of the dispensing unit so that you will know where to reattach them, then disconnect the wires from the switch terminals.
5. Set an ohmmeter on the R × 1 scale and attach the probes of the instrument to the terminals of the switch. Do not press the button on the switch. (This is the button against which the handle of the dispenser presses to activate the unit, causing it to discharge ice or water.) If the needle of the ohmmeter points to infinity (∞), there is a faulty (open) circuit inside the switch. Replace the switch.
6. If the switch passes this test, continue to keep the probes of the ohmmeter connected to the terminals of the switch. Press the button on the switch. The needle of the ohmmeter should swing to zero. If it doesn't, replace the switch.

2

RANGES

M̲ost of the problems encountered with a range or oven, whether gas or electric, are easily repaired. Here we address the most frequently occurring malfunctions. Since many problems of ranges and ovens are related to incorrect usage, consult the owner's manual you received when you purchased the range to make certain you are using it correctly.

• ELECTRIC RANGES AND OVENS •

Safety Precautions

Electric ranges and ovens are easy to work on, but you can put yourself in danger if you do not abide by the following important safety precaution:

• *Disconnect the range from the electrical supply.* Before attempting any repair on an electric oven or range, you must disconnect the appliance from the electrical system. Either pull the power cord plug from the wall outlet (if you can reach it), switch off the circuit breaker, or remove the fuse serving the range/oven in the main electrical circuit breaker or fuse panel. To make certain that the range/oven has been disconnected, turn the surface and/or oven elements to their highest temperature settings and wait one minute. Carefully bring the palm of your hand close to the elements. If you feel any warmth, you have not disconnected the electricity. Do not proceed with the repair until you are absolutely sure the unit is disconnected from the power source.

• RANGE/OVEN REPAIRS •

Following is a list of the repairs presented in this chapter, along with the tools and materials necessary to make them.

REPAIR	TOOLS AND MATERIALS
1. Cleaning a continuous-cleaning oven	Commercial oven cleaner, nylon bristle brush or pad
2. Cleaning between oven door glass panels	Screwdriver, nut driver, putty knife, silicone sealing compound
3. Tracking down oven noise	None
4. Replacing a defective oven light	Bulb, pencil eraser, nut driver, screwdriver, masking tape or self-adhering labels
5. Self-cleaning oven door latch failure	None
6. Repairing an oven timer	Nut driver, mineral spirits, cotton swab
7. Replacing a defective electric range cooktop element	Screwdriver, nut driver
8. Testing an electric range cooktop element	Ohmmeter
9. Troubleshooting control switches and burner blocks	Nut driver, masking tape or self-adhering labels
10. Replacing a control switch	Nut driver, screwdriver
11. Replacing an electric oven element	Nut driver, screwdriver, masking tape or self-adhering labels, ohmmeter
12. Replacing an electric oven temperature control	Nut driver, screwdriver, masking tape or self-adhering labels
13. Resetting an electric oven thermostat	Oven thermometer, screwdriver, adjustable wrench
14. Adjusting gas range burners for maximum efficiency	Screwdriver
15. Repairing a burner pilot	Screwdriver or adjustable wrench
16. Replacing a defective spark igniter	Screwdriver, nut driver, masking tape or self-adhering labels, knife, electrician's tape

REPAIR · 1

CLEANING A CONTINUOUS-CLEANING OVEN

PROBLEM: Your continuous-cleaning oven fails to clean itself completely.

In most continuous-cleaning ovens, only the interior sides and top have a continuous-clean finish; the bottom and door liner are porcelain, and only resemble the continuous-clean finish. Check your owner's manual first. If the bottom and door liner of your oven are *not* continuous-clean, you can safely clean these surfaces with a commercial oven cleaner.

The ingredients used in oven cleaners may cause damage to the continuous-clean finish or to the door gasket, so cover these surfaces before you use the cleaner. *Caution:* Most oven-cleaning products contain sodium hydroxide (lye). Any product that contains lye must be used with extreme caution. Before using any cleaner containing lye, put on safety goggles, a long-sleeved shirt, and rubber gloves. If you're using an aerosol, wear a paper dust mask, to keep from inhaling the droplets, and protective goggles. Also protect nearby floors, counters, and other surfaces. To avoid taking all these precautionary steps, buy an aerosol cleaner without lye in the ingredients.

If the continuous-clean areas have become so heavily coated with burnt-on residue that they won't come clean in the normal cleaning operation of the oven, do *not* spray the buildup directly with an oven cleaner. Instead, rub the area gently with a regular household cleaner and a nylon-bristle brush or pad. Then place a paper towel over the buildup and saturate the towel with an ordinary household cleaner. Allow the cleaner to work on the residue for 30 minutes. Remove the towel and rub the spot with the nylon brush or pad. Using a sponge, rinse with cold water. When the area is as clean as you can possibly get it, set the oven temperature to 450 degrees. Turn on the oven. At the end of 2½ hours, the oven should be completely clean.

REPAIR · 2

CLEANING BETWEEN OVEN DOOR GLASS PANELS

PROBLEM: The window in your oven door is so dirty you can hardly see into the oven.

The glass in an oven door consists of two panes held together by a gasket or bead of chemical sealer. Hot grease can get between the two panes, resulting in smoking and streaking. To separate and clean the inside surfaces of the panes, do the following:

1.   Open the door to the first stop and try to lift it off its hinges. This sometimes takes some gentle adjusting and moving of the door, especially in regard to the angle of closure. Some doors, however, won't come off unless screws that hold hinges are removed (Figure 2.1). Do not try to yank the door out.

2.   Once you have removed it, place the door on a surface that will not scratch or damage it. Unscrew the handle (Figure 2.2). Then re-

Figure 2.1 If an oven door doesn't come off easily, look to see if a screw holds each hinge. Remove the screws, one on each side of the door.

Figure 2.2 To reach the glass, remove the screws holding the door handle.

Figure 2.3 Working around the perimeter of the door, remove all other screws. For safekeeping, put the screws into a receptacle.

Figure 2.4 When all the screws have been taken out, separate the outer panel from the inner panel that holds the glass.

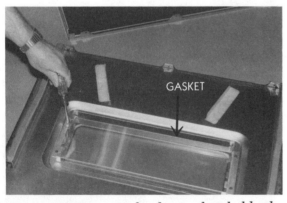

Figure 2.5 Remove the frame that holds the glass. In this unit, the two panes come apart easily for cleaning. They do not have to be sealed because the manufacturer has installed a gasket (arrow). Try not to damage this gasket.

move the screws that hold the panels together (Figure 2.3).

3. With the panels separated, you can see the frame holding the glass (Figure 2.4). Remove the frame (Figure 2.5). Using a thin-bladed tool, such as a putty knife, remove the gasket to separate the panes or pry the panes apart if they are held by a chemical sealer.

4. Clean the glass. If the application of reasonable amounts of ammonia, water, and energetic cleaning fail to remove the streaks, they have probably been caused by heat and not by grease. There is nothing you can do about this.

5. Place the panes of glass together and put them back in position in the frame.

6. Press the gasket back in place with a putty knife, or seal around the panes with silicone sealing compound. Do not leave gaps, or you will have to repeat the entire job within a short time.

7. Reassemble door panels and handle. Put the door on its hinges, again easing it into place gently.

R E P A I R · 3

TRACKING DOWN OVEN NOISE

PROBLEM: As you bake or roast, you hear strange noises coming from your oven, like a series of pops.

Popping sounds coming from an oven are usually caused by a metal part—pan, rack, door panel, or interior panel—expanding and contracting as the oven temperature changes.

To trace the source of the noise, take out one removable part at a time and turn on the oven. When the oven heats up and you don't hear the noise, you have found the offending part. If you remove all the metal parts and the noise persists, it is caused by a door panel or one of the other interior panels. You have the choice of putting up with the annoying sound or replacing the panels, one by one.

REPAIR · 4

REPLACING A DEFECTIVE OVEN LIGHT

PROBLEM: Your oven light does not go on when you press the light switch.

Failure of an oven light to operate properly can have three possible causes: (1) the bulb has failed; (2) receptacle contacts are corroded; or (3) the light switch is defective.

Burned-out bulb. The first step is to test the bulb itself. An oven bulb is smaller than most household bulbs and fits into a tightly recessed area in most ovens. As a consequence, you may not be able to use an ordinary household bulb as a tester, but will have to purchase a new bulb from an appliance parts store. Screw the new bulb into the receptacle. Turn on the switch. If the new bulb lights, the original oven bulb has burned out.

If the light still does not go on, the problem is not a burned-out bulb. Remove the new bulb and save it for when the old bulb does burn out.

Corroded receptacle contacts. Turn off electricity to the range at the main electrical service panel. After you have done so, examine the contacts inside the bulb receptacle. If they are corroded or grease-filled, rub them clean with a rubber pencil eraser. Blow any loose particles from the receptacle. Install the bulb, and turn on electricity. If the bulb still does not work, ask your hardware store for a stronger cleaner to remove the corrosion.

Defective light switch. If neither the bulb nor the receptacle contacts are at fault, the on-off switch is probably worn out. This is almost certainly the problem if the switch feels loose and sloppy, or catches as you flip it on and off. To replace the switch, do the following:

1. Turn off electricity to the range.
2. Disassemble the door (see Repair 2, above) or open the console panel; the switch is located in one or the other.
3. Using self-adhering labels or strips of masking tape, label the wires so you can tell which one connects to each terminal of the switch, then disconnect the wires. In most

ranges, wires are held to the switch by push-on, pull-off spade connectors. When handling these parts, grasp the connector itself. Do *not* pull the wire, or it may separate from the connector.

4. Buy a matching switch from an appliance parts dealer. Install the new switch, making sure that the wires are connected to the proper terminals.

H E L P F U L   H I N T

Setting Clocks Correctly

If the self-cleaning feature of an oven fails to work, your first step is to make sure the clocks are set in accordance with the instructions in the owner's manual. Manufacturers identify the failure to set clocks correctly as the main cause for a non-working self-cleaning feature. Many homeowners learn this only after they have called in a technician and paid the cost of a service call.

REPAIR · 5

SELF-CLEANING OVEN DOOR LATCH FAILURE

PROBLEM: The door latch on your self-cleaning oven no longer securely locks the oven door.

First check your owner's manual to make sure that some operational error is not the cause of the door latch failure. If that is not the case, this is one problem you will be unable to fix on your own. A number of parts make up the locking mechanism, including the oven-temperature control switch, lock solenoid, and door-lock switch. The wiring is also intricate, so training and special tools are needed to work on this system successfully. Furthermore, upsetting or bypassing any of the safety factors engineered into these locking mechanisms can create an unsafe situation in which it is possible for someone to open the oven door accidentally while the oven is at extremely high self-cleaning temperatures.

If you don't wish to incur the expense of having a service technician repair the problem, you will have to do without the self-cleaning feature. To keep the oven clean, you will first have to wipe up spills as soon as they occur. Second, use a commercial oven cleaner periodically (see cautions on page 25), but be sure to rinse all the cleaner off the self-clean surfaces. This is important, for if you eventually have the locking mechanism repaired and start to use the self-cleaning feature again, the high oven-cleaning temperature will cause damage to that portion of the liner that still has some residue of the oven cleaner on it.

REPAIR · 6

REPAIRING AN OVEN TIMER

PROBLEM: Your oven timer does not buzz.

When oven timers turn themselves off, they usually emit a buzzing sound to warn you that the cooking process has been completed. The buzzing is supposed to continue until you manually turn the timer off. If the signal doesn't work properly, there may be grease or dirt on the buzzer vibrator. To clean the vibrator, do the following:

1. Turn off electricity to the range.
2. Remove the screws of the control console and open the console.
3. The vibrator is attached to the timer, which is located behind the clock. Moisten a cotton swab with mineral spirits and clean off the vibrator.

HELPFUL HINT

Preventing Cooktop Element Failure in an Electric Range

Failure to insert an element fully into the burner block receptacle of an electric range can cause carbon to form in the gap between the terminals of the element and burner block. Eventually this carbon will create a wall of insulation between the parts, and the element will fail to heat.

To prevent this damage, connect an element in the following way:

1. When inserting the terminals into the burner block, hold the element as closely parallel to the range as possible.
2. Press in the elements firmly until they are correctly seated all the way into the burner block.

REPAIR · 7

REPLACING A DEFECTIVE ELECTRIC RANGE COOKTOP ELEMENT

PROBLEM: One area of a cooktop element on an electric range glows more brightly than the rest of its surface.

Cooking elements of most electric ranges are resistance wire made of nickel and chromium (often referred to as Nichrome resistance wire) that is inside a sheath containing magnesium oxide.

A glowing spot indicates that the sheath has broken down in that area, and the exposed wire is burning hotter than the rest of the element. The element will soon fail completely, and any cookware coming into contact with the red-hot spot may be scorched.

To replace a cooktop element, first make sure the element is cold, then grasp the element and carefully pull it out of the range. Most elements are plugged into a burner

Figure 2.6 When reinstalling electric range cooktop elements, hold the element as close to the range top as possible. Press the terminals firmly and securely into the burner block.

Figure 2.7 If an element is one of a kind in size, you will have to use an ohmmeter to establish whether the element is faulty. An infinity reading (∞) indicates that a new element is needed.

block, so tugging gently on the element should cause it to come free (Figure 2.6). Buy a new element of the same type from an appliance parts dealer. Plug it securely into the burner block by holding it as low as possible and pushing in forcefully.

The terminals of some elements are secured to wires with screws. If you have this type of element, turn off current to the range, and carefully pull the element toward you until the terminals are revealed. Loosen the terminal screws, disconnect the wires from the damaged element, and screw a new element to the wires.

REPAIR · 8

TESTING AN ELECTRIC RANGE COOKTOP ELEMENT

PROBLEM: One element on your electric range does not get warm.

You must test the nonworking element to make certain it, and not some other part, has failed. To do so, follow these steps:

1.   Most electric ranges have two cooktop elements that measure 5½ inches in diameter, and two that measure 7½ inches in diameter. To test a nonworking element, first be sure the burner elements are turned off and are cold. Then transfer the nonworking element

into the burner block of a working element of the same size. Turn on the power. If the element still doesn't glow, the defective element must be replaced.

2.   If the nonworking element is one of a kind in size, remove the element from the range. Hold the probes of an ohmmeter to the ends of the element (Figure 2.7). If the ohmmeter needle points to infinity (∞), the element is defective and must be replaced.

REPAIR · 9

TROUBLESHOOTING CONTROL SWITCHES AND BURNER BLOCKS

PROBLEM: The cooktop element heats up in another position, but will not work when returned to its original position in the range.

If testing a cooktop element (see Repair 8, above) proves that the element is in good working order, its failure to operate lies with the control switch or the burner block into which the element is plugged. To find out which one is causing the trouble, do the following:

1.   Turn off the electricity at the main electrical service panel. Don't touch any wire until you are certain that all current to the range is off.

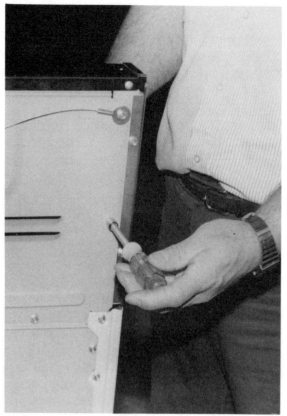

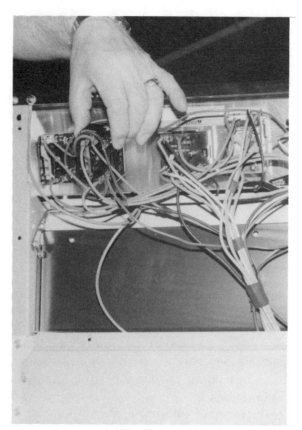

Figure 2.8 Open the control panel—in this case, by removing the cover at the back of the range.

Figure 2.9 Use self-adhering labels or strips of masking tape to mark each wire and the terminal of the switch to which it attaches.

2.   Open the control panel (Figure 2.8).

3.   To find out whether you are dealing with a bad control switch or a bad burner block, transfer the wires of the burner block serving the nonworking element to the control switch of a comparably sized element that is working. Although the wires are probably color-coded to make them easier to identify, use self-adhering labels or strips of masking tape to mark them and their terminals so that you can distinguish one wire and its control-switch terminal from another set (Figure 2.9).

4.   Restore power. *Caution:* As you proceed further in this test procedure, remember that the power is *on.* Do not touch any wire or component other than the knob of the control switch.

5.   Turn on the control switch. If the non-operating element now glows, the control

switch should be replaced. Follow the instructions below to replace it. If the element still doesn't glow, the burner block is defective or worn. In that case, turn off the electricity and reconnect the wires to their correct switch terminals. Close the control panel. You must have a service technician install a new burner block.

R E P A I R · 10

REPLACING A CONTROL SWITCH

PROBLEM: The cooktop element of an electric range does not work and the control switch is at fault.

Replacing a faulty control switch is a relatively simple task. Do the following:

1.   Jot down the make and model number of

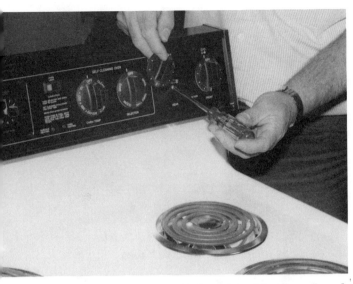

Figure 2.10 Pull off the control knob and undo the screws that hold the switch.

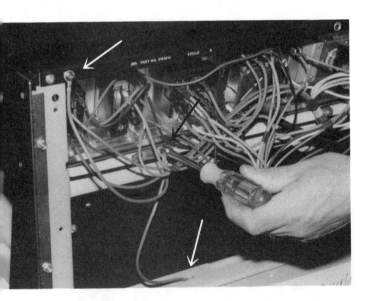

Figure 2.11 Every electric range or appliance is grounded. If you have to disconnect a ground, reconnect it tightly after making a repair, or someone using it later can get a serious shock. The appliance here is grounded with three wires. The wires are attached to the metal frame (arrow).

the range. Take this information to an appliance parts store and get the correct control switch for your unit.

2. Turn off the electricity at the main electrical service panel. Do not proceed until you are sure the electricity has been disconnected.

3. Pull off the control switch knob. If there is a rubber pad under the knob, remove that, too.

4. If this is a freestanding range, remove the screws holding the control panel. Open the panel; you will see the row of switches. Identify the one you have to replace by matching the physical characteristics of the new switch to that of the malfunctioning switch. Hold the new switch next to the one you are replacing and transfer wires from the terminals of the damaged switch to the corresponding terminals of the new switch. Lay the new switch aside. Unscrew the damaged switch from the range, and install the new switch in its place (Figure 2.10). Make certain that wires are secure, including ground wires (Figure 2.11). Close the control panel. Attach the control knob to the stem of the new switch.

5. If this is a countertop range, open the doors of the oven cabinet under the counter. (Note that the inside bottom of the range is covered by an access panel.) Undo the screws holding this panel in place and remove the panel. Identify the faulty switch. Hold the new switch next to it so that each feature coincides, and transfer wires from the old switch to the new one. Remove the screws that hold the old switch in place. Then push the old switch through the hole and let it fall under the counter where you can retrieve it. Maneuver the stem of the new switch through the vacated hole and screw the switch to the counter. Before reattaching the access panel, push the wires well back into the counter so that a wire won't be cut by a sharp edge of the access panel.

6. Replace the rubber pad and knob, if any, and restore electricity.

R E P A I R · 11

REPLACING AN ELECTRIC OVEN ELEMENT

*PROBLEM: An oven element appears damaged, or
does not work.*

An electric oven element that has failed will
often show damage, either in the form of a
hole in the element or by a drooping appearance, almost as if it has melted.

To replace a defective oven element, do the
following:

1.   Turn off the electricity to the range at the
main electric service panel. To be certain that
current is no longer reaching the range, turn
on the cooktop and oven elements. If you feel
warmth on a hand held close to any of them,
current is still present. *Do not proceed until
you are sure the current is off.*

2.   Open the oven door.

3.   Take the racks out of the oven.

4.   Remove the two screws securing the element bracket to the back wall of the oven (Figure 2.12).

5.   Pull the element away from the back wall
until the terminals are accessible.

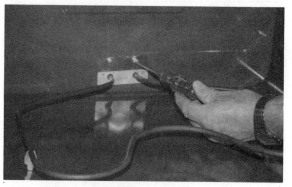

*Figure 2.12 Undo the screws and slowly pull
the element away from the back wall.*

6.   Using a screwdriver or nut driver, undo
the screws holding the wires to the element.
Use self-adhering labels or strips of masking
tape to label the wires. Then you can tell which
one connects to each element. If you do not
see any screws, the wires are secured by push-
pull spade connectors. Grasp these by the
metal when pulling them apart or pressing
them together (Figure 2.13). Do *not* pull or
press on the wires; this can pull them loose
from their connectors.

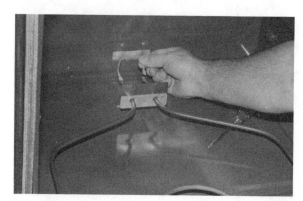

*Figure 2.13 In many electric ovens, bake and
broil element wires are attached with spade
connectors. These are designed to be pulled
off and pushed onto the terminals.*

7.   Remove the element. To make certain it
is faulty, hold the probes of an ohmmeter to
the terminals. A reading of infinity (∞) iden-
tifies a burned-out element.

8. Attach wires to the new element by tightening the screws or pushing on the spade connectors.

9. Attach the element to the back wall of the oven. Tighten screws.

Caution: Handle wires gently. Over time, heat may have made the insulation covering the wires brittle. If a wire falls apart, you must have a service technician rewire the element.

R E P A I R · 12

REPLACING AN ELECTRIC OVEN TEMPERATURE CONTROL

PROBLEM: The electric oven does not get hot.

One of the elements may be damaged (see Repair 11, above, for replacement instructions) or the temperature control may have to be replaced. To replace the temperature control, do the following:

1. Turn off electricity to the range at the main electrical service panel. To make sure electricity has been turned off, turn on all cooktop and oven elements. If you feel warmth on a hand placed near any of the elements, do not proceed until the electricity is completely disconnected.

2. Remove the screws holding the control panel. Open the panel.

3. Release the temperature sensing rod inside the oven (Figure 2.14). Do this by removing the rod from the bracket and, if necessary, unscrewing the plate covering the hole in the back wall of the oven through which the rod passes.

4. At the console, using self-adhering labels or strips of masking tape, label each wire and the terminal of the oven temperature control to which it attaches. Disconnect wires. Unscrew the oven temperature control of the console.

5. Pull the oven temperature control out of the console. The sensing rod should come with it.

6. Take the entire assembly to an appliance parts dealer and buy a replacement.

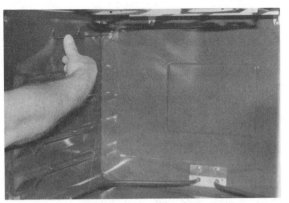

Figure 2.14 This is the temperature sensing rod. As you withdraw the switch from the console, the sensing rod will come out of the oven with it. The switch and sensing rod are usually replaced as a unit.

7. Loosely screw the new oven temperature control into the spot vacated by the old one. Do not tighten the screws. Insert the new sensing rod through the hole in the oven wall. Then, working inside the oven, secure the sensing rod to the bracket. The sensing rod must not rest against the oven wall, or its ability to monitor temperature accurately will be impaired.

8. Connect wires, tighten screws, and install the control panel and knobs. Restore power.

R E P A I R · 13

RESETTING AN ELECTRIC OVEN THERMOSTAT

PROBLEM: Even though you follow the correct cooking times carefully, food comes out of the oven either undercooked or overcooked.

Consistently undercooked or overcooked food is often the result of a maladjusted oven thermostat. You can check the thermostat by using an oven thermometer. Place the thermometer in the center of the oven, set the temperature control to 400 degrees, turn on the oven, and allow the oven to heat until the indicator light goes off. Record the thermometer reading. Wait for the indicator light to come on again, and record the thermometer reading. Do this three times. The average reading should be between 390 and 430 degrees. If not, you will have to reset the thermometer. Follow these steps:

1.   Pull off the oven temperature control knob. Look for an adjustment mechanism on its back. If present, it will be in the form of a dial. Loosen the screw holding the dial and turn the dial the number of notches necessary to bring the temperature to the desired level. (Each notch represents a 10-degree advance.) After making the adjustment and tightening the screw, check the oven temperature with the oven thermometer again. Continue with this procedure until the temperature falls within the normal range.

2.   If there is no dial on the knob, the adjustment mechanism is inside the shaft on which the temperature control knob sits. Insert a thin screwdriver into the hole in the shaft to engage the adjustment screw. Holding the shaft with a wrench, turn the adjustment screw to increase or decrease temperature. Each one-eighth turn usually increases or decreases oven temperature by about 25 degrees. After making the adjustment, test the oven with the thermometer again to determine whether the desired temperature has been reached. If the test shows that you have turned the screw in the wrong direction, make the adjustment again, in the opposite direction.

• GAS RANGES AND OVENS •

Safety Precautions

Observe these two safety precautions when doing repairs to a gas range:

• *Turn off the gas.* Find out where the main gas valve is located (usually close to the gas meter). If you smell gas, turn off the gas supply to the home. If you think the leak is coming from a gas-fed pilot, and you attempt to make the repair, you will have to close this valve before making the repair, and then reopen it to restore the gas supply in order to check results. If you again smell gas, turn off the supply until you can have a check made by a utility company or independent technician.

• Disconnect electricity if you are working on electrical components. If your gas range has spark igniters rather than gas-fed pilots, and you are going to replace one that has failed, remember that a spark igniter is an electrical component. You must turn off all electricity to the range before you start to replace the faulty spark igniter. This repair should be attempted only if your range is equipped with nonsealed spark igniters. Nonsealed spark igniters are not encased, but are positioned in a bracket that you can unscrew on the range.

REPAIR • 14

ADJUSTING GAS RANGE BURNERS FOR MAXIMUM EFFICIENCY

PROBLEM: The flame on one of the burners of your gas range has changed color.

A gas range normally gives off a blue flame. A yellow flame indicates that a burner is not functioning properly. A yellow flame also burns cooler than a blue flame, so food will take longer to cook. One of two malfunctions will cause a burner to show a yellow flame: either the ports of the burner are clogged by food that has spilled onto the burner, or the air control shutter needs adjustment.

To restore a burner to peak efficiency, do the following:

1.   Remove the affected burner from the range by pulling it from its place, and wash it in soapy water (Figure 2.15).
2.   There are a series of tiny holes, called *ports,* around the base of the burner. Use a toothpick to loosen and remove food deposits that may be clogging these ports.
3.   Let the burner dry fully before placing it back into the range. Turn on the range. If the

Figure 2.15 *Remove and clean the gas burner. Since air-control shutters (arrows) are set at the factory, do not readjust them unless all other efforts to repair the problem have failed.*

flame is still yellow, adjust the air-control shutter as follows:

    a.   Turn the burner control to High.

    b.   Loosen the air-control shutter screw.

    c.   Slide the air-control shutter in one direction and then in the other, until the flame turns blue.

    d.   Tighten the air-control shutter screw.

4.   With the burner control still on High, place a pan containing a little water onto the burner and check the height of the flame. It should end just below the bottom of the pan, no more than ⅛ inch away. If the flame touches the pan, it means receptacles placed on the burner (with the burner control on High) can be scorched and food will burn. Conversely, if the length of the flame is too short, food will take longer to cook. To adjust the height of the flame, locate (if you can) the orifice-control screw on the gas delivery tube to the burner. Turn this control screw clockwise to increase the length of the flame. Turning this screw counterclockwise will lower the flame.

REPAIRING A BURNER PILOT

PROBLEM: One of the pilots on your gas range is out. You relight it with a match, but it constantly needs relighting.

If your gas range doesn't have spark igniters, the burners are ignited by a gas-fed pilot. In some ranges, each burner has its own pilot; in others, two burners share a pilot. If the pilot doesn't get enough gas, the pilot will keep going out. Turn the pilot adjustment screw 1/16 inch counterclockwise at a time, using a screwdriver or an adjustable wrench (Figure 2.16). If the pilot won't stay lit, call a utility company or independent technician to make the repair.

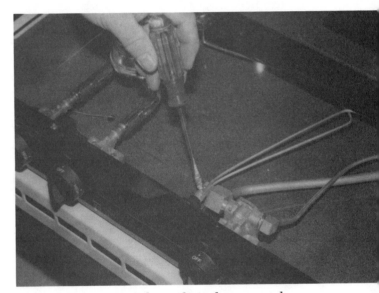

Figure 2.16 *To readjust the pilot, turn the pilot adjustment screw 1/16 inch counterclockwise.*

REPLACING A DEFECTIVE SPARK IGNITER

PROBLEM: Two burners on one side of the range won't ignite, although the two on the other side of the range operate normally.

If the spark igniter on the nonworking side doesn't make a ticking sound when you turn on a burner, it means the igniter is defective.

As long as the igniter is uncovered (that is, a nonsealed unit), you can replace it by following these steps:

1. Disconnect electricity to the range by turning off the circuit at the main electrical service panel. You do not have to turn off the gas.

2. Remove rangetop grates and pans. With some ranges, this will allow access to the spark igniter. With other ranges, you can swing open the top of the range. Be careful not to catch wires under the back edge of the top when you are closing it. A cut wire can knock out power to a spark igniter.

3. Remove the bracket holding the nonworking spark igniter to its spot between the gas feed tubes of the two burners. In a typical four-burner range, one spark igniter serves the front and rear burners on one side of the range and a second spark igniter serves the front and rear burners on the other side.

4. To reach the control module that feeds current to the spark igniters, move the range away from the wall and take off the rear panel. The range is tethered to a vertical gas supply pipe by a gooseneck line that has a certain amount of flexibility to it. *Be careful that you do not try to move the range so far away from the wall that you jeopardize the integrity of the connections.* Once you have the range away from the wall, you should spot the control module—a rectangular metal box.

5. To find one wire you are seeking—the one that is connected to the nonworking spark igniter—have an assistant pull gently on the nonworking igniter. The wire that moves at the control module is the one you want. Using a self-adhering label or strip of masking tape, mark its location before disconnecting it.

6. After purchasing a new spark igniter, cut the wire that leads from the nonworking igniter back to the control panel. Cut it close to the igniter so that you'll have enough of the wire going back to the control panel to work with. Remove the old igniter from its position and replace it with the new one. Don't tighten down the new one yet.

7. Note that the new igniter comes with its own new wire, already fitted with a terminal end. Use tape to tie together the terminal end of the new wire securely to the cut end of the old wire. Make sure the tape protects the terminal end of the new wire.

8. At the control module, slowly pull the old wire from the range, bringing the new wire with it. If it sticks as you pull, the taped splice you made may be catching somewhere. Pull it back the other way, smooth out your splice, and try again. With the new wire in position at the module, and the new igniter sitting in its bracket (not yet screwed down tight), undo your splice so that the two wires separate. Discard the old wire. Connect the terminal of the new wire to the spot you marked for it in the control module.

9. Replace the control module cover and rear panel.

10. The new igniter must be spaced evenly between the feed tubes of the two burners. To do this, use two dimes held together as spacers. Place them first on one side of the igniter and then on the other. Shift the igniter to get an even spacing between it and the burner pilot tubes. When you are satisfied about the spacing, tighten the bracket. Check the spacing once more to make sure you didn't disturb it in tightening the bracket, and restore electricity to the range.

3

WASHING MACHINES

A washing machine is among the most reliable of home appliances. It's also one of the easiest to repair, because most problems usually involve a water leak or damage to the interior clothes basket. Both of these problems are easy to repair, and only rarely require the help of a trained technician.

Safety Precautions

• *Disconnect the washing machine from the electrical supply.* If the wall outlet is not accessible, switch off the electricity to the appliance at the main electrical service panel by switching the circuit breaker off or removing the fuse. To ensure that electricity is not present, turn the machine on. If you hear any noises or if any lights go on, you haven't dis-

connected the correct circuit breaker or fuse. Do not proceed with any repairs until you are sure that you have done so.

Another precaution, not related to safety, may help you avoid a most unpleasant situation. You will notice two shut-off valves near the point where the washing machine hoses are connected to the home's water lines—one on the hot water line and another on the cold water line. It makes sense always to take the time to turn these shut-off valves off when the washer has completed its cycle. Why? The weakest links in a washing machine are the water hoses. If you leave the shut-off valves open, and a hose bursts while you are away from home, you will return to a flooded basement or utility room and an enormous water bill. This could happen whether or not the washing machine was in operation when you left.

• WASHING MACHINE REPAIRS •

Following is a list of the repairs presented in this chapter, and the tools and materials to make them:

REPAIR	TOOLS AND MATERIALS
1. Troubleshooting the cause of overly wet clothes	Nut driver, adjustable pliers, adjustable wrench
2. Analyzing a leak	Screwdriver
3. Replacing the water-level switch	Screwdriver, masking tape or self-adhering labels, ohmmeter or 12-volt test light
4. Replacing a water pump	Screwdriver, nut driver, adjustable pliers, adjustable wrench
5. Stemming an overflow from the standpipe	Garden hose
6. Removing a burr in the basket	Nylon stocking, fine-grit sandpaper
7. Repairing a rusted basket	Fine-grit sandpaper, nontoxic epoxy compound, waterproof porcelain enamel paint
8. Replacing a basket	Adjustable pliers, penetrating oil, rubber or wooden mallet, chisel, hammer, screwdriver, adjustable wrench, stiff bristle brush, silicone lubricant
9. Replacing damaged water-intake hoses	Adjustable pliers
10. Testing and replacing the water-intake valve	Adjustable pliers, nut driver, screwdriver, putty knife, masking tape or self-adhering labels, ohmmeter, adjustable wrench
11. Getting rid of a squeal	Nut driver, drive-belt lubricant, adjustable wrench, wire brush, multipurpose grease
12. Adjusting a basket that bangs against the chassis	Carpenter's level, pliers, adjustable wrench, nut driver, socket wrench, screwdriver
13. Overcoming sluggish agitation	None
14. Straightening a dented lid	Rubber mallet
15. Getting rid of black stains in the basket	Vinegar, acetic acid, baking soda

REPAIR · 1

TROUBLESHOOTING THE CAUSE OF OVERLY WET CLOTHES

PROBLEM: Clothes come out of the washer too wet.

Clothes coming out of a washing machine should be damp, not dripping wet. If they are too wet, and the machine is not being overloaded, there is a mechanical problem with the washer. Either the drain hose is not clear, the drive belt needs replacement, or lint is impeding the flow of water out of your washer. To determine the cause of the problem and correct it, do the following:

1. Check the drain hose leading from the machine to the standpipe or sink. If it is twisted, straighten it out. (You may have to replace the hose if you can't uncoil it.)

2. If the problem isn't caused by a twisted drain hose, turn off electricity by pulling the power cord of the washing machine from the wall outlet. Move the appliance away from the wall and take off the rear panel. Disconnect the drain hose from the pump and then from the standpipe. Using the handle of a mop or broom, push a clean rag all the way through the hose. Then reinstall the hose.

3. Adjust or replace the drive belt. With the electricity turned off and the rear panel removed, press down on the belt at a point midway between the motor and pump pulleys. If there is more than ½ inch deflection, the belt has been stretched. Inspect the belt for damage, such as a shiny glaze on the inner surface or cracks. Replace a damaged belt by loosening (not removing) the bolts holding the motor. This will allow the motor to slide toward the pulley. Buy a new belt of the correct size for the machine. Place it around the pulleys and then pull back on the motor until pressing down on the belt midway between the pulleys causes the belt to deflect no more than about ¼ inch. Tighten the bolts to hold the motor in place. Adjust a stretched belt the same way—that is, by loosening and pulling back on the motor.

4. Clear lint blockage. Even if your washing machine has a self-cleaning filter, lint can still accumulate on the filter and restrict the flow of water out of the machine. Trace the drain hose to find the filter, which is probably located on the basket side of the pump. Remove the filter and clean or replace it.

REPAIR · 2

ANALYZING A LEAK

PROBLEM: Your washing machine discharges a small quantity of water on the floor after each use.

A small quantity of water on the floor indicates that the washing machine may need a new water-level switch. (A significant quantity of water probably would be caused by a worn-out water pump [see Repair 4, below].)

To find the source of the leak, do the following:

1. Disconnect the power cord from the wall outlet and move the machine away from the wall.

2. Open the control panel (Figures 3.1 and 3.2). Look for the part to which the hose is attached (Figure 3.3). This component is the water-level switch and overflow hose. The water-level switch is supposed to turn off the water-intake valve when the water in the basket reaches a preset level. If the water-level

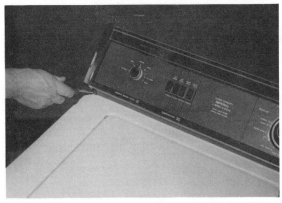

Figure 3.1 *To reach the controls of a washing machine, unscrew the control panel. Turn off electricity first.*

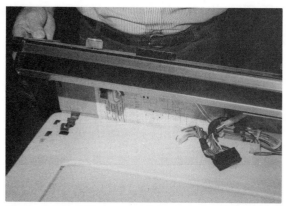

Figure 3.2 *When you lift the control panel, disconnect wire couplers, if necessary, by unplugging them so you can reach the components, such as the water-level switch.*

Figure 3.3 *The water-level switch. The hose is connected to it.*

switch is maladjusted, and the water in the basket is going higher than it should, the excess is being expelled out of the basket through the overflow hose to the floor.

3. Test the water-level switch by placing a receptacle on the floor under the overflow hose that is connected to the water-level switch. Turn on the washer. If water appears in the receptacle, it confirms that the leak is coming from the overflow hose. Either replace the water-level switch (see Repair 3, below) or keep the receptacle in place to save yourself the cost of a new switch. Remember to empty it periodically.

REPAIR · 3
REPLACING THE WATER-LEVEL SWITCH

PROBLEM: The washing machine won't fill, the motor won't go on, or the motor won't shut off.

If the water-level switch goes bad, water on the floor is not the only problem that can result. If one of these three problems is the result of a defective water-level switch, the switch will have to be replaced.

To perform the diagnostic test described in the following steps, you will need an ohmmeter or a 12-volt test light. If you use a test light, make sure it is battery-powered. Do not use a test light that must be plugged into a wall outlet. The test is to be done only under the conditions noted in this section.

To find out if the water-level switch has failed, do the following:

1. Unplug the washer from the wall outlet. Find the water-level switch (see Repair 2, above). Using self-adhering labels or strips of masking tape, label wires so you can tell which one connects to each terminal, and pull the wires off the terminals.

2. Pull the overflow hose up from the bottom.

3. Attach one lead of the ohmmeter or the 12-volt test light to the main terminal of the switch. Attach the other lead of the ohmmeter or test light to one of the remaining (secondary) terminals of the switch. You can distinguish between the main terminal and the two secondary terminals by the fact that the main terminal is isolated from the others.

4. Move the ohmmeter or test light lead to the other secondary terminal and blow into the hose (Figure 3.4). The ohmmeter should show infinity (∞) in one of the positions and zero or a reading slightly above zero in the other. If you are using a test light, it should glow when one of the secondary terminals is touched; it should not glow when you move the lead to the other secondary terminal. If it does, the water-level switch is faulty.

6. Remove the water-level switch; use masking tape or self-adhering labels to note the

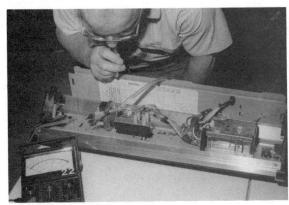

Figure 3.4 Test the switch with an ohmmeter or 12-volt test light. Blow into the overflow hose.

placement of all wires; and put a new one in its place. Be sure that you reattach the wires correctly.

7.   Before attaching the overflow hose to the switch, pour some water down into the hose. A hose completely empty of water may cause a flooding problem when you use the washing machine for the first time after installing a new water-level switch.

R E P A I R · 4

REPLACING A WATER PUMP

PROBLEM: A large puddle of water collects under the washing machine, or water remains in the washing machine basket.

These symptoms usually indicate water pump failure. However, a water-intake or drain hose also may be defective. So inspect the hoses first—a visual examination may reveal a cracked hose. To replace a hose, loosen the clamps and pull the hose off at both ends (Figure 3.5). You can find a replacement hose at any appliance parts store.

If the hoses are in good working order, then the water pump is probably at fault. To check and, if necessary, replace the pump, do the following:

1.   Disconnect the power cord from the wall outlet. Turn off the water.

2.   Remove the rear or front panel of the unit,

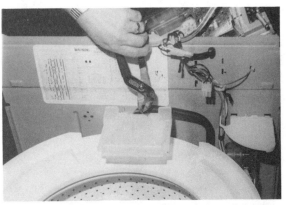

Figure 3.5 Hoses should be examined before a pump is replaced. There are three water-intake hoses. One is the hose seen here, which goes from the water-intake valve to the water inlet of the basket.

whichever is necessary to reach the pump.

3.   There will be at least two hoses connected to the water pump. Dirty water flows from the basket to the pump through one hose and from the pump to the standpipe or sink drain through the other. Examine each hose for leakage. Then use adjustable pliers to squeeze the hose clamps open so you can slide the clamps up onto the hoses (Figure 3.6). Pull the hoses

Figure 3.6 Release the clamps that hold the drain hoses to the pump. Slide the clamp up onto the hose.

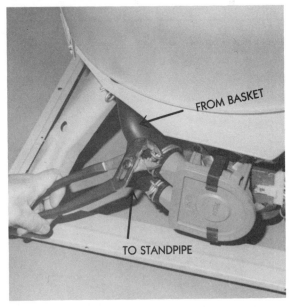

FROM BASKET

TO STANDPIPE

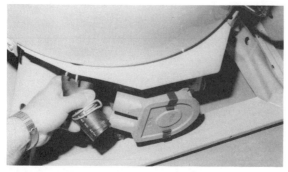

Figure 3.7 With the clamp out of the way, twist and pull on the hose to release it from the pump.

off the ports of the pump (Figure 3.7).

4. If the pump is driven by a belt, loosen the motor bracket bolts and take off the belt.

5. Remove the bolts or release the clamps holding the pump in place and take the pump out of the washer (Figures 3.8 and 3.9).

Figure 3.8 Disconnect the pump from the motor by releasing the clamps or removing the bolts that hold it in place. The pumps in some models are separate from the motor and are driven by a belt that stretches between a pulley on the motor and a pulley on the pump.

Figure 3.9 Take the pump off the motor.

HELPFUL HINT
How to Load a Washer

Proper loading is essential for the most efficient use of a washing machine. Put in the detergent first, the clothes next, and then add the water. If you put in the detergent first, the detergent becomes submerged by the fill water and promptly dissolves. On the other hand, if detergent is dumped on top of clothes, it remains on the clothes in a dissolved or partially dissolved state until agitation starts, causing fading or streaking.

Load the clothing loosely in the machine until clothes come to just below the top of the agitator. If a washing machine is overloaded, the speed at which the basket spins may be reduced, thus decreasing the amount of water extracted during the spin cycle. These abnormally wet clothes will impose an unnecessary burden on your clothes dryer.

6. Examine the pump to verify that it has gone bad; for example, look for a crack in the case. Then move the pump lever (if there is one) up and down to examine the inside of the ports to see if they are closing. Inside a port, you may find a sock or some other item that is preventing drainage. Pulling out the obstruction will probably restore the pump to service if no other defects are present. To make sure, shake the pulley (if there is one) to see if it has excessive "play" or wobble. If the pump is cracked, the ports won't close or the pulley will be loose. In either case, the pump must be replaced with a new one.

7. After the pump has been replaced, adjust the drive belt (if there is one). To adjust, pull back on the motor until pressing down on the belt midway between the pump and motor pulleys makes the belt deflect ¼ inch.

8.   Tighten the motor and check belt deflection again. If a belt is left too loose, agitation and/or spin speed will be affected. A too-tight belt can damage the pump or motor.

STEMMING AN OVERFLOW FROM THE STANDPIPE

PROBLEM: *Water draining out of your washing machine overflows the standpipe.*

To remedy this problem, do the following:

1.   Remove the drain hose from the standpipe.
2.   Aim a garden hose (with its nozzle removed) down the standpipe and turn on the water at a slow flow. If the water backs up and overflows the standpipe, the plumbing system is clogged. If you can't relieve the blockage yourself, call in a plumber.
3.   If the water from the garden hose does not overflow the standpipe, the problem may be the result of an oversize drain hose or undersize standpipe. For drainage to take place, air has to flow freely between the hose and the sides of the standpipe. If the drain hose is too wide, or the standpipe is too narrow, the escape of air is restricted, and water will back up. Replacing the hose with one having a smaller diameter than the standpipe should resolve the problem.

REMOVING A BURR IN THE BASKET

PROBLEM: *Clothes come out of a washing machine showing rips and tears.*

Ripped or torn clothes indicate that you're either using too much bleach, which weakens fabrics over time, or a burr or "catch" has developed in the basket and is snagging clothes. To repair a burr:

1.   Wrap a piece of nylon stocking around your hand and wipe it over every inch of the basket. The stocking will snag on the burr, if there is one.
2.   Rub the burr gently with a piece of fine-grit sandpaper. Then test the spot with the stocking to see if it is smooth.

REPAIRING A RUSTED BASKET

PROBLEM: *Spots of rust appear on the basket of your washing machine.*

Signs of rust mean the basket needs to be refinished before its structure is seriously weakened. Ask an appliance parts dealer to recommend a nontoxic epoxy compound and a waterproof porcelain enamel paint that can withstand a water temperature of 200 degrees.

These products come with complete instructions that must be carefully followed if the repair is to be a success. Be sure to remove all rust with fine-grit sandpaper before applying the epoxy and paint.

REPLACING A BASKET

PROBLEM: *Leaks have developed in the basket of your washing machine.*

To replace a damaged basket (or agitator), you first have to take out the agitator. To proceed, do the following:

1.   Unscrew the agitator cap by turning it counterclockwise. Large adjustable pliers may be needed to remove the cap. If the agitator is held to the shaft with a nut, remove the nut.
2.   Try to lift off the agitator. It should come straight up, held in place on the shaft by vertical splints. If it won't budge, screw the agitator cap back on, but not all the way down. Leave ½ inch of space between the base of the cap and the top of the agitator. Fill the basket with hot water and let the agitator oscillate back and forth for a few minutes. Drain the water, turn off the machine, remove the cap,

and try to lift the agitator. *Caution:* Wear heavy rubber gloves to keep water from scalding your hands.

3. If the agitator still won't loosen, let it sit in the hot water for 30 minutes. Then turn on the machine to the drain cycle. After the water drains out, grasp the agitator along its bottom edge and rock it from side to side as you try to lift it off the agitator shaft.

4. If the agitator is really stuck, squirt penetrating oil around the crown of the agitator. Allow 30 minutes for the oil to work down the shaft. Then tap the agitator with a rubber or wooden mallet. Get your fingers around the bottom lip of the agitator and lift it off the shaft.

5. Finally, if you find it impossible to remove the agitator, you will have to resort to a hammer and chisel. With the chisel held in position so that it will make vertical cuts in the agitator, strike the crown of the chisel with a hammer. Eventually the agitator should break open. Now, in addition to the basket, you will need a new agitator.

6. Once the agitator has been removed, release the screws holding the basket. Lift out the basket.

7. Use a stiff bristle brush and hot water to clean deposits from the agitator shaft.

8. Apply a thin layer of silicone lubricant to the shaft. Install a new basket, and then the agitator.

REPAIR · 9

REPLACING DAMAGED WATER-INTAKE HOSES

PROBLEM: *The cold- or hot-water-intake hose of your washing machine begins to bulge or leak.*

Replace defective hoses as quickly as possible, or you will have a flood if one should break unexpectedly. *Note:* If one hose starts to leak, replace them both, since you can be sure that the other hose will soon fail. Here's how to do it:

1. Shut off the water.
2. Unscrew the hose from the water faucet by unscrewing the ferrule (the female cuff in the hose).

3. Unscrew the other end of the hose from the water-intake valve.

4. Buy replacement hoses that are built to withstand the pressure and temperature of water flowing into a washing machine.

5. Install the new hoses, but do not overtighten them.

REPAIR · 10

TESTING AND REPLACING THE WATER-INTAKE VALVE

PROBLEM: *Water either trickles into the washing machine basket or does not flow in at all.*

Check hoses and filters. If hoses are not kinked and filters aren't clogged, you will probably have to replace the water-intake valve. Here's how to do it:

1. Pull the power cord from the wall outlet. Turn off the water.

2. After making certain the hoses are not kinked, unscrew them and look for the filters in the hoses or in the ferrules of the water-intake valve. Clean the filters. Reattach hoses and test the unit. If this procedure hasn't resolved the problem, test the water-intake valve by doing the following:

a. Raise the top of the machine by inserting a putty knife in the crevice where the top and front panels meet and prying up. If the top is part of the cabinet, you will have to disassemble the cabinet. Using a nut driver, take out all fasteners holding the panels together.

b. A water-intake valve is electronically operated, so it will have one or two solenoids (a coil of wire commonly in the form of a long cylinder). A coil solenoid, which allows the ports in the water-intake valve to open and close, has two terminals. Before disconnecting any wires, label them and their terminals with self-adhering labels or

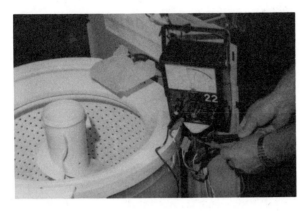

Figure 3.10 To determine whether a valve is bad, test it with an ohmmeter. Note that in order to test the valve of this machine, the cabinet had to be disassembled.

strips of masking tape so that later you know how to reattach them correctly.

c. Hold the probes of an ohmmeter to the terminals of the solenoid (Figure 3.10). If the ohmmeter shows a reading of infinity (∞), the water-intake valve is defective. Test the second solenoid this same way. If either solenoid is defective, the water-intake valve must be replaced.

3. Remove a faulty water-intake valve by releasing the clamp or bracket (if there is one) to which the valve is attached inside the washer. On the outside of the washer, undo the screws holding the valve to the panel (Figure 3.11).

Figure 3.11 Release the water-intake valve by undoing the screws that hold the valve to the inside of the washing machine's rear panel.

4. Reverse this procedure when you install a new water-intake valve.

REPAIR · 11

GETTING RID OF A SQUEAL

PROBLEM: Your washing machine emits a squeal when it enters the spin cycle.

This problem is often caused by a glazed (shiny) drive belt used in a machine that has a belt to drive the water pump.

Here's how to get rid of a squeal:

1. Buy a tube of drive-belt lubricant at a hardware or appliance parts store, or an automotive parts supply store.

2. Unplug the power cord from the wall outlet and move the washing machine away from the wall. Take off the rear panel.

3. Spread a thin layer of the lubricant on the underside of the belt. Don't use too much.

4. Restore electricity. Turn the control dial to Spin, and turn on the machine. Has the squeal disappeared or lessened in intensity? If it has, the problem was caused by the glazed belt. If the noise recurs later, you may have to replace the belt.

5. If the intensity of the noise is the same as before, check the adjustment of the drive belt. First, turn off electricity. Press down on the belt with your thumb at a spot approximately midway between the water pump and motor pulleys. The belt should deflect no less than ¼ inch and no more than ½ inch. If the belt is not adjusted properly, loosen the motor and shift it until belt deflection is ¼ inch. Tighten the motor and restore electricity. Turn on the machine. If the noise is still present, the support bracket for the motor may need cleaning.

6. Turn off electricity. Using a wire brush, clean the support bracket on which the motor rests. Then, spread a thin coat of multipurpose grease on the bracket. This treatment should eliminate the noise.

R E P A I R · 12

ADJUSTING A BASKET THAT BANGS AGAINST THE CHASSIS

PROBLEM: The machine makes knocking noises as it washes.

Obviously the basket in your washing machine is striking some other part of the machine as it rotates. Here are several reasons that a basket will hit the chassis, and what you can do about each one:

The machine is poorly loaded. Make sure clothes are distributed evenly around the agitator when you load the machine.

The washing machine is not level. To ensure that the washer is positioned correctly, place a carpenter's level along the side-to-side axis and then front to back on the top of the machine. If the unit isn't level, check to see if the washer is resting on an uneven patch of floor. If so, shift the washer around until it is level, or adjust the legs to make it level. If the machine has movable legs, the front washer legs are threaded into the machine frame. Turn them out or in to lengthen or shorten the legs, until the carpenter's level shows that the machine is sitting evenly on the floor.

The snubber is worn out. The snubber prevents the basket from oscillating from side to side and hitting the chassis. If the snubber wears out, it loses its ability to control the movement of the basket. (Not every washing machine has a snubber.) To replace a snubber, do the following:

1. Open the top of the washing machine. Find the snubber, which is located in one of the rear corners. It's a hard, rubberized, round object that is bolted to the top of the basket. A large metal spring, attached on one end to the chassis of the washer, fits over the snubber and restricts the movement of the basket.
2. Push the spring off the snubber, and unscrew it. Buy a new snubber and snubber spring that is made for your particular brand of washing machine.
3. Install the new parts by using a socket wrench or nut driver to take off the fastener

holding one end of the spring to the chassis. If your machine is like most, the other end of the spring is hooked into a hole in the chassis. Unhook it. Attach the new spring the same way as the old one and install the new snubber. Press the spring onto the snubber, close the lid, and restore power.

R E P A I R · 13

OVERCOMING SLUGGISH AGITATION

PROBLEM: Your washing machine slows down during the wash cycle.

The most likely cause of sluggish action in a washing machine is that the area where the machine sits is too cold. A washing machine that's kept in an unheated basement, for example, is often sluggish, because the lubricant in the transmission thickens up in cold weather. To confirm this diagnosis, do the following:

1. Turn the temperature-control dial to Hot. Turn on the machine. Allow the basket to fill with hot water.
2. Turn off the machine.
3. Wait 15 minutes to give the heat from the water time to act upon the lubricant.
4. Do a load of wash. If the machine runs normally, you have pinpointed the problem. If having to do all these steps every time you do a wash will turn your automatic washer into a semiautomatic, find some way to provide a little heat to the laundry area. Or move the unit to a warmer location.

R E P A I R · 14

STRAIGHTENING A DENTED LID

PROBLEM: Something has dropped on the lid of your top-loading washing machine and put a dent in it.

To fix a dent, do the following:

1. Raise the lid to an angle of about 45 degrees.

2. With your left hand, tightly grasp the left rear corner of the lid. With your right hand, grasp the right front corner.

3. Pull the lid forward and down with your right hand as you push up with your left hand. The dented spot should pop back into place.

4. If the above procedure doesn't work, rap the dent gently from the underside of the lid with your fist, or tap it with a rubber mallet.

REPAIR · 15

GETTING RID OF BLACK STAINS IN THE BASKET

PROBLEM: The basket of your washing machine is coated with black stains.

A black coating on the surface of a washing machine basket indicates that your water is high in manganese. This condition affects well water in particular, since water utility companies usually filter objectionably high levels of minerals at the pumping station. Although manganese is not harmful, the resulting black residue can stain your clothes.

If your water comes from a well, have it tested. If manganese levels are high, install a filtering system to reduce the amount of the mineral in the water. In the meantime, if washing the surface of the basket with soap and water doesn't remove the stains, try washing it with straight vinegar.

If vinegar doesn't do the job, buy a container of acetic acid from a hardware or home supply store. Mix one part of the chemical with four parts of water. If the residue is particularly heavy, mix two parts of the acid with two parts of water.

Put on rubber gloves and goggles and wash the basket with the solution.

Whichever of the cleaning steps you try, use only rags to apply the cleaning solution. Do *not* use an abrasive material, such as steel wool, which could damage the porcelain. When stains are gone, toss two tablespoons of baking soda into the appliance and run it, empty, through a complete cycle.

4

CLOTHES DRYERS

Whirlpool
large capacity
4 Cycle - 3 Temp
HEAVY DUTY
Permanent Press
Cool Down Care

Almost all of the repairs in this chapter are within the capabilities of most homeowners, even the seemingly complex one of replacing the defective motor of an electric dryer. That's because a clothes dryer, especially one that runs on electricity, is a simple machine.

Safety Precautions

There are, of course, precautions to follow in handling an electric or gas clothes dryer:

• *Electric dryer.* Disconnect the dryer from the home's electrical system before you begin to work. First unplug the dryer power cord from the wall outlet. If the outlet isn't accessible or the dryer is wired directly into the electrical system, switch off the circuit breaker or remove the fuse that serves the dryer in the main electrical circuit breaker or fuse panel.

• *Gas dryer.* Find and turn off the shut-off valve on the gas pipe leading to your gas dryer before attempting any repairs. Unlike the water shut-offs to your washer, which are small rotating wheels or knobs, the gas shut-off valve has a bar that in operation is in line with the gas pipe. To turn the gas off, rotate the bar 90 degrees only, so that it lies perpendicular to the gas pipe. If you move the dryer from its position, do not put stress on the gas line, which might cause it to rupture.

• CLOTHES DRYER REPAIRS •

Following is a list of the repairs presented in this chapter, and the tools and materials needed to make them:

REPAIR	TOOLS AND MATERIALS
1. Replacing a drive belt	Screwdriver, nut driver, putty knife, block of 2 × 4 lumber
2. Repairing the vent system	Screwdriver, panty hose, duct tape, broom or mop
3. Testing the thermostats in an electric dryer	Screwdriver, nut driver, duct tape, putty knife, masking tape or self-adhering labels, ohmmeter, electric skillet
4. Fixing an electric dryer that won't shut off	Liquid dishwashing detergent
5. Replacing a door seal	Silicone spray, screwdriver, putty knife
6. Replacing the drum support rollers	Putty knife, screwdriver
7. Replacing a stuck timer	Nut driver, screwdriver
8. Installing a new motor in an electric dryer	Screwdriver, putty knife, nut driver, masking tape or self-adhering labels, wrenches

REPAIR · 1

REPLACING A DRIVE BELT

PROBLEM: *The drum doesn't rotate when the dryer motor is running.*

This problem indicates that the drive belt has snapped. A dryer usually has one or two belts. To find out how many are in your dryer, raise the top of the dryer and shine a flashlight along the sides of the drum. If you spot a split belt, it confirms that you will have to replace a single belt. If you don't see a belt at all, your dryer is the type that has two belts located in the rear of the dryer, behind the motor and drum.

To install a single belt, follow these steps:

1. Disconnect the dryer from its electrical supply. If you are working on a gas dryer, close the shut-off valve on the gas-feed pipe behind the dryer.

2. If the lint screen is inserted in the top of the dryer, take out the screws inside the lint screen housing (Figure 4.1). Remove the screen.

3. Slip a putty knife under the top of the dryer, about two inches from a corner. To release the clip, push in on the putty knife as you lift up on the corner (Figure 4.2). Do the same at the other corner to release the other clip. Lift the top and lean it back against the wall. Do you see the single belt (Figure 4.3)? If it's lying alongside the drum, proceed to step 4. If you don't see a belt, close the top and proceed to step 5.

4. Use a nut driver or screwdriver to remove the screws holding the front panel of the dryer.

Figure 4.1 *If the lint screen is in the top of the dryer, remove the screws in the lint-screen housing. Leave the screen in place until you've removed the housing, just in case you lose your grip on a screw. The screen will keep the screw from falling into the dryer.*

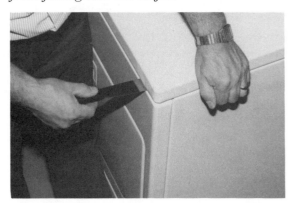

Figure 4.2 *Use a putty knife to release the top of the dryer.*

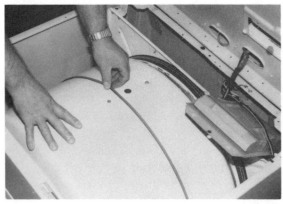

Figure 4.3 *In most clothes dryers, the drum is driven by a single belt. Look down alongside the drum to see if the snapped belt is lying there.*

If there is a toeplate, remove that also. If the toeplate is held by a clip instead of screws, use a putty knife to spring it free. Place a block of 2 × 4 lumber under the drum to keep it level.

Retrieve the broken belt. Place a new belt of the right size for your dryer around the drum. The old belt probably left a mark on the drum, so if you place the new belt within the boundary of this mark, you will place it in the right spot. At the motor, form the end of the belt into a loop. Slide the belt under the idler pulley and around the motor pulley (Figure 4.4).

5.   If the drum is driven by two belts, remove the rear panel. You will notice that one of the belts probably extends from the motor pulley to an idler pulley. The other belt extends from the idler pulley to the drum pulley. Release the idler pulley tension spring, and remove the old belts. Attach new belts and reconnect the tension spring. (*Note:* It is advisable to replace both belts even if only one has snapped. The other belt has probably sustained enough wear that it too will soon give way.)

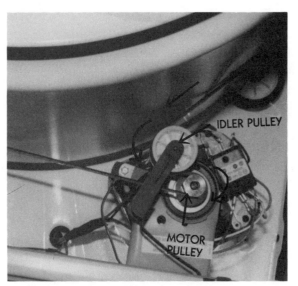

Figure 4.4 *The belt is wrapped around the idler and motor pulleys.*

R E P A I R · 2

REPAIRING THE VENT SYSTEM

PROBLEM: The lint screen is clean, but clothes remain damp after going through the drying cycle.

Damp clothes usually indicate that the vent system of the dryer is clogged with lint (Figure 4.5). Follow these steps to confirm the problem and to fix it:

Figure 4.5 The main reason that clothes take longer to dry is a lint-clogged filter. Clean this screen before or after each cycle.

1.   Move the dryer away from the wall so you can reach the exhaust outlet at the back of the appliance.
2.   Disconnect the duct from the exhaust outlet and place a sealed fine-mesh "bag" around the outlet (a discarded pair of panty hose is ideal). Dry a load of clothes. If clothes still don't dry, the cause of the problem is *not* the vent system, but an internal problem with a thermostat or a gas burner component (see Repair 3, below). Dry clothes, however, confirm a malfunctioning vent system. To clear the system, continue with the following steps.
3.   Remove the duct. If the duct consists of a series of attached aluminum sections with duct tape wrapped around the joints as a seal, pull off the duct tape and take the sections apart. If the duct is a one-piece accordion type, simply disconnect it at both ends.
4.   Remove and discard the fine-mesh bag. Clean any lint out of the dryer exhaust outlet. Then, using the end of a broom or a mop

handle, push a cloth down the length of the one-piece duct or down each duct section to dislodge any remaining lint.
5.   Reconnect the duct. Wrap duct tape around the joints of a multisectional system, if you have that type of duct.
6.   Turn on the dryer and go outside to where the hood covers the exhaust damper. Place your hand under the hood. Do you feel a surge of warm air? If you don't, slide the hood off the damper. Clean out any lint and dirt from the flapper section, which has to open freely to allow the hot, moist air to escape when the dryer is in operation.
7.   If all of the above steps don't help, you may have a defective thermostat (see Repair 3, below).

H E L P F U L H I N T
Preventing Fire

Some manufacturers caution that the high temperature produced in a clothes dryer sometimes can cause fabrics soiled with vegetable oil to ignite. To be on the safe side, do not put newly washed items that were soiled with vegetable oil into your dryer. Hang them up to dry instead.

R E P A I R · 3

TESTING THE THERMOSTATS IN AN ELECTRIC DRYER

PROBLEM: Clothes are damp at the completion of the drying cycle.

If the reason for damp clothes is not a clogged vent system (see Repair 2, above), the cause of the problem is in the dryer itself, probably with a thermostat. To test a thermostat, do the following:

1.   Disconnect the dryer from its electrical supply. The dryer should be cold, so don't

perform this test for at least one hour after the dryer has been running.

2. If your model has a lint screen inserted in the top of the dryer, remove the screws from the housing.

3. Lift the top of the dryer by inserting a putty knife in the crevice between the top and front panel, about two inches from a corner. To release the clip, push in on the putty knife as you lift up. Do the same at the other corner. Raise the top and lean it back against the wall.

4. Using a nut driver or screwdriver, remove the screws holding the front panel (Figures 4.6 and 4.7). If there is a toeplate, remove that too. If the toeplate is held by a clip instead of screws, use a putty knife to spring it free.

Figure 4.6 Raise the top of the dryer and unscrew the front panel.

Figure 4.7 If the front panel doesn't come free, look for hidden bolts. Remove the toeplate and look under the panel.

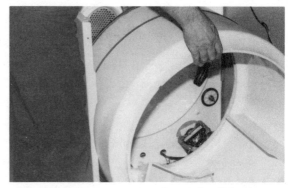

Figure 4.8 Remove the drum by lifting it up and out.

5. Remove the drum (Figure 4.8). Release the drive belt if it extends around the drum. If your dryer uses two belts, remove the rear panel and take off both belts, then remove the drum. You will now be able to find the thermostats. One, two, or three thermostats may be contained in your unit; they are found near the blower housing.

6. Disconnect the wires from one of the thermostats. Using self-adhering labels or strips of masking tape, label each wire and the terminal to which it attaches. Hold the probes of an ohmmeter to the terminals. Note the position of the ohmmeter needle (Figure 4.9). If the thermostat is working properly, the needle will probably show zero resistance. If a reading other than zero is recorded, remove the ther-

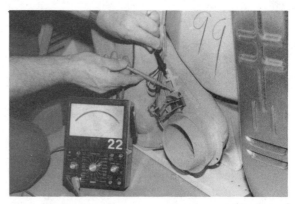

Figure 4.9 The thermostats are usually found on the blower housing. Disconnect the wires and test each thermostat with an ohmmeter.

mostat by unscrewing it from the dryer and have it tested by an appliance parts dealer. In some dryers thermostats work in a manner opposite of the norm. The dealer will know if yours is one of them.

HELPFUL HINT

How to Vent a Gas or Electric Dryer in an Apartment

A clothes dryer always must be vented. If you live in an apartment building or complex that prohibits venting to the outdoors, use an indoor vent system to trap the lint.

You can buy an indoor vent from an appliance parts store. Vent systems come in different styles, but one of the easiest to install utilizes a container that you fill with water and attach to the exhaust outlet at the rear of the dryer. However, this lint trap must be cleaned after drying each load. You do this by detaching the container from the exhaust outlet, pouring the lint-laden water into the sink or toilet, refilling the container with water, and reattaching it to the exhaust outlet.

Caution: Never run a dryer that doesn't have a properly designed venting system. Lint is highly flammable and can create a fire hazard if it vents into the air.

REPAIR · 4

FIXING AN ELECTRIC DRYER THAT WON'T SHUT OFF

PROBLEM: Your electric dryer won't stop running.

An electronically controlled clothes dryer uses sensors embedded in the drum to monitor the moisture in clothes and to determine when the clothes are dry. The sensors transmit a signal to the electronic control unit (or processor),

which then orders the dryer motor to shut itself off.

Fabric softeners sprayed on clothes, or anti-static-electricity strips tossed in the dryer with clothes, can coat the sensors. This coating impedes their ability to monitor moisture, resulting in a dryer that keeps running even after the clothes are dry. (Another reason for excessive drying time, of course, is a clogged lint screen. Make sure your lint screen is clean each time you use the dryer.)

Before calling a technician to service the unit, do the following:

1. Wash the lint screen in hot water until water flows freely through the mesh.
2. Mix dishwashing liquid detergent, or washing machine detergent, with hot water—the hotter the better. (Wear rubber gloves to keep from burning your hands.)
3. Dip a swatch of terry cloth in the solution and wash the baffles (the raised projections) on the drum, which usually hold the sensors. *Important: Do not clean baffles with any abrasive material. This may damage the sensors.*
4. Dry a load of clothes to determine whether this treatment has had an effect. If not, the reason for the extended drying period is probably a defective electronic component, and you will have to call in a service technician.

REPAIR · 5

REPLACING A DOOR SEAL

PROBLEM: The dryer takes an excessive amount of time to dry clothes.

Many clothes dryers have a seal around the door opening to keep the heat in. This seal can crack, causing an increase in drying time.

To make the repair, do the following:

1. Loosen the screws around the door opening. Pull off the defective seal.
2. Get a new seal of the same design at an appliance parts store. (You will need the make and model number of the dryer.)
3. Spray the new seal with silicone or dip it in soapy water to make it more pliable.

4.   Insert the seal into the groove at the top of the door opening. Then press it into place all around the opening, using a putty knife, if necessary, or a screwdriver with a dull, worn-out tip. Don't press down too hard.

5.   Tighten loosened screws.

REPAIR · 6

REPLACING THE DRUM SUPPORT ROLLERS

PROBLEM: The dryer emits a loud scraping or squeaking noise as the drum revolves.

Deterioration of the rubber rollers on which the drum rides is usually the reason for a scraping or squeaking noise in the dryer. To replace rollers, do the following:

1.   Disconnect the dryer from its electrical supply. If you are working on a gas dryer, close the shut-off valve on the gas-delivery pipe.

2.   If the dryer has a single-belt arrangement, use a putty knife to raise the top (see step 3, page 49) and remove the belt from around the drum. If the dryer has two belts, remove the rear panel to take them off. Lift out the drum. The rollers are found on the rear bulkhead.

3.   One of the rollers is probably held by a bracket. Remove the screw holding the bottom of the bracket to the frame (Figure 4.10).

4.   The rollers are probably held to their

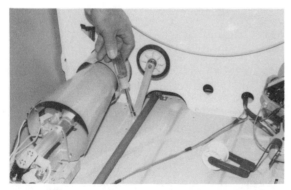

Figure 4.10 *Unscrew the bracket and release the roller.*

Figure 4.11 Remove each roller by releasing the clip that holds it on the shaft.

shafts by C-clips. Pry the clips off the shafts with a screwdriver. Release the rollers (Figure 4.11).

5.   Examine the rubber on the rollers to determine whether there are flat or hard spots that indicate deterioration. If there are no obvious signs of damage, it is difficult to determine whether the rollers are the reason for the noise. But as long as you have come this far, you might as well replace them.

6.   Install new rollers by attaching them to their shafts and pressing new C-clips onto the shafts with a screwdriver.

7.   Position the drum so it is supported by both rollers, reinstall the belt(s), and reassemble the rest of the unit.

REPAIR · 7

REPLACING A STUCK TIMER

PROBLEM: The dryer's timer sticks and doesn't advance.

A stuck timer has to be replaced. Follow these steps:

1.   Disconnect the dryer from its electrical supply.

2.   Pull the knobs off the console panel and open the console (Figure 4.12).

3.   Buy a new timer for your particular machine from an appliance parts store. Hold it alongside the old timer so that the terminals and distinguishing marks of one line up with

those of the other. Then remove the screws that hold the bad timer in place. Remove the timer (Figures 4.13 and 4.14). Transfer one wire at a time from the old timer to the corresponding terminal of the new timer.

4. Discard the old timer, and screw the new timer into place.

Figure 4.12 To replace a faulty timer, disconnect electricity and open the console.

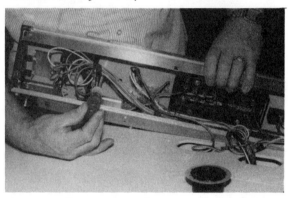

Figure 4.13 Unscrew the timer from the console.

Figure 4.14 Match the new timer to the faulty timer. Transfer one wire at a time from the old timer to the corresponding terminal of the new timer.

H E L P F U L   H I N T

If Your Gas Dryer Fails to Dry

The three parts of a gas clothes dryer that become suspect when clothes remain soaking wet after the dryer has completed its cycle are the thermocouple, the gas-valve solenoid, and the gas valve. All these parts work together to ignite the main burner and to ensure that the unit operates in a safe manner.

If one of these parts is malfunctioning, you will have to call a service technician. If the technician traces the trouble to the gas-valve solenoid or thermocouple, the part will have to be replaced. On the other hand, a faulty gas valve can usually be disassembled, cleaned, and restored to service. In any case, you should *not* try to test or repair gas burner components yourself.

Before spending your money on a service call, however, make sure that the vent system is clean and all thermostats are working properly.

R E P A I R · 8

INSTALLING A NEW MOTOR IN AN ELECTRIC DRYER

PROBLEM: *The motor of your electric clothes dryer burns out.*

Having a technician install a new motor could cost you almost as much as a new dryer. If you want to try replacing the motor yourself, here's how to proceed:

1. Disconnect the dryer from its electrical supply.

2. If the lint screen is positioned in a housing in the top of your dryer, undo the screws in the housing.

3. Slip a putty knife under the top of the dryer about two inches from a corner. To release the clip, push in on the putty knife as you lift up on the corner. Do the same at the other corner. Lift the top and lean it back against the wall.

4. The drums of most electric dryers are driven by a single belt that stretches around the drum. If this top view shows a belt, lift the drum out of the cabinet and remove the belt. You will now be able to reach the motor by using a nut driver or screwdriver to remove the screws holding the front panel. Take off the front panel. If there is a toeplate, remove that too.

5. If you see no belt around the drum, the dryer uses two belts. Take off the rear panel to release the belt from the motor. You will probably be able to remove the motor without taking out the drum.

6. Using self-adhering labels or strips of masking tape, label the wires so you can tell which one connects with each terminal of the motor. Disconnect the wires from the motor.

7. Unbolt the motor. To do this, hold the hub of the blower wheel on the back end of the motor with one wrench while using a second wrench to turn the motor shaft clockwise.

When the motor and blower wheel have been separated, lift the motor out of the dryer. If the motor doesn't come free, check around the bottom of the motor for clamps that may be holding it to the floor of the cabinet. Unscrew the clamps.

8. Before buying a new motor, have the old motor tested just to be sure it is defective. An attendant at an appliance parts store can do this for you.

9. Install the new motor and connect the wires to the correct terminals of the motor. Make sure the dryer is properly grounded by attaching the ground wire (a green or bare wire) to the ground terminal. The ground terminal is usually identified by the letters GRD or GRN or by the color green.

10. Install the drum so it rests squarely on the two rubber rollers at the rear of the cabinet.

11. When installing the belt of a dryer that uses a single belt, place the belt within the boundary of the mark it has left on the drum. Then, at the motor, form a loop in the belt, slide the belt under the idler pulley, and place it around the motor pulley.

12. Reinstall panels, close the top, and restore electricity.

5

DISHWASHERS

None of the repair jobs described in this chapter require the services of a professional technician—not even the repair that involves disassembling the pump.

Obviously, some of the repairs are more involved than others. In most instances, the difference between an easy repair and a more complex one depends on the extent of the disassembly needed. But many components are accessible from inside the dishwasher and found by simply opening the door of the unit. Those components located beneath the unit are accessible by removing a bottom access plate or by taking off the front panel. Seldom will you have to pull the dishwasher out from under the counter to make the repair.

Safety Precautions

To prevent injury, take the following steps before starting a repair to your dishwasher:

• *Disconnect the dishwasher from the electrical supply.* Turn off the electricity to the dishwasher by turning off the appropriate circuit breaker or removing the appropriate fuse in the home's main electrical service panel. To make certain that the electricity has been turned off, latch the door and turn on the dishwasher. If the dishwasher responds, you have not deactivated the correct circuit breaker or fuse. Do not make the repair until you have done this.

• *Turn off the water to the dishwasher.* If there isn't a shut-off valve on the water line extending to the appliance (as there should be), close the main water shut-off valve at the water meter—if water is supplied by a water utility company—or turn off the pump if you have a private water well.

- *Do not work on the dishwasher immediately*

after the unit has been in operation. Both water and the heat-drying element get very hot, and touching certain parts can cause you a severe burn.

• DISHWASHER REPAIRS •

Following is a list of the repairs presented in this chapter, and the tools and materials needed to make them:

REPAIRS	TOOLS AND MATERIALS
1. Testing for a clogged or damaged water-intake valve.	Indelible grease pencil or crayon
2. Replacing the water-intake filter and water-intake valve	Screwdriver, nut driver, adjustable pliers, masking tape or self-adhering labels
3. Replacing the float (overfill) switch	Screwdriver, nut driver, masking tape or self-adhering labels, ohmmeter
4. Troubleshooting a hose breakdown	Screwdriver, nut driver, adjustable wrench, adjustable pliers
5. Repairing a spray arm	Adjustable wrench, screwdriver
6. Treating rust spots	Fine-grit sandpaper, nontoxic epoxy repair compound, waterproof porcelain enamel paint
7. Repairing the prongs of a dishwasher rack	Prong-tip repair kit
8. Fixing a detergent dispenser that doesn't open	Vinegar, screwdriver, nut driver, masking tape or self-adhering labels
9. Replacing a heater element	Screwdriver, nut driver, masking tape or self-adhering labels, ohmmeter, adjustable wrench
10. Repairing a leaky pump	Pump resealing kit, nut driver, screwdriver, adjustable wrench
11. Repairing a leak from the air-gap system	Pail, adjustable wrench, screwdriver, nut driver, adjustable pliers
12. Replacing hoses on a portable dishwasher	Screwdriver, nut driver, adjustable pliers, nippers, utility knife
13. Replacing casters on a portable dishwasher	Pliers, electric drill, caster-repair kit, hammer, adjustable wrench

REPAIR · 1

TESTING FOR A CLOGGED OR DAMAGED WATER-INTAKE VALVE

PROBLEM: Your dishes come out of your dishwasher still soiled or dirty.

If your dishwasher no longer gets dishes spotlessly clean, make the following checks:

Proper loading. Scrupulously follow the loading procedure given in the owner's manual and run a test cycle.

Old detergent. Are you using old or adulterated dishwasher detergent? Although you may have purchased it recently, detergent that is kept under the kitchen sink is subject to contamination by moisture. Try a newly purchased product to determine if it makes a difference.

Low water temperature. Water temperature should be no less than that recommended by the manufacturer in the owner's manual. If the dishwasher has performed adequately until now, it's unlikely that this is the reason for the trouble unless someone has tampered with the temperature-control dial of your gas or oil water heater. Or perhaps the thermostat or heating element of the electric water heater isn't working properly.

Clogged filter. The dishwasher may not be taking in enough water because of a clogged water-intake filter or because the water-intake valve is damaged. To determine whether the water-intake valve is involved, do the following:

1. Remove the bottom rack. Pour 9 quarts of water into the dishwasher.
2. Using an indelible grease pencil or crayon, make a reference mark at the water line on a side or back wall of the tub.
3. Latch the door and turn the control dial to Drain. Turn on the dishwasher so the water is pumped out.
4. When the draining cycle is over, set the control dial to Fill. Turn on the dishwasher so it will take in water.
5. When you hear the water-intake valve click off just before the dishwasher is to begin

the washing cycle, unlatch and partially open the door. Look to see where the water has settled. If it isn't on or above the reference mark, the reason for dishes not being clean is an inadequate amount of water. You will have to replace the water-intake filter and/or the water-intake valve (see the following repair).

REPAIR · 2

REPLACING THE WATER-INTAKE FILTER AND THE WATER-INTAKE VALVE

PROBLEM: Your dishwasher doesn't take in a full supply of water.

Insufficient water usually means that the water-intake filter is clogged and has to be cleaned. A dishwasher that doesn't take in any water at all suggests a water-intake valve that has to be replaced. Here's how to do both jobs:

1. Turn off the circuit breaker or remove the fuse serving the dishwasher. Turn on the dishwasher to make certain that current has been shut down; otherwise do not proceed.
2. Turn off the water to the dishwasher. There should be a valve on the hot water line under your sink.
3. Unscrew the lower access panel (Figure 5.1). Find the water-intake valve located at the end of the water-intake hose (Figure 5.2).
4. Loosen the clamp holding the water-intake hose to the water-intake valve by

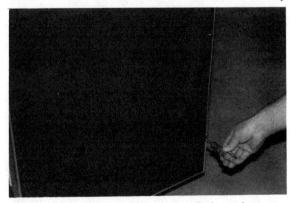

Figure 5.1 Most repairs to a dishwasher are done inside or under the unit. To get under the unit, remove the lower access panel.

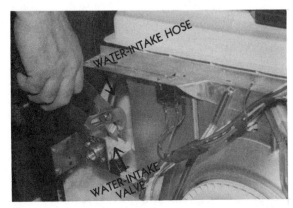

Figure 5.2 To illustrate how to test and replace the water-intake valve and screen, the unit has been turned on its back.

squeezing it and sliding it up on the hose; then pull off the hose (Figure 5.3).

5.   Find the filter, which will be in the valve. You will probably have to remove the valve to reach the filter and clean it (Figure 5.4). If so, be sure to label the wires connected to the

Figure 5.3 Squeeze the intake hose clamp and slide it up on the hose. Then take the hose off the water-intake valve.

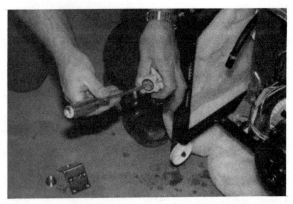

Figure 5.4 To reach the filter inside this water-intake valve, it was necessary to take the valve off the dishwasher, remove the bracket from the valve, and pry the filter out of the valve.

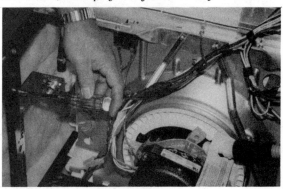

Figure 5.5 When installing a water-intake valve, make sure wires are connected correctly, the water-intake hose is attached properly and securely, and the valve is screwed tightly into place.

valve, so that you can tell which wire connects to each terminal. You will also have to detach another hose from the valve—the one that carries from the valve into the dishwasher.

6.   Brush and flush deposits away from the filter. Then reconnect the wires, reinstall the filter, reconnect the hoses, and restore power and water (Figure 5.5).

7.   Test the performance of the dishwasher. If the flow of water is still sluggish (or there is no flow to begin with), disassemble the unit again. Make sure the wires connected to the terminals of the water-intake valve are properly labeled, then pull the wires off the terminals, and test the valve with an ohmmeter (Figure 5.6). If the valve fails the test, pur-

Figure 5.6 *Test the water-intake valve with an ohmmeter. If the ohmmeter displays infinity (∞), the water-intake valve is defective.*

chase a new valve and install it. Be sure to connect wires and hoses correctly.

If the water-intake valve passes the ohmmeter test, it may still be defective, because the ohmmeter won't record a mechanical malfunction but only an electrical one. Before replacing the valve, however, test the float switch (see the following repair). A defective switch may be the reason that the water flow into the dishwasher is so poor.

R E P A I R · 3

REPLACING THE FLOAT (OVERFILL) SWITCH

PROBLEM: Water overflows the dishwasher, or no water at all comes into the dishwasher.

The purpose of the float or overfill switch is to prevent water from overfilling the dishwasher and flooding the kitchen. If a malfunction keeps the dishwasher from draining, if the timer sticks in the Fill position, or if the float switch fails to open and shut off current to the water-intake valve, water can overflow the dishwasher. Conversely, a float switch that gets stuck in the open position (impeding current to the valve) will prevent the dishwasher from filling with water at all.

Here is how to check the float switch:

1.   Open the door of the dishwasher and note

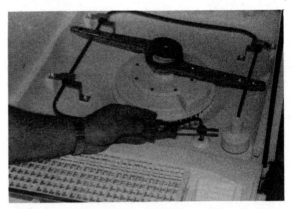

Figure 5.7 *The float is in one of the front corners of the dishwasher, and the float switch lies right beneath the float.*

the location of the float. The float is the plastic dome-shaped component standing in one of the two front corners (Figure 5.7). The switch is under the dishwasher, directly beneath the float.

2.   Test the float first. To determine whether the float is sticking, try moving it up and down by hand. If the float seems to stick, pull it off its stem. Clean the stem and the float. Then run the dishwasher through a cycle to determine whether the water intake problem has been resolved.

3.   If not, turn off the circuit breaker or remove the fuse serving the dishwasher. Try to turn on the dishwasher. Do not proceed unless the electricity has been disconnected.

4.   Remove the access panel and take off the float switch (Figure 5.8). Notice how the

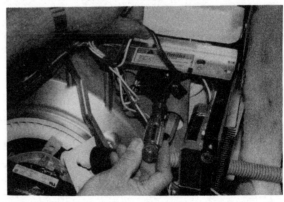

Figure 5.8 *To reach the float switch, remove the access panel. Make sure the appliance is disconnected from its electrical supply before unscrewing the switch from the frame of the dishwasher.*

switch is assembled, especially the leaf-type breaker point that controls the electrical signal to the water-intake valve. Test the movement of this part (Figure 5.9).

5.   Finally, test the switch with an ohmmeter by holding the probes of the ohmmeter to the wire terminals. (You don't have to disconnect the wires.) As the breaker point is lifted, the ohmmeter should register infinity (∞), indicating an open circuit (Figure 5.10). When you hold the breaker point closed, the ohmmeter should display a reading of zero or slightly above zero. Any other reading indicates a bad float switch.

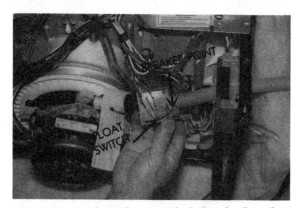

Figure 5.9 *When the switch fails, the breaker point (arrow) could be causing the trouble. If the breaker point gets stuck in the open position, the dishwasher won't fill. If it sticks in the closed position, water will overflow the dishwasher. If the point doesn't move freely, replace the switch.*

Figure 5.10 *When the point is closed, the ohmmeter needle should read zero or slightly above. When the point is open, as here, the ohmmeter needle should give a reading of infinity (∞).*

6.   If you have to replace the float switch, label each wire and the terminal to which it attaches (using self-adhering labels or strips of masking tape) before disconnecting them. Take off the switch, attach the wires to a new switch, secure the switch to the dishwasher, and install the access panel. Restore electricity.

REPAIR · 4

TROUBLESHOOTING A HOSE BREAKDOWN

PROBLEM: Dishes come out of your dishwasher with black streaks on them.

Black streaks on dishes can be caused simply by aluminum utensils that rub against them in the operation of the dishwasher. That's easy to fix.

Load dishes so they don't come in contact with aluminum knives, forks, spoons, pots, and serving pieces. And don't put throwaway aluminum pans in the dishwasher. The thin aluminum will break down under heat, leaving hard-to-remove black stains on the dishes.

If aluminum utensils are not a factor, the cause of the trouble may be the result of a breakdown of the interior of the hose that goes from the water-intake valve to the inside of the dishwasher. To find out, do the following:

1.   Turn off the circuit breaker or remove the fuse serving the dishwasher. Try to turn on the dishwasher. Do not proceed until you have made sure the electricity has been disconnected.

2.   Take off the access panel at the base of the dishwasher.

3.   Find and remove the hose between the water-intake valve and the dishwasher. If this can't be done with the dishwasher in position under the counter, you will have to turn off the water, disconnect the water line to the dishwasher, and pull the dishwasher out from under the counter.

4.   Push a wad of cloth through the hose. If particles of matter come out, the hose has de-

teriorated. These particles are getting into the dishwasher and smudging the dishes.

5. Buy a new hose at an appliance parts store. Install the hose and restore the dishwasher to service.

REPAIR · 5

REPAIRING A SPRAY ARM

PROBLEM: Your dishwasher seems to go through the washing cycle normally, but the dishes are not clean.

If dishes come out from a dishwashing cycle as soiled as when they were loaded, the reason may be a swollen motor housing cover that is keeping the spray arm from revolving. Before proceeding with the repair, first check your owner's manual to make sure the dishwasher is being loaded properly. Next, make sure water intake is not the problem (see Repair 1, above). If the problem does not result from any of these factors, do the following:

1. Turn off the circuit breaker or remove the fuse serving the dishwasher. Try to turn on the dishwasher. Do not proceed until you have made sure the electricity has been disconnected.

2. Remove dishwasher racks and strainer(s).

3. If the spray arm has a cover and/or is held to the motor shaft by a nut, remove the cover and/or the nut (Figure 5.11). Then pull off the spray arm.

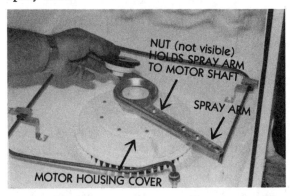

Figure 5.11 *The spray arm may release quickly from the shaft, or you may first have to remove a cover and/or nut.*

4. Pour a kettle full of very hot water over the motor housing cover that fits around the motor shaft; then rotate the motor shaft by hand a few times.

5. Reinstall the spray arm. Load the dishwasher with dirty dishes, restore electricity, turn on the dishwasher, and let it run through a complete cycle. Do the dishes come clean? If they do, you have found the cause of the trouble.

6. If the dishes still don't come clean, you will have to replace the cover. Disassemble the dishwasher as before. When you reach the cover, take off the screws holding it in place, and remove the part. Take it to an appliance parts store and get a replacement. Install the new cover and reassemble the dishwasher.

REPAIR · 6

TREATING RUST SPOTS

PROBLEM: Some of the interior surfaces of your dishwasher are chipped.

Utensils accidentally dropped on the porcelain enamel of a dishwasher can chip the porcelain. The unprotected spot may then become a target for rust. If rust is allowed to spread, it can eventually eat its way through the dishwasher and cause leaks.

To keep this from happening, you must treat rust spots early. Do the following:

1. Using fine-grit sandpaper, rub the rust lightly until the bare underlying metal is exposed.

2. Wash the area and dry it thoroughly.

3. Buy a nontoxic epoxy and a jar of waterproof porcelain enamel paint from an appliance parts dealer. Carefully following the product directions, apply the epoxy to the spots and let it cure. The epoxy puts a protective coating over the bare metal. Then paint the spot with enamel. *Caution:* Be sure the epoxy and enamel are rated to resist temperatures up to 200 degrees.

HELPFUL HINT

Removing Stains from a Dishwasher

A black coating that builds up on the sides and bottom of a dishwasher is a sign that the water may be high in mineral content, especially manganese. This is a problem that usually affects water coming from private wells, since water supplied by a municipal water company is routinely filtered to remove excessive minerals. If you have this problem, buy a container of acetic acid from a hardware or home supply store. Mix one part of the acetic acid to four parts of water.

If the black residue is heavy, increase the amount of acetic acid to two parts, and reduce the quantity of water to two parts.

Put on rubber gloves and goggles. Wash the inside of the dishwasher with the solution. Then throw two tablespoons of baking soda into the empty unit and run it through a complete cycle.

Caution: Do not clean the dishwasher with an abrasive cleanser, such as scouring powder. This will rub off the finish, whether it is porcelain or plastic.

For stubborn stains. If the stains don't come off with the acetic-acid treatment, do the following:
1.   Buy a water-softener resin cleaner from a dealer of plumbing and heating supplies.
2.   Pour 8 ounces of the cleaner directly into the empty dishwasher, and fill the detergent cup with detergent. If the dishwasher has two detergent cups, fill the one that opens during the *second* washing. (If only one cup has a lid, that is the second-wash cup. If both cups have lids, consult the owner's manual to find out which one is the second-wash cup.)
3.   Close and latch the door. Turn on the dishwasher. Run it through a complete cycle.
4.   Open the door. If some stains remain, repeat the procedure only one more time. Overusing a water-softener resin cleaner can result in damage to the plastic parts of a dishwasher.

REPAIR · 7

REPAIRING THE PRONGS OF A DISHWASHER RACK

PROBLEM: The prongs of the dishwasher rack are broken off and beginning to rust.

Often, when cups and glasses are placed over the prongs of a rack, the weight of the glass is on the tips of the prongs instead of on the floor of the rack. This continued stress can cause the tips to break off and rust.

If this advice comes too late and you see rust on prong tips, don't rush out to buy a new rack. You can purchase a prong-tip (or tine) repair kit from a dealer of appliance parts. The rubber tips in the kit fit snugly over the ends of prongs. Use the silicone sealer in the kit to secure the tips.

To put on the rubber tips, do the following:

1.   Dry the ends of the prongs.
2.   Put a *tiny* dab of silicone sealer on the end of a prong.
3.   Press a rubber tip in place.
4.   Wipe off any of the sealer that oozes from around the bottom of the rubber tip. Do this *before* the sealer hardens.

Caution: Do not use the dishwasher for 12 hours after making the repair. This time is needed for the sealer to cure properly.

When the weather is cold, dishwasher detergent powder often cakes and adheres to the detergent dispenser. The cause may not lie with the detergent or the dishwasher, but with the home's hot water system. If your main hot water pipe has a very long run in an uninsulated, unheated basement, the temperature of the water may drop too much before it reaches the dishwasher.

To check, turn on the hot water faucet at the sink next to the dishwasher. Let the water run until it gets as hot as possible. Fill a glass with the hot water. Place a meat or photographic thermometer into the filled glass and place the glass back under the tap. Read the temperature while the hot water is running into the glass.

Caution: Wear heavy rubber gloves to prevent burning your hands.

If the thermometer shows that the temperature is less than 140 degrees, the water is not hot enough to dissolve detergent. To solve your problem, you will have to raise the temperature on your water heater for the winter.

Note: If your dishwasher is equipped with a heater that raises the temperature of the water to a normal preset level established by the manufacturer, obviously you won't experience this problem.

REPAIR · 8

FIXING A DETERGENT DISPENSER THAT WON'T OPEN

PROBLEM: At the end of the cycle, you find the automatic dispenser lid still closed, with detergent still in it.

Crusty, dried-out detergent may be causing the lid to stick. Before taking apart a detergent dispenser because its lid doesn't open automatically, try using vinegar to dissolve the crust.

1. Pour undiluted white vinegar into the dispenser cup with the sticking lid. Do *not* add detergent.
2. Close the lid and latch the door. Turn on the dishwasher, and let it run through a complete cycle.
3. Open the door. Put soiled dishes into the dishwasher, add detergent to the cup or cups, and run the machine through a complete cycle to determine whether the vinegar has resolved the problem. If it hasn't, you will have to overhaul the dispenser.

Note: The following repair should not be attempted if the detergent dispenser is molded into the interior door panel. A molded dispenser is an integral part of the panel—not a separate component. If your dishwasher has a molded detergent dispenser that isn't opening, have a service technician make the repair.

To overhaul a dispenser, do the following:

1. Turn off the circuit breaker or remove the fuse serving the dishwasher. Try to turn the dishwasher on. Do not proceed until you are sure the electricity has been disconnected.
2. Remove the outside door panel. This will uncover the backside of the detergent dispenser.
3. Using self-adhering labels or strips of masking tape, label the wires attached to the bimetallic element of the dispenser that controls the lid, so that you can tell which wire connects to each terminal. Then disconnect the wires.

4.   Undo the screws holding the dispenser to the inside door panel, then push the dispenser out of the panel.

5.   Retrieve the gasket that was between the door panel and the dispenser.

6.   Wash the dispenser in hot water to remove the hardened detergent.

7.   Remove the bimetal element and buy a new element and gasket from an appliance parts dealer.

8.   Place the gasket around the hole into which the dispenser fits. Install the dispenser against the gasket. Insert the retaining screws, and screw the dispenser securely to the inside door panel.

9.   Install the bimetal element so that the space between it and the actuating lever, which is the part that pushes open the cover, is $1/32$ to $1/64$ inch. Reconnect wires.

10.   Install the front panel and restore electricity.

REPAIR · 9

REPLACING A HEATER ELEMENT

PROBLEM: Your dishes come out wet from the dishwasher.

If dishes don't dry, the heater element in the dishwasher has probably burned out. To troubleshoot and replace a heater element, do the following:

1.   Turn off the circuit breaker or remove the fuse serving the dishwasher. Try to turn the dishwasher on. Do not proceed until you are sure the electricity has been disconnected.

2.   Take off the access panel at the foot of the dishwasher. Pinpoint the terminals of the heater element issuing from the bottom of the dishwasher. The terminals will have wires leading to them (Figure 5.12).

3.   Using self-adhering labels or strips of masking tape, label each of the two wires and the terminals to which they connect, so that you will be able to tell which wire connects to each terminal. Then disconnect the wires from the terminals.

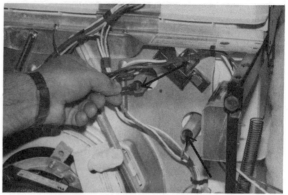

Figure 5.12 Remove the lower access panel, and disconnect wires attached to the terminals of the element (arrows).

Figure 5.13 If the ohmmeter needle points to zero or slightly above, the heater element is not defective. If it gives a reading of infinity (∞), replace the element.

Figure 5.14 Unscrew the heater element nuts.

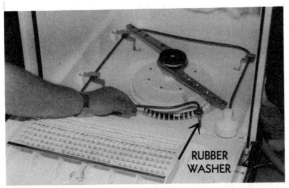

Figure 5.15 Pull the burned-out element from the holes in the floor of the dishwasher, and release the element from the brackets. If the new element doesn't come equipped with rubber washers (arrow), use the ones from the old element, if they are in good condition.

4. To determine whether the element has burned out, hold ohmmeter probes to the terminals (Figure 5.13). If the ohmmeter needle gives a reading of infinity (∞), replace the element.

5. From below, remove the nuts holding the element to the dishwasher (Figure 5.14).

6. Working inside the dishwasher, lift the old element from its seat. Purchase a new element from an appliance parts dealer. If the new element doesn't come with the thick rubber washers needed for insulation, take the washers off the old element and use them if they are still in good condition (Figure 5.15). If they aren't, buy new washers from the dealer.

7. Install the new element. Tighten the nuts that hold it to the dishwasher, and attach wires to their proper terminals. Reinstall the access panel and turn on electricity.

R E P A I R · 10

REPAIRING A LEAKY PUMP

PROBLEM: Puddles show up under your dishwasher.

Practically all dishwashers have the pump and motor combined into a single assembly. A defective seal results in puddles under the dishwasher. A water leak can also cause a burned-out motor. You will then have to replace the

motor, so don't wait too long to reseal the pump.

The job is done from inside the dishwasher, as follows:

1. From an appliance parts dealer, buy a pump resealing kit for your type of dishwasher.

2. Turn off the circuit breaker or remove the fuse serving the dishwasher. Try to turn on the dishwasher. Do not proceed until you are sure the electricity has been disconnected.

3. Turn off water to the dishwasher. Then remove the racks, pull off the spray arm, and take out the filter.

4. The job now involves unscrewing one part after another until you reach the seals (Figure 5.16). The number of seals you have to replace is the number in the pump resealing kit. This is not a particularly difficult job, and doesn't require special tools or training. However, the following tips will make the task easier:

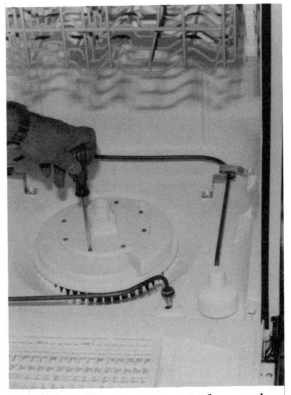

Figure 5.16 Unscrew one part after another, starting with the motor cover, until the seals are reached. Lay out parts and their fasteners in order.

- Make notes of the order in which you remove parts.

- Note the way in which each part is attached to its adjacent part.

- Lay parts out in an orderly fashion, and keep their screws right with them.

5.   When you have replaced the bottom seal, make sure all new seals are seated securely before you begin to reassemble the pump. If you have difficulty getting a seal into place because it's too stiff, put it in warm water for a few minutes to soften it up.

REPAIR · 11

REPAIRING A LEAK FROM THE AIR-GAP SYSTEM

PROBLEM: A stream of water runs from under the dishwasher after each drain cycle.

Some building codes require that under-the-counter dishwashers be equipped with an air-gap system that prevents draining water from backing up and reentering the dishwasher. The system consists of an air-gap baffle, which usually extends from the countertop above the dishwasher, a hose that extends from the output end of the dishwasher pump to the inlet side of the baffle, and another hose that extends from the output end of the baffle to the drain pipe.

When the dishwasher is not in use, the air-gap baffle separates the hoses from one another, thereby preventing any backflow from the drainpipe into the baffle, and from the baffle back through the hose into the dishwasher. As the dishwasher operates and drains, the force of the water causes the baffle to open so that drainage can proceed from the pump into the drainpipe.

A stream of water that runs from under the dishwasher after each drain cycle points to the possibility of a leak in this air-gap system. Use the following steps to check it out:

1.   Place a pail under the kitchen sink drain trap, which also serves as a trap for the dish-washer. Unscrew the trap and clean it out. Debris in the trap may be impeding the flow of water into the drain system, causing water to back up into the air-gap baffle. This backflow may be the reason for the leak. Reinstall the trap and wash a load of dishes. If the leak is still present, continue with the repair.

2.   Turn off the circuit breaker or remove the fuse that serves the dishwasher. Try to turn on the dishwasher. Do not proceed until you are sure the electricity has been disconnected.

3.   Remove the access toeplate from the bottom front of the dishwasher so you can reach the pump.

4.   Trace the hose from the kitchen sink drainpipe to the air-gap baffle; then trace the hose from the air-gap baffle to the dishwasher pump. If you can't gain access to one or more parts of the system, you will have to pull the dishwasher out from under the counter.

5.   Make sure the hoses are connected tightly at each end. Also see that they are in sound condition. (If the hoses are cracked, replace them.)

6.   Disconnect the hoses to make certain there is nothing inside one that is obstructing the flow of water.

7.   Connect the hoses. Make certain that the connections are tight and that the hoses are not kinked.

REPAIR · 12

REPLACING HOSES ON A PORTABLE DISHWASHER

PROBLEM: Water leaks out from your portable dishwasher.

One of the most common problems faced with a portable dishwasher is a leak from the water-intake or water-drain hose. With many portable dishwashers, both hoses are attached to a coupler that is connected to the kitchen sink faucet when the dishwasher is in use. During the draining phase of the cycle, water intake is automatically stopped by a valve so that water can't enter the dishwasher. Pushing the coupler onto the faucet and pulling it off after dishes have been washed eventually takes its toll on the hoses, which begin to leak.

To replace these hoses, do the following:

1. Disconnect the power cord of the dishwasher from the wall outlet.

2. If the dishwasher has a one-piece front panel, remove the panel to reach the pump. Do this by unscrewing or pulling off the control dial and removing the screws that are holding the panel. If there is a toeplate at the foot of the dishwasher, the main panel doesn't have to be removed, only the toeplate.

3. Trace the hoses to the pump. Place a pan under the pump to catch any water that may issue from the hoses when you loosen them.

4. Loosen the clamps holding the hoses to the pump, and twist the ends of the hoses back and forth until you release them from the pump. In many dishwashers, clamps are of a spring design. These have to be squeezed together with pliers and slid onto the hoses, which can then be pulled off the pump.

5. Examine the hose clamps. Are they in good condition? If so, reuse them. If not, you will need to buy new ones.

6. To get the hoses off the faucet coupler, unscrew the cover over the coupler to gain access to the ends of the hoses.

7. Using metal-cutting nippers, cut the clamps holding the hoses to the coupler. Then use a screwdriver to spread the clamps apart so you can release the clamps from the hoses.

8. Pull the hoses off the coupler. Do not use so much force that you damage the coupler. Instead, with a sharp utility knife, slice stubborn hoses off just below where they are attached to the coupler. To remove the small section of hose still secured to the coupler, use the same utility knife to make several shallow horizontal slices around the perimeter of the pieces of hose, which should allow you to peel the pieces off the coupler. *Caution:* Don't slice all the way through the hoses, because the knife may cut into and ruin the coupler.

9. Purchase new hoses and clamps from an appliance parts dealer, if needed.

10. Slide clamps onto the hoses. Place the ends of the hoses in hot water to make them pliable. Then push them onto the nibs of the pump and coupler.

11. Slide clamps into position about ⅛ inch from the ends of the hoses. Tighten the clamp to hold hoses in place.

12. Reinstall the front panel and control dial, and restore electricity. Run the dishwasher through a water intake and drain cycle to find out if there is a leak around the end of the hose. If there is, turn off the electricity and tighten the clamp some more.

REPAIR · 13

REPLACING CASTERS ON A PORTABLE DISHWASHER

PROBLEM: Your portable dishwasher doesn't roll smoothly across the floor.

Old or broken casters should be replaced. Get a repair kit from an appliance parts dealer. Use this procedure to replace the casters and, if necessary, the sleeves into which they fit.

1. Unplug the dishwasher from the wall outlet. Latch the door.

2. Spread an old quilt or mattress cover on the floor, and tip the dishwasher over so that its back panel rests on the quilt or mattress cover, with the casters facing you.

3. Pull the casters out of their sleeves. Push in the new casters. If they don't fit the sleeves securely, but keep falling out, you will have to replace the sleeves as well.

4. To replace the sleeves, use an electric drill to drill out the weld spots securing the sleeves to the dishwasher. Then get each sleeve off by tapping it with a hammer.

5. Place one of the small washers from the repair kit onto the threaded end of a caster. Insert the end of the caster through the hole in the dishwasher frame and place the other washer on it. Then screw the nut onto the ferrule by hand until you can't turn it any farther. Use a wrench to tighten the nut. Do the same at all the other corners of the dishwasher.

6

MICROWAVE OVENS

*A*lthough we strongly discourage the disassembly of a microwave oven unless it is done by a professional technician, there are some minor repairs that you can safely undertake. They are described in this chapter. We also discuss certain internal repairs commonly made during the life of a microwave oven. The intent is to enable you to understand and discuss each one with a professional technician.

Safety Precautions

Two precautions must be observed when you handle a microwave oven, even though the repairs in this chapter are performed on the outside of the cabinet:

• Some repairs call for handling a dish after it has been heated inside the oven. Use a pot holder to avoid burning your fingers.

• Some repairs require that you take the precaution of pulling the power cord from the wall outlet.

• MICROWAVE OVEN REPAIRS •

Following is a list of repairs presented in this chapter, and the tools and materials needed to make them:

REPAIRS	TOOLS AND MATERIALS
1. Testing dish response to microwaving	Pot holder
2. Getting rid of a burnt odor or other food odors	Lemon, lemon rind, cloves, microwave-proof receptacle, concentrated lemon juice
3. Removing hardened residue	None
4. Eliminating a sparking problem	Liquid dishwashing detergent
5. Reducing excessive cooking times	None
6. Checking a chip on the inside of the cabinet for danger	Microwave-proof receptacle
7. Repairing a rusty panel	Razor blade or utility knife, enamel paint, RTV (room temperature vulcanizing) sealer

REPAIR • 1

TESTING DISH RESPONSE TO MICROWAVING

PROBLEM: *You want to determine whether a dish can withstand the heat generated in a microwave oven.*

To make sure a dish can be safely used in a microwave oven, do the following.

1. Place the dish in the microwave. Set the control for full power, and the timer for 20 seconds.
2. Turn on the microwave.
3. When the microwave turns off, remove the dish with a pot holder.
4. *Carefully* touch the outside of the dish to determine which of the following is true:

- The surface of the dish is so hot that you can't keep your finger on it. If so, do not use the dish in the microwave, because it could crack.

- The surface of the dish is warm, but not too hot to touch. In this case, limit the

exposure of the dish to microwaving to a maximum of 5 minutes.

- The surface of the dish is cool. There are no limitations as to how long you can expose this dish to microwaving.

REPAIR • 2

GETTING RID OF A BURNT ODOR OR OTHER FOOD ODORS

PROBLEM: *You overcooked some food in the microwave, and a burnt odor still lingers in the oven.*

To get rid of a burnt odor in a microwave oven, do the following:

1. In a microwave-proof receptacle, mix together a cup of water, the juice of one lemon, grated lemon rind, and five whole cloves. Put the receptacle in the microwave.
2. Set the control for full power, and the timer for 5 minutes.
3. Turn on the oven.
4. When the oven turns off, remove the re-

HELPFUL HINT
Microwave Cookware

You change a lot of old habits when you get into microwave cooking. One of them is what you cook food in. For instance, you'll make hot chocolate in the same cup you drink it from. You'll heat dinner right on your dinner plate.

But leave your stainless-steel saucepan hanging on the wall. Metal pots and pans don't work in a microwave oven because the metal reflects the microwave energy. If you use a metal pot in a microwave oven, at best you'll have a cold meal. At worst, you'll have a damaged oven. But you may be able to use a small amount of foil in your oven, especially if the oven is a fairly recent model (see page 74).

You probably already own several items suitable for microwave cooking: plastic freezer containers, straw serving baskets, glass or ceramic casseroles and baking dishes, and paper towels. You can also buy a full line of glass, ceramic, and plastic cookware marketed specifically for microwave cooking: roasting racks, soufflé dishes, baking pans, bacon racks, pie plates, muffin rings, ring molds—just about every form of pan you would find in conventional cookware.

When you buy cooking equipment for your microwave oven, observe the following tips:

- For convenience, make sure the cookware is dishwasher safe.

- The shape of a pan affects its performance in a microwave oven. Round pans are generally superior to rectangular pans, as food tends to overcook in corners. Food also cooks more evenly in a shallow pan, where it's spread out, than in a deeper dish.

- Bacon racks are generally no better than paper towels. However, racks are the more environmentally sound choice, since paper towels are simply tossed out after cooking the bacon, while racks only need to be cleaned after each use.

- Some roasting pans come with a cover to help keep food from drying out and spattering during cooking. Check the depth of the pan itself so that once the lid is on, it doesn't make the container so shallow that it won't hold a roast or a whole fowl. And a lidded roaster should have an opening somewhere for inserting a microwave oven's temperature probe into the food.

- Be careful of pottery; it may have metal in the glaze or impurities in the clay.

ceptacle and wipe the cabinet with a paper towel or dry cloth.

5. If some odor still remains, repeat the procedure.

Lingering odors. Odors from foods previously cooked in a microwave oven can be eliminated as follows:

1. Pour ½ cup of concentrated lemon juice into a microwave-proof bowl or measuring cup. Add 1 cup of cold water.

2. Place the bowl or measuring cup in the oven, close the door, and set the timer for 5 minutes. Turn on the oven at full power.

3. At the end of this time, remove the bowl

or measuring cup, and wipe up condensation. If vestiges of odor remain, repeat the procedure.

REPAIR · 3

REMOVING HARDENED RESIDUE

PROBLEM: Food residue has hardened on the floor or sides of the cabinet.

Do not use steel wool or scouring powder to get hardened food residue off the interior of a microwave—these can rub away the finish.

Instead, do the following:

1. Place a cup of water in the oven. Turn the oven on at full power for 3 minutes.
2. When the oven shuts off, do not open the door for 5 minutes. This will allow steam to work on the residue.
3. Open the door and let the steam dissipate. Use a damp cloth to remove the soft spots.
4. If some residue remains that is too hard to wipe away, repeat the procedure.

REPAIR · 4

ELIMINATING A SPARKING PROBLEM

PROBLEM: Your microwave oven sparks even when there is no metal in the oven.

If sparks in the microwave oven aren't the result of using metal utensils (see sidebar), the cause may be one of the following:

- *Grease.* Use a sudsy mixture of warm water and liquid dishwashing detergent to wash off grease that has collected on supporting shelf screws, or that has collected in crevices.

- *Temperature probe.* The presence of a temperature probe with an exposed probe end can cause sparking. The probe should be fully inserted in food or removed from the cooking chamber when the oven is in use.

- *A loose cooking rack.* Make sure a cooking rack is secured firmly when the oven is in use or removed when it isn't needed.

If these conditions don't apply, sparking indicates either a damaged magnetron, a faulty wave guide cover, or a badly chipped or rusted cabinet. Cooking in a damaged microwave can be dangerous, so don't use the unit until you have it checked out by a service technician.

REPAIR · 5

REDUCING EXCESSIVE COOKING TIMES

PROBLEM: Your microwave doesn't cook food as quickly as it once did.

Though fixing the cause of excessive cooking time is not a repair you can safely undertake, it is usually a simple and fairly inexpensive procedure to have done.

Before calling a service technician, check the instructions in the owner's manual to be sure you are programming the proper power level and length of cooking time. If you are, the technician should do the following to try to restore more rapid cooking times:

1. Remove the main cooking shelf and clean beneath it. An accumulation of moisture and grease under the shelf can be a reason for increased cooking time.
2. Try to restore the energy of the power transformer by switching its circuit. Many microwave ovens have a spare power transformer terminal. The power transformer can be restored to full energy by switching it from the sluggish power circuit to the unused, lively circuit. Two power terminals—the one that has been in use and the spare—will be similarly marked: for example, 4 and 4A. If the technician finds this to be the case with your microwave, he or she will disconnect the transformer wire from terminal 4 and reconnect it to terminal 4A.
3. If the preceding two steps do not reduce cooking time, your problem is that the magnetron tube has lost power. If you wish to restore full power, you will have to consider having a new magnetron tube installed.

How to Use Aluminum Foil in a Microwave Oven

If your microwave is a fairly new product, you can probably use a small amount of aluminum in it. That's because the design of more recently manufactured magnetron tubes (the part that emits microwaves) reduces the feedback of energy so that it won't reflect off aluminum and cause sparks inside the unit.

To find out, place a two-inch-square piece of aluminum foil on a microwave-proof dish. Place the dish in the oven, and turn on the appliance for three minutes. Is there sparking during this period? If not, a small amount of foil can be used safely in your oven. A "small amount" means an amount equivalent to that used to cover the legs and wings of a whole chicken or covering the corners of an oblong casserole dish. When you put on the foil, be careful that it doesn't rest against the sides of the oven.

You can also put aluminum foil pans, including TV dinner pans, in a modern microwave oven, as long as the pans are less than ¾ inch deep. The first time you do this, however, observe the inside of the oven. If sparks appear, turn the oven off at once.

Other metal utensils. Here are some guidelines for other types of metal utensils:

- It is safe to use skewers and poultry clamps in an oven if a large quantity of food is being cooked, but do not allow them to come into contact with the sides of the oven while the oven is on.

- It is safe to use any metal item that has been specifically manufactured for a microwave, including a food thermometer and food sensor.

- Don't place pewter, silver, stainless steel, or aluminum (other than that specified above) into a microwave. This restriction applies also to any dishes having gold, silver, platinum, or other metal trim.

- Remove twisters from plastic or paper cooking bags before placing bags into a microwave. The metal in a twister can get hot enough to melt a plastic bag or set fire to a paper bag.

REPAIR · 6

CHECKING A CHIP ON THE INSIDE OF THE CABINET FOR DANGER

PROBLEM: Your microwave oven has a chip in the surface of the floor, and you wonder if it poses a health hazard.

A tiny chip in the floor surface of a microwave cabinet may or may not be cause for concern. To find out, do the following:

1. Put a cup of water in a microwave-proof receptacle into the oven. Do not place it on top of the chip.
2. Set the control on full power for 30 seconds. Turn on the appliance.
3. At the end of the time, open the door and move your finger close to the chip. If you feel any heat, call a service technician, who will check the unit for radiation leakage.

REPAIR · 7

REPAIRING A RUSTY PANEL

PROBLEM: Your microwave oven has developed some rust on interior surfaces.

Rust that develops on a panel inside the cabinet of a microwave oven can eat through the panel and lead to radiation leakage. It should be repaired as soon as possible.

Do the following:

1. Unplug the unit.
2. Wipe the damaged surface with a soft rag to remove loose flakes of rust.
3. If the rust is under a glass shelf, remove the shelf. If the shelf is held by sealer, use a razor blade or utility knife to slice through the sealer. After the shelf has been removed, clean off any strips of sealer that remain.
4. Buy a spray can of enamel paint for your make of microwave oven from a dealer who sells your type of oven. Also buy a tube of RTV (room temperature vulcanizing) sealer if the unit has a glass shelf.

HELPFUL HINT

Protection Against Lightning

Most microwave ovens are equipped with a fuse that prevents damage to the appliance if lightning causes a surge of current to pass through your home's electrical system. When a surge hits the fuse, it burns apart (opens) to keep the overload from getting to the capacitor, magnetron tube, timer, and other electronic components that could be damaged.

Once the fuse has done its job, it has to be replaced, because without an intact fuse a microwave oven won't operate. Replacing the fuse involves disassembling the cabinet, so this is not a job for someone not familiar with microwave oven circuitry. Even with the electricity turned off, it is possible for someone poking around inside the cabinet to receive a severe shock from the capacitor, which stores electrical energy even when the unit is turned off.

To keep a surge from destroying an internal fuse, plug the oven into a surge protector, which is available in any hardware, appliance, or electronic parts store. If lightning should strike, the circuit breaker inside the surge protector will trip to keep electricity from damaging the fuse and other components of the microwave.

Most surge protectors have a circuit breaker that can be reset to restore the device to service after the breaker has done its job. Not only will you not have to call in a service technician to replace the fuse in your microwave oven; you won't even have to buy a new surge protector. Surge protectors are a good investment, not only for your microwave but for many of your other home appliances as well.

5.   Following directions on the can of paint, refinish the damage. Let the paint dry.

6.   Install the glass shelf. Then, following directions on the tube of sealer, apply a bead around the edges of the shelf.

7.   Before using the oven, let the sealer cure for the length of time specified in the instructions on the sealer tube.

H E L P F U L   H I N T

Common Internal Microwave Oven Repairs

If your microwave oven stops running, the fan motor, thermal cut-out switch, or interlock switch is probably the cause. All these components are easily replaced by a service technician.

The fan and thermal cut-out switch work as a team. The fan cools the magnetron, which is the part that does the cooking. The thermal cut-out switch shuts the oven off if the fan malfunctions, so no damage will occur as the temperature rises.

After the service technician checks to see if the fan is rotating, he or she should test the thermal cut-out switch. When the oven operates for a few minutes, heat can cause a faulty thermal cut-out switch to open prematurely. When the thermal cut-out switch opens, the microwave shuts down. The technician will use an ohmmeter to determine whether resistance in the thermal cut-out switch circuit is within the bounds set for it by the manufacturer. If not, the switch has to be replaced.

The interlock switch shuts off the oven if someone opens the door while the unit is running. It also interrupts operation if one of the terminals is overly sensitive to heat. As heat rises, the effect on the switch is similar to what happens when someone opens the oven door. The circuit is broken and the switch shuts off the oven, even though the door is still closed. If the interlock switch is faulty, it too has to be replaced.

7

APPLIANCE CABINETS,
WINDOW AIR CONDITIONERS,
FOOD WASTE DISPOSERS,
DEHUMIDIFIERS,
and TRASH COMPACTORS

*T*his chapter covers a potpourri of topics, including repairs to window air conditioners, food waste disposers, dehumidifiers, and trash compactors. Other than a major breakdown, such as a refrigerant leak in a window air conditioner or dehumidifier, or a burned-out motor, the repairs described are not particularly difficult.

Safety Precautions

• Before using any product mentioned in this chapter, such as spray cans of primer and paint, read and observe the cautionary instructions printed on the container. Most important, keep the area where you work well ventilated.

• If you move an appliance to another location, make sure you can handle the weight or ask someone to help you. Attempting to lug a heavy appliance yourself can result in a serious injury.

• Before you begin to work on any appliance, disconnect the unit from the home's electrical system. Pull the power cord from the wall outlet, turn off the circuit breaker, or remove the appropriate fuse at the house's main electric service panel.

• Never place your hand into the drain opening of a food waste disposer.

· VARIOUS APPLIANCE REPAIRS ·

Following is a list of repairs presented in this chapter, and the tools and materials needed to make them:

REPAIR	TOOLS AND MATERIALS
1. Touching up scratched appliance panels	Primer, enamel paint, blending agent, no. 360 wet-or-dry sandpaper, masking tape, auto-body rubbing compound, dishwashing detergent
2. Finding the origin of noise from a window air conditioner	Wood wedges, glazing compound, tape
3. Tuning up a window air conditioner	Vacuum cleaner, fin comb
4. Freeing a food waste disposer that has seized	Special food waste disposer wrench, broomstick or hammer
5. Repairing a food waste disposer that stalls	Flashlight, tongs, special food waste disposer wrench
6. Troubleshooting a dehumidifier's deicer switch	Screwdriver, nut driver, vacuum cleaner
7. Troubleshooting a dehumidifier that doesn't draw enough moisture	Screwdriver, nut driver
8. Repairing a sluggishly operating trash compactor drawer	Silicone lubricant, nut driver, screwdriver, adjustable pliers, adjustable wrench, no. 000 steel wool, rust remover, rust-inhibiting paint

R E P A I R · 1

TOUCHING UP SCRATCHED APPLIANCE PANELS

PROBLEM: You notice a scratch on your appliance and wonder if you should go to the trouble of refinishing it.

Refinishing a scratched appliance will prevent it from rusting. To treat incipient rust, do the following:

1. Go to an appliance parts dealer and purchase the following materials:

- Spray can of enamel paint primer (white if the appliance is a light color, gray if the appliance is a dark color)

- Spray can of enamel paint that matches the color of the panel

- Spray can of blending agent

- Sheet of no. 360 wet-or-dry sandpaper

- Sandpaper pad

- Masking tape (½-inch width)

- Auto-body rubbing compound

2. Mix a little dishwashing detergent (*not* dishwasher detergent, but the liquid kind of detergent used for hand-washing dishes) with hot water and rub the panel with the suds. Then rinse the panel with clear, cold water. Use clean rags only—not a brush or an abra-

sive such as steel wool, which can cause more scratches.

3. Attach a piece of no. 360 wet-or-dry sandpaper to the sandpaper pad. Dip it in cold water. Sand the scratched area and two inches on each side of it until paint and primer are removed, and bare metal is exposed. *Note:* Dip the sandpaper in cold water frequently during the sanding process.

4. Wipe the surface dry with a clean cloth. Try to remove all dust left by sanding.

5. Mask the area that is being refinished by taping newspaper around it, leaving exposed the bare metal and a border of about ¼ inch of the original finish.

6. Hold the spray can of primer about 12 inches from the area. Keeping the can in constant motion, spray on one light coat of primer. Sweep the can across the spot in one direction only—either to the left or right. Then wait for the primer to dry. Examine the result. If bare metal still shows through, spray on another light coat of primer. Continue spraying one coat at a time, allowing each coat to dry, until there is no show-through.

7. Attach a clean piece of no. 360 wet-or-dry sandpaper to the sandpaper pad and dip it in cold water. Sweep it gently over the primed area once or twice. This procedure serves to roughen the primer a little and provide the enamel paint with some "tooth" on which to adhere. Wipe off dust left by the sandpaper.

8. Apply the enamel paint by making only one sweep with the spray across the surface and one sweep back. Then let the paint dry before judging the results. If another coat of finish paint is needed, again sweep the paint once across the spot and once back.

9. When the enamel has dried, remove the newspaper and masking tape.

10. Spray a light coat of blending agent on the refinished surface. Extend the coat a couple of inches beyond that area onto the original paint. Let the agent dry. Do not rub it off.

11. Place a little auto-body rubbing compound on a clean cloth and *gently* wipe it over the area, using a circular motion. Use a clean rag to wipe off the residue.

HELPFUL HINT

Changing the Color of an Appliance

You may have redecorated your kitchen and find that the color of the appliances no longer fits in. Before you consider buying a new refrigerator/freezer, range, or dishwasher, you might want to investigate the possibility of having the present unit refinished by a company that specializes in such work. Companies that refinish appliances are listed in the yellow pages of many phone books under "Appliances, Household—Refinishing." Most of these services are able to do the job right in your home, charging between $100 and $200 per appliance. But there are some caveats: Don't expect to use the appliance until approximately 48 hours after it has been painted. And, no matter what the company may say, paint sprayed on a range may in time take on a yellowish tinge in areas affected by heat.

If you can't locate a refinishing company in your area, an automobile body shop can do the job. However, there are two disadvantages to having the job done by a body shop: first, the cost may almost equal, or perhaps exceed, the price of a new appliance, so make sure you understand all the charges you have to pay before proceeding; and second, you will probably have to haul the appliance to the shop to have the work done.

H E L P F U L   H I N T

What Size Air Conditioner Do You Need?

The first step in achieving air-conditioned comfort without spending more than necessary is to match the air conditioner's capacity to the room it will serve. The Cooling Load Estimate Form that follows will help you determine how large an air conditioner you need.

WORKSHEET: COOLING LOAD ESTIMATE FORM: CALCULATING THE SIZE THAT'S RIGHT

This worksheet, adapted from one published by the Association of Home Appliance Manufacturers, can help you estimate how much cooling capacity you need.

Preliminaries

1. Measure the length of each wall in the room.   24 x 11 = 264

2. Determine the area (length × width, in feet) of the floor and the ceiling.

3. Measure the area (width × height, in feet) of each window.   3x4 = 12

4. Measure the width of all permanently open doors. Rooms connected by a door or archway more than 5 feet wide should be considered one area. Take measurements for both rooms.

Calculations

Multiply the appropriate measurement by the factor given. Use factors in parentheses if the air conditioner will be used only at night.

1. _____ × 300 (200) = _____   1
    width of permanently open doors, ft.

2. _____48_____ × 14 = _____   672   _____   2
    areas of all windows, sq. ft. (multiply by 7, not 14, for double glass or block)

3. Use only the line that's appropriate for your house.
    Uninsulated ceiling, no space above: _____ × 19 (5) = _____   3
                                          ceiling area, sq. ft.

    Uninsulated ceiling, attic above: _____ × 12 (7) = _____   3
                                      ceiling area, sq. ft.

    Insulated ceiling, no space above: _____ × 8 (3) = _____   3
                                       ceiling area, sq. ft.

    Insulated attic above: ___260___ × 5 (4) = __1300__ (1040)__   3
                           ceiling area, sq. ft.

    Occupied space above: _____ × 3 (3) = _____   3
                          ceiling area, sq. ft.

4. Enter length of all walls, in feet, as directed, and multiply by appropriate factor. Consider walls shaded by adjacent buildings as facing north.

Wall Facing	Uninsulated Frame or Masonry up to 8 in. Thick		Insulated Frame or Masonry over 8 in. Thick	
Outside, north _____	× 30 (30)	or	× 20 (20) =	_____ 4
Outside, other _____	× 60 (30)	or	× 30 (20) =	276 (138) 4
Inside ____24____	× 30 (30)	or	× 20 (20) =	72 4

5. If floor is on ground or over basement, omit this step and go to step 6.

    _____260_____ × 3 = _____780_____ 5
    floor area, sq. ft.

6. If air conditioner will be used only at night or if all windows in the room face
    north, omit this step and go to step 7. Otherwise, enter the area for each window
    on the appropriate line. Do the multiplication. Multiply factor by 0.5 for any
    window with glass block; by 0.8 for double glass or storm window. Enter only
    largest number.

Window Facing	Window Area	No Shades		Inside Shades	Outside Awnings	
Northeast	_____	× 60	or ×	25	or × 20 =	_____
East	12	× 80	or ×	40	or × 25 =	480
Southeast	_____	× 75	or ×	30	or × 20 =	_____
South	24	× 75	or ×	35	or × 20 =	840 X.
Southwest	_____	× 110	or ×	45	or × 30 =	_____
West	12	× 150	or ×	65	or × 45 =	780
Northwest	_____	× 120	or ×	50	or × 35 =	

Largest number _840_ 6

7. **Subtotal.** Add lines 1 through 6. Enter sum here:_____3940_____ 7

8. Climate correction

    _____3940_____ × _____.8_____ = ____3160.____ 8
    figure from line 7   factor from map

9. _____2_____ × 600 = _____1200_____ 9
    people in room (min. 2)

10. _____ × 3 = _____ 10
    wattage of all lights and appliances in room (not including air conditioner)

11. **Total cooling load.** Add line 8 to 10. Enter sum: 4350
    This number tells you how many Btu of heat build up in the room each hour.
    The air conditioner's cooling capacity (Btu/hour) should nearly match the heat
    buildup you calculated. A difference of about 5 percent between the number
    you calculate and the air conditioner's capacity should not be significant.

• AIR CONDITIONERS •

REPAIR • 2

FINDING THE ORIGIN OF NOISE FROM A WINDOW AIR CONDITIONER

PROBLEM: Your window air conditioner makes odd noises when it's in operation.

Many such noises are cabinet- or window-related and easily repaired. Do the following to find the source of the disturbance:

1. Turn on the air conditioner. Press your hand against the window sash. If the noise ceases, the sash is the source. To fix it, insert small wooden wedges between the sash and window frame.
2. With the air conditioner running, press on the glass panes. If the noise then ceases, reglaze the glass so it's tight.
3. With your hand, press the front grille of the cabinet to see if that reduces the noise. If the grille is making the noise and is attached to the unit, tape it securely against the cabinet to cut down on the vibration.

REPAIR • 3

TUNING UP A WINDOW AIR CONDITIONER

PROBLEM: Your air conditioner doesn't seem to be working at peak efficiency.

The following services done at the beginning of the air-conditioning season will allow your window air conditioner to provide the most efficient service:

1. Remove and wash the replaceable (aluminum or plastic) filter in the unit. Replace a filter that can't be washed.
2. Vacuum areas inside the unit that you can reach with a straight-nozzle vacuum cleaner attachment.
3. Straighten aluminum evaporator fins with a special tool called a fin comb. You can buy a fin comb from any company listed in the yellow pages of the telephone book under "Air Conditioning Equipment and Systems—Supplies and Parts."

• FOOD WASTE DISPOSERS •

REPAIR • 4

FREEING A FOOD WASTE DISPOSER THAT HAS SEIZED

PROBLEM: When you turn on the waste disposer after returning from a vacation, it does not respond.

It is not unusual for a food waste disposer to seize or bind if it isn't used for a period of time. To fix, do the following:

1. Check the electric service panel to make certain the circuit breaker is on or that the fuse protecting the waste disposer circuit is intact.
2. Turn the disposer on-off switch to On. Press the reset button in the base of the disposer housing for about 10 seconds. After re-

leasing the button, wait 5 seconds for a response. If there is none, repeat the procedure once more. If nothing happens, turn the on-off switch to Off.
3. Some manufacturers put a hexagonal hole in the base of the disposer housing and provide a wrench that fits the hole. The wrench allows you to rotate the turntable manually, an action that might free up the unit. If your disposer is so equipped, first turn the on-off switch to Off. Insert the wrench, turn it in one direction, and then in the other direction. Remove the wrench and your hands and flip the on-off switch to On. Press the reset button. If there isn't any response, try a few times more. If nothing happens, the motor bearings have probably frozen, in which case the unit will require an overhaul.

4.   If the disposer doesn't have the hexagonal hole mentioned above, be sure the on-off switch is turned to Off. Insert the end of a broomstick or hammer handle into the hopper and hold it against one of the impellers on the flywheel. Using as much force as necessary, push against the impeller until the turntable turns. If you get no movement by pushing in one direction, move the position of the pole and push in the other direction.

Remove the pole and your hands. Flip the switch to On and press the reset button. If the appliance doesn't start, turn the switch to Off and repeat the procedure several more times before giving up.

How to prevent seizing. If your food waste disposer isn't used for some time, hardening food residue can cause the turntable to seize. To prevent this, be sure to flush the unit properly whenever you use it:

1.   Turn on the water, turn on the disposer, and grind waste.
2.   Turn off the disposer, but allow water to continue running through the disposer for no less than 30 seconds.

H E L P F U L   H I N T

Using Your Food Waste Disposer Correctly

You can safely grind almost all food waste in a disposer, except for oyster and clam shells, and dense-fiber matter such as corn husks. You can even grind steak and poultry bones and coffee grounds.

Metallic objects, however, including the comparatively soft flip tops from aluminum soda cans, should *never* be thrown into a disposer. Metal will damage the shredder, which is the part that chops waste into fine particles so they can flow easily down the drain. If the shredder is damaged, the disposer will probably have to be replaced.

H E L P F U L   H I N T

Water Overflows: The Disposer's Fault?

If water backs up into the sink when your dishwasher is running, and the dishwasher is connected to the food waste disposer, the disposer is not at fault. Disposers are designed not to clog. Instead, look for a blockage in the drainpipe.

R E P A I R · 5

REPAIRING A FOOD WASTE DISPOSER UNIT THAT STALLS

PROBLEM: Your food waste disposer comes to a stop after running only a few seconds.

When a disposer stalls, there is usually something lodged between the teeth of the shredder, or the motor may be damaged. To check, do the following:

1.   At the main electrical service panel, turn off the circuit breaker or remove the fuse serving the disposer.
2.   Push aside the rubber baffle over the disposer, in the mouth of the sink drain hole. Using a flashlight, examine the ring encircling the turntable. This ring is the shredder. Look closely between its teeth for an object that may be lodged there.
3.   If you spot such an object, use a pair of tongs to pull it out. Restore electricity and test the disposer.
4.   If the disposer still does not operate, the motor may be damaged. If your disposer came equipped with a hexagonal wrench, you can test the motor. First, turn the on-off switch to Off. Insert the wrench into the hole in the base of the disposer and turn. Is there free move-

ment, or do you have to use force? If the latter, the bearings of the motor are probably damaged. The disposer will have to be disassem-

bled to determine whether repairing the unit is economically practical. This is a task that should be left to a trained technician.

• DEHUMIDIFIERS •

REPAIR • 6

TROUBLESHOOTING A DEHUMIDIFIER'S DEICER SWITCH

PROBLEM: Your dehumidifier shuts down prematurely.

To find out why your dehumidifier is not working properly, you must first understand how it operates. Many dehumidifiers are equipped with a deicer switch. This switch is clipped to the evaporator coil, through which the refrigerant circulates and draws moisture from the air.

The deicer switch works in this way: Moisture from the humid air condenses on the cold coil and drips into a pan. When the ambient temperature drops below 65 degrees, the moisture that forms on the evaporator coil will turn to frost. If an excessive amount of frost builds up on the coil, dehumidification ceases but the compressor motor keeps on running. The deicer switch keeps this from happening by interrupting the electricity that runs the compressor motor, thus shutting off the dehumidifier.

If the evaporator coil of your dehumidifier frosts up at an ambient temperature *higher* than 65 degrees, the compressor motor will shut down prematurely. This is a sign that one of three conditions exists:

1. *The position of the dehumidifier is blocking the flow of air.* Nothing should obstruct the front, rear, or sides of a dehumidifier. Keep objects large enough to block airflow at least two feet from the unit and keep the unit positioned at least two feet from a wall.

2. *The evaporator coil is covered with dirt.* Dirt acts as an insulator and keeps air from

reaching the coil. Pull the unit's power cord plug from the wall outlet and remove the cabinet to reach all sides of the evaporator coil (Figure 7.1). Vacuum or brush the coil (Figure 7.2). Reinstall the cabinet.

3. *The deicer switch is damaged.* Replace the switch with one made for your unit. Unscrew it from the evaporator coil, release the wires, and put a new switch in its place. You can obtain a new deicer switch from an appliance parts dealer.

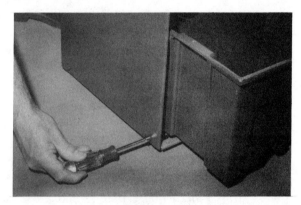

Figure 7.1 Turn off electricity, remove cabinet screws, and lift the cabinet off to reveal internal components.

Figure 7.2 Clean evaporator coils. Dirt-covered coils can frost and cause premature shutdown of the compressor.

HELPFUL HINT
How Big a Dehumidifier Do You Need?

Dehumidifiers are available in many sizes. Size is measured by how many pints of water the unit can draw from the air in a 24-hour period. To determine the size of the unit you need, do the following:

1. Measure the length and width of the room where the dehumidifier is going to be placed. Multiply the two figures to get the square footage.

2. When a period of warm and humid weather hits your area, measure the relative humidity with a hygrometer. You can buy this instrument in a hardware or home supply store. After 12 hours, record the reading.

3. The following chart can help determine the size of the dehumidifier that will best serve your needs. When in doubt, a large-capacity model is quicker and more efficient than a smaller unit.

Humidity level	Capacity of dehumidifier (in pints)				
	500 sq. ft.	1,000 sq. ft.	1,500 sq. ft.	2,000 sq. ft.	2,500 sq. ft.
75–85% RH. Area feels moderately damp and has a musty odor only when the weather outside the house is humid.	10	14	18	22	26
85–95% RH. Area feels damp and has a musty odor on humid days and at times on nonhumid days as well; during these periods, pipes and water tank sweat.	12	17	22	27	32
95–100% RH. Area feels and smells damp all the time; pipes and water tank sweat all the time; even walls and/or the floor gets wet.	14	20	26	32	28

REPAIR · 7

TROUBLESHOOTING A DEHUMIDIFIER THAT DOESN'T DRAW MOISTURE ADEQUATELY

PROBLEM: Your dehumidifier runs, but doesn't seem to draw much moisture from the air.

The failure of a dehumidifier to draw enough moisture from the air may be related to one of the following conditions:

1. *Restricted air circulation.* The dehumidifier is too close to walls or other obstructions, such as furniture. Maintain a minimum of two feet of cleared space in the front, at the rear, and to the sides of the appliance.

2. *Frosted evaporator coil.* Frost on the evaporator coil indicates that the dehumidifier is being asked to draw humidity when the ambient temperature of the area is lower than 65 degrees. Dehumidifiers function only when the ambient temperature is higher than this. Turn off the unit until the ambient temperature rises and frost melts.

3. *Burned-out deicer switch.* Replace the switch as described in Repair 6, above.

4. *Burned-out motor.* A dehumidifier has two motors: a fan motor and a compressor motor. Both must operate for the dehumidifier to draw moisture from the air. To check the motors, pull the plug of the dehumidifier power cord from the wall outlet. Remove the cabinet. The fan and compressor motors will be visible. Plug the power cord into the outlet. Turn on the unit. *Caution:* Keep your hands away from electric wires and connections as long as the power cord is plugged into the wall outlet; also, make sure you aren't standing in water or on a damp floor. To check the operation of the fan motor, look at the fan blade. If it isn't rotating, the fan motor is damaged or worn out. Turn off the electricity, and make sure wires are securely plugged into their connecting points. Turn on the electricity and see if the problem has been resolved. If wires loosened by vibration are not the cause of the trouble, call an appliance parts dealer to find out if a replacement fan motor is available. If it is,

Figure 7.3 If the fan isn't revolving, the fan motor has probably burned out. Remove the motor and have it tested by an appliance parts dealer before purchasing a new motor.

turn off the electricity and unscrew the burned-out fan motor from the appliance (Figure 7.3). Take the motor with you to the appliance parts store and ask the dealer to test it. If the test proves that the motor is defective, buy a new motor. Once home, plug the wires into it, attach the new motor to the dehumidifier, and reassemble the appliance.

5. *Burned-out compressor.* If the fan motor is working normally, check out the compressor motor (Figure 7.4). Do you feel it running? If not, the compressor may be burned out. After finding out the cost of installing a new compressor, you may decide to buy a new dehumidifier.

6. *Loss of refrigerant.* If all the above parts are working, and you have checked for bad positioning and dirt, the cause of the problem is lack of refrigerant. Take the dehumidifier to a service technician who has the special tools needed to find and repair a refrigerant leak and to recharge the unit.

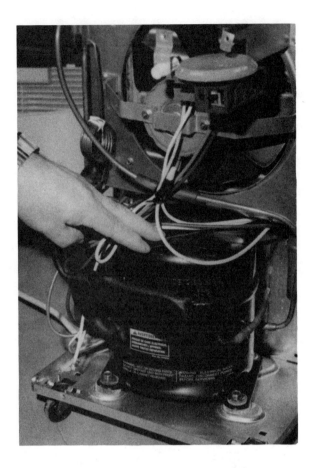

Figure 7.4 To determine whether the compressor motor is working, turn on the dehumidifier and place your fingers on the compressor. You should feel vibration.

• TRASH COMPACTORS •

REPAIR • 8

REPAIRING A SLUGGISH TRASH COMPACTOR DRAWER

PROBLEM: The drawer of your trash compactor fails to open all the way.

First, consult your owner's manual. It gives several explanations for this problem, including failure to use the controls properly and improper installation of the trash bag.

If the trouble cannot be solved by closely following procedures in the manual, the jammed drawer may be caused by dirty or rusted slides on which the drawer rides.

To check and solve, do the following:

1. Disconnect the power cord from the wall outlet.
2. Take out the drawer (Figure 7.5).

3. Use a rag to wipe dirt off the frames and bearings. Then spray a light coating of silicone lubricant on each slide frame and bearing (Figure 7.6).
4. Replace the drawer. Restore electricity. Open the drawer a few times to determine whether the cleaning and lubrication have made a difference.
5. If the above repair has no effect, the frames and/or bearings are probably corroded. Disconnect the power cord from the outlet. Remove the drawer, and examine the damaged slide frame and bearing unit. Are the two riveted together? (If not, skip step 6 and read on.)
6. If they are riveted together, you can replace them as a unit. Unscrew both slide frame and bearing assemblies from the cabinet. Purchase new ones from an appliance parts store

Figure 7.5 *Turn off electricity and remove the compactor drawer.*

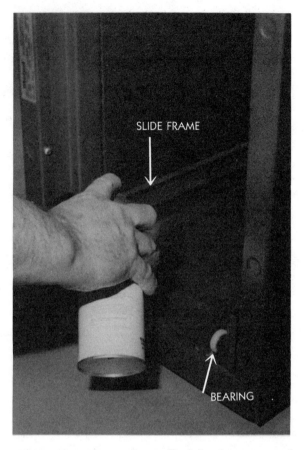

SLIDE FRAME

BEARING

Figure 7.6 *Wipe dirt off slide frames, and spray frames and bearings with a light coating of silicone.*

and screw them into the cabinet. Reinstall the drawer, and restore electricity.

Most trash compactors, however, have separate slide frames and roller bearings. In that case, you may want to replace only the bearings and try to restore the slide frames. Here's how:

1. Place your finger down behind a slide frame and put pressure on the nut of the screw that holds the frame to the cabinet. Undo the screw with your other hand (Figure 7.7).
2. Raise the free slide frame up away from the bearing (Figure 7.8).
3. Use adjustable pliers or a wrench to turn the bearing counterclockwise, releasing the part from the cabinet. When the bearing is free, retrieve the nut behind it (Figure 7.9).

Do the same thing on the other side of the cabinet.
4. Buy new bearings from an appliance parts dealer. Screw them tightly to the cabinet. Spray the slide frames with a light coating of silicone lubricant, screw them back into place, install the drawer, and restore electricity. If the slide frames are corroded, saturate a pad of no. 000 steel wool with liquid rust remover. Rub the frames with the steel wool until they are clean. Then apply silicone lubricant, reattach the frames to the cabinet, install the drawer, and turn on electricity. *Caution:* Don't press down too hard on the steel wool—too much pressure might remove the paint on the slide frames; if this happens and bare metal is exposed, repaint the frames with rust-inhibiting paint.

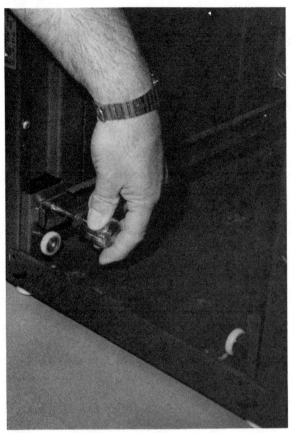

Figure 7.7 *Remove screws and nuts holding the slide frames to the cabinet.*

Figure 7.8 *Lift the slide frame up away from the bearing.*

Figure 7.9 *On this unit, the bearings are released by removing nuts with a wrench. On other units, you can unscrew the bearings using adjustable pliers.*

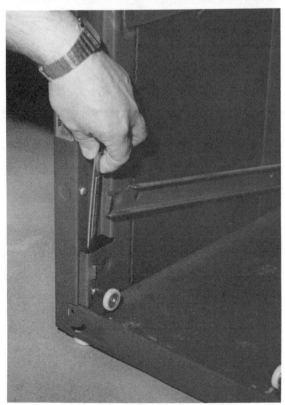

8

SMALL
GASOLINE ENGINES

The category of outdoor power equipment covers a wide range of tools, from large power lawn mowers and snow throwers to small items that you can hold in your hand, such as grass trimmers and chain saws. The common denominator is that each piece of equipment described in this chapter is equipped with a small gasoline engine.

Small gasoline engines fall into two categories: two-cycle and four-cycle. In many cases you would use the same troubleshooting and repair procedures for one or the other. But there are differences in the two, as we will point out, and those differences are significant.

Safety Precautions

The safety precautions you must follow when working on a small gasoline engine are obvious and easily observed. They are necessary because you will either be handling or working in close proximity to gasoline, an extremely volatile substance. Gasoline engines, unlike electric motors, do not have to be plugged into a power source to run. Once started, they generate their own ignition power, provided only that there is gasoline in the fuel tank. So be very careful to follow these rules:

• *Disconnect the spark plug cable from the spark plug.* This will ensure that you do not accidentally start the engine by inadvertently cranking the engine shaft while working. To make sure that the spark plug cable does not accidentally come into contact with the spark plug and complete the ignition circuit, you must short-circuit the ignition system by grounding the cable to the engine. To do this, buy a jumper wire, which is a short length of cable with an alligator clip on each end. (An

90

alligator clip has serrated, spring-type jaws that allow a positive grip.) Grasp the boot or metal sleeve at the end of the spark plug cable and twist and pull it off the spark plug. Attach one alligator clip of the jumper wire to the metal terminal inside the boot of the cable, or to its metal sleeve. Attach the other alligator clip to a metal part of the engine, such as a cylinder-head bolt (Figure 8.1). Make sure the clip has a good grip on the bolt.

• If a procedure instructs you to handle gasoline, bring all the equipment you're working on outdoors for ventilation. Try not to inhale the fumes. *Do not smoke.* Do not allow any object near the gasoline that may create a spark or flame.

• If the procedure instructs you to drain fuel from the fuel tank and then discard it, take the precautions noted above. In addition, pour fuel to be discarded into a receptacle that you cap tightly. For proper disposal, take it to a waste-management disposal site or to a service station you patronize. Do *not* pour the fuel on the ground, down a drain, or down a toilet, or do anything else with it that is environmentally damaging.

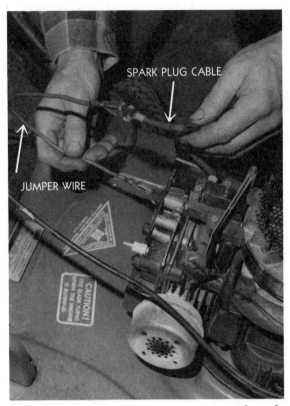

Figure 8.1 Ground the ignition system by taking the cable off the spark plug. Attach one end of a jumper wire to the terminal on the end of the cable. Attach the other end of the jumper wire to a cylinder-head bolt.

• REPAIRS TO SMALL GASOLINE ENGINES •

Following is a list of repairs presented in this chapter, and the tools and materials needed to make them:

REPAIR	TOOLS AND MATERIALS
1. Replacing a horizontal-pull recoil starter rope	Nylon starter rope, jumper wire, screwdriver, open-end or socket wrenches, awl
2. Replacing a vertical-pull recoil starter rope	Nylon starter rope, jumper wire, open-end or socket wrenches, screwdriver, needle-nose pliers, awl
3. Repairing a vertical-pull recoil starter	Jumper wire, open-end or socket wrenches, screwdriver, safety goggles, rust remover, no. 2 multipurpose grease, sealer
4. Troubleshooting a gas engine that stalls	Pliers, open-end or socket wrenches, syringe, spark plug, flywheel puller

REPAIR	TOOLS AND MATERIALS
5. Removing the engine flywheel	Flywheel holder and puller, clutch remover, propane torch, deep-socket and open-end wrenches
6. Decreasing engine vibration	Jumper wire, socket wrenches, flywheel puller, flywheel pin
7. Preventing the engine from overheating	Paintbrush
8. Troubleshooting a two-cycle engine that is hard to start	Syringe, two-cycle engine oil, gasoline, gasoline can, spark plug, spark plug feeler gauge, air filter, SAE 30 oil, carburetor cleaner, spark plug or socket wrench
9. Troubleshooting a four-cycle engine that is hard to start	Jumper wire, gasoline, spark plug, spark plug feeler gauge, spark plug or socket wrench
10. Troubleshooting the ignition system of an engine that doesn't start	Insulated pliers
11. Testing engine compression	Compression gauge, spark plug wrench, socket wrenches, carbon solvent
12. Troubleshooting an engine that runs too fast	Carburetor solvent, screwdriver, throttle cable
13. Restoring a frozen engine	Jumper wire, socket wrenches, breaker bar, clutch remover

R E P A I R · 1

REPLACING A HORIZONTAL-PULL RECOIL STARTER ROPE

PROBLEM: You pull the starter rope of a piece of outdoor equipment, and it breaks off in your hand.

Constant tugging on a starter rope will eventually cause the rope to fray and then to snap. But installing a new rope is easy and doesn't require special tools or training.

Note: This discussion is about recoil starter ropes that are located inside the engine cover and are pulled *horizontally*. How to replace recoil starter ropes that are pulled *vertically*, and the recoil starter ropes of grass trimmers, is discussed in Repair 2, below.

To replace a horizontal-pull recoil starter rope, do the following.

1. Buy the correct nylon rope from a dealer who sells your make of equipment. Starter ropes come in various lengths for different models, so be sure you get the length you need.
2. Using a kitchen match, burn each end of the rope until it chars. Don't overdo it, because the rope can ignite. Place a wet cloth against the charred ends to cool them down. (Charring the ends will prevent the unraveling of individual strands.)
3. Disconnect the spark plug cable from the spark plug. Ground the engine by connecting an alligator clip of a jumper wire to the cable

terminal, and securely connecting the other alligator clip to a metal part of the engine, such as a cylinder-head bolt.

4. If the throttle cable is held to the engine cover by a bracket or clip, loosen the bracket or clip and release the cable (Figure 8.2).

5. Remove the bolts or any other parts necessary in order to remove the engine cover. The accompanying photographs indicate how to remove a particular engine cover. Your type of engine may require the same or less work (Figures 8.3–8.8).

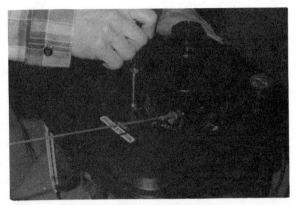

Figure 8.4 Loosen the fuel tank.

Figure 8.2 Release the throttle cable prior to removing the engine cover, which contains the horizontal recoil starter and rope.

Figure 8.5 If the fuel tank won't lift off after you take out visible bolts, look for hidden bolts.

Figure 8.3 You must usually remove several parts of the engine to reach the horizontal recoil starter rope. Begin by taking off the ventilation cover.

Figure 8.6 To release and remove the fuel tank, disconnect the fuel line.

Figure 8.7 *Release the recoil starter rope and handle from the handle of the mower.*

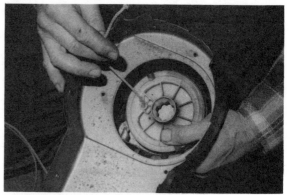

Figure 8.9 *Be sure to keep your thumb on the pulley so that the pulley doesn't unwind and cause the rope to wrap itself around the pulley again.*

Figure 8.8 *Take off the engine cover, which houses the horizontal recoil starter rope and pulley.*

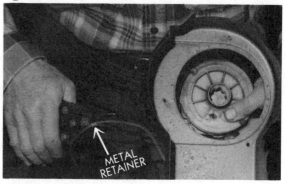

Figure 8.10 *This kind of engine possesses a starter rope that has a metal retainer. Cut off the old rope on the cover side of the retainer. Then pry the retainer off the old rope. Press it onto the new rope at about the same spot it was on the old rope.*

6.   Pull the starter rope out of the engine far enough to enable you to cut off the handle. Lay the handle aside.

7.   Pull on the rope until the pulley stops you. Press your thumb tightly against the pulley. Note that there is a knot in the end of the rope securing the rope to a slot in the pulley (Figure 8.9). Still holding the pulley tightly with your thumb, pull the knot from the slot and cut off the knotted end of the rope (Figure 8.10). (Certain cautionary steps, indicated in the caption, apply to the ropes in many of today's small engines.)

8.   The rest of the rope, now free of the pulley, can be pulled off and the rope discarded. When this is done, release your grip on the pulley and let it ease back slowly to an unwound position.

9.   Make a tight knot about ⅛ inch away

from one end of the new rope.

10.   Turn the pulley counterclockwise until you can't turn it any farther. Then rotate it back two revolutions.

11.   Holding the pulley tightly with your thumb as you did before, feed the *unknotted* end of the rope into the hole in the pulley and draw the rope through until the knot hits against the hole.

12.   Keeping the rope taut, let the pulley unwind slowly, which allows the rope to wrap itself around the pulley. When the pulley is unwound most of the way, thread the unknotted end of the rope through the hole in the engine cover. Pull this end of the rope out to take up slack; then, holding onto it, release

your grip to let the pulley unwind fully.

13. Before releasing the rope, make a temporary knot about 6 inches from the end of the rope. Then release your hold on the rope to let the knot come against the engine cover. The knot is there to keep some of the rope extended so you can attach the handle.

14. Using an awl, pry out the metal pin in the crevice of the handle. Take note of the kind of knot that was used to tie the old rope to the pin. (You may want to make a sketch of it.) Then untie the strands of rope around the pin and discard them.

15. Feed the unknotted end of the new rope through the hole in the handle. Secure the new rope to the pin using the same knot as on the old rope (consult your sketch, if necessary).

16. Press the pin into the crevice of the handle and pull the rope taut. Undo the knot holding the rope against the engine cover, and allow the rope to retract fully.

17. Screw the engine cover and all other parts back on, and reconnect the spark plug cable to the spark plug.

REPAIR · 2

REPLACING A VERTICAL-PULL RECOIL STARTER ROPE

PROBLEM: The vertical-pull recoil starter rope on a small gasoline engine has snapped.

As you make this repair, keep in mind that there are always variations between engines, and that you may have to alter the procedure somewhat from the steps described here.

1. Follow steps 1, 2, and 3 of Repair 1, above.

2. Remove the fuel tank and air filter housing, if necessary (Figure 8.11).

3. If you need to remove the engine cover to reach the rope, pull the rope out far enough so you can cut off the handle. Then, unbolt the recoil starter housing from the engine (Figure 8.12).

4. Examine the housing in which the pulley sits (Figure 8.13). Unlike the type of vertical-

Figure 8.11 Because the construction of engines varies, you may have to remove some parts, such as the air filter housing, that you would not have to remove from other engines.

Figure 8.12 Many vertical-pull recoil starter ropes (like the one illustrated here) are easier to replace than the type described in the text. Begin by removing the recoil starter housing.

Figure 8.13 This particular recoil starter pulley takes up the entire housing. Notice the knot in the starter rope (arrow). The rope is wrapped around the pulley, which receives its springiness from the starter mechanism in the center of the assembly.

pull starter illustrated in the photograph, there could be a notch above the pin that holds the pulley in the bracket. The notch will allow you to replace the rope without removing and disassembling the pulley.

5. If this is the first time the engine starter rope is being replaced, the rope may be secured to the pulley by a fastener that resembles a large staple. Grasp the end of the rope and pull it out slowly until this fastener comes into view. Hold onto the pulley and use a screwdriver to pry out the fastener. Then, pull the rope off the pulley, but keep hold of the pulley so it doesn't unwind. If the rope isn't secured to a fastener, its end will be knotted to secure it to a flange in the pulley. If this is the case, cut off the knot, and pull the rope out of the flange and off the pulley (Figure 8.14). (*Important:* If the pulley unwinds, in

Figure 8.14 *Pull the rope partially out and cut it off. Keep your thumb on the pulley so it doesn't recoil.*

order to install the new rope you will have to rewind it by hand, which is a nuisance. Therefore, either you or an assistant should keep pressure on the pulley at all times to keep it from unwinding. If you're doing the job by yourself, wedge a thin screwdriver or an awl through the slot in the pulley to keep the pulley secure after the rope has been cut off. You can then release your grip on the pulley.)

6. Holding the pulley, remove the screwdriver or awl (if you've used one), and wind the pulley up the extra turn or two necessary to get it fully wound. Then back it off slowly until the flange comes into view. It will be

positioned 180 degrees from the spot where the staple-like fastener appeared (again, assuming this is the first replacement rope installed in this engine).

7. To reuse the handle, take the retainer off the short piece of rope left in the handle, place the handle on the end of the new rope, and secure it with the retainer (Figure 8.15).

Figure 8.15 *Pull the old rope out of the handle and cut it off. Retrieve the retainer and use it to attach the new rope to the handle.*

8. Keeping a grip on the pulley, feed one end of the new rope through the hole in the flange (Figure 8.16). Tie a secure knot in the

Figure 8.16 *With the pulley wound up, thread the new rope onto the pulley. Make a knot in the end of it, and then allow it to wind itself onto the pulley.*

end of the rope and pull the rope taut. Make sure the knot doesn't rub against the interior wall of the bracket as the pulley unwinds. If it looks as if it might do this, trim enough off the end of the rope to provide clearance.

9. Allow the pulley to unwind all the way so the rope wraps around it.

10. Thread the rope through the hole in the engine cover and bolt the cover to the engine.

11. Reassemble engine parts and reconnect the spark plug cable to the spark plug.

REPAIR · 3

REPAIRING A VERTICAL-PULL RECOIL STARTER

PROBLEM: The rope on your recoil starter fails to return all the way into the housing after it has been pulled to get the engine started.

If this happens, the recoil starter mechanism is binding and has to be repaired. Note that there are two different types of vertical recoil starters. One type has all the parts discussed here *inside* the cover, the other has the pawls (clutches) *outside* the housing; the accompanying photographs illustrate the latter (Figures 8.17–8.19).

Here is how to fix the rope when the components are inside the housing:

1. Remove the spark plug cable from the spark plug. Ground the engine by attaching one alligator clip of a jumper wire to the cable terminal in the boot, and the other clip to a bolt on the engine.

2. Remove the fuel tank and air filter housing; then remove the cover over the recoil starter.

3. Remove the screws holding the recoil starter to the engine. Take off the assembly.

4. Place the recoil starter on a workbench and take the handle off the rope.

5. Turn the recoil starter over to remove the bolt in the center of the assembly. You are now able to take off the pawl retainer, pawl, pawl spring, and center spring. Lay components out in an orderly manner and draw a

Figure 8.17 The pulley of this vertical-pull recoil starter is controlled by an assembly that contains a spring and pawls. To repair it, first remove the cover of the mechanism.

Figure 8.18 If the spring doesn't feel as if it has sufficient tension, replace it. Examine the pawls and replace them if they are rusted.

Figure 8.19 Apply a drop of no. 2 multipurpose grease to the pivot points of the pawls.

sketch of how each part fits to avoid confusion when you reassemble the unit.

6. When all the parts mentioned above have been removed, take off the pulley, which has the rope wrapped around it, and also the recoil starter spring. (Wear safety goggles as you do this part of the job.) Hold the spring tightly to keep it from uncoiling in a whiplike fashion and possibly causing an injury.

7. Slowly let the recoil spring unravel. Then inspect it. Is the spring rusted? If so, the spring is the part that's keeping the rope from returning fully into the recoil starter housing. You may be able to remove the rust by cleaning it with a rust remover. But the spring also may have lost tension and you may need a new one. Purchase the part from a dealer who sells your particular make of equipment.

8. Spread a thin layer of no. 2 multipurpose grease (also available from the dealer) on the new (or old) spring.

9. Wind the spring up and place it into the spring retainer in the pulley. Then install the pulley and rope, center spring, pawl spring, and pawl retainer, in that exact order.

10. When the recoil starter has been put back together, place a dab of sealer on the threads of the bolt and screw it tightly back into position.

11. Attach the recoil starter to the engine and replace the rope handle. Then remove the jumper wire from the spark plug boot and engine bolt, and push the spark plug cable tightly back onto the spark plug.

REPAIR · 4

TROUBLESHOOTING A GAS ENGINE THAT STALLS

PROBLEM: The gasoline engine of your lawn mower or snow thrower stalls constantly.

The following information will help you find the source of the stalling problem. Try each procedure in turn until the problem is solved.

1. If this is a two-cycle engine that uses a mixture of gasoline and oil, make sure the fuel

tank contains the correct fuel combination. The amount of gasoline and oil must be in accordance with the manufacturer's instructions found in the owner's manual.

2. Remove the fuel tank cap and see if it has a small breather hole. If it does, insert a thin piece of wire through the hole to make sure nothing is blocking it.

3. Install a new spark plug (see box, opposite). To do this, you will need a deep-socket wrench of the diameter proper for your type of spark plug.

4. Determine whether the gasoline (four-cycle engine) or gasoline-oil fuel mixture (two-cycle engine) is contaminated. To do this, drain some fuel into a glass cup by pressing the drain valve or removing the plug in the bottom of the carburetor (see Figure 8.20). If there is no drain or plug, disconnect the fuel line at the carburetor and allow fuel to flow into the cup; or insert a syringe all the way into the fuel tank and draw out a sample. Allow the sample to set for 15 minutes, then hold the glass cup up to the light. The presence of particles on the bottom of the cup indicates that the fuel is contaminated with rust from the fuel tank, which means the fuel tank must be replaced. To do so, remove the screws holding the housing. Lift off the housing. Unclamp the fuel hose that lies between the carburetor and the fuel tank. You can now lift out the fuel tank. Install a new tank in the same manner.

Figure 8.20 *Carburetors of most small engines have a drain valve or drain plug that can be removed to get a gasoline sample to check for contamination.*

Gapping a New Spark Plug

For a spark plug to operate correctly, the distance between its outer and inner electrodes must be "gapped" or positioned correctly. A new plug must always be gapped before it is installed. To confirm that an old plug is properly gapped, first remove it from the engine, using the correct size deep-socket wrench (Figure 8.21).

To determine the proper spark plug gap for your engine, consult the owner's manual that came with your engine (it is the make and model of the engine that determines proper gap, not the type of spark plug). The width of the gap will be given in thousandths of an inch, such as .030 or .050.

Choose the correct feeler on a spark plug feeler gauge and slip it between the electrodes of the spark plug. The gap is properly set if you feel slight resistance as you move the appropriate feeler finger back and forth between the electrodes (Figure 8.22). If the gap is too tight or too narrow, use the adjustment tang on the spark plug feeler gauge to bend the outer electrode to make the adjustment (Figure 8.23). Don't use pliers, or you will ruin the spark plug.

Check the gap again, and repeat the process until the correct feeler meets slight resistance as it moves between the electrodes.

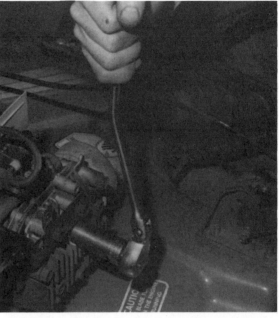

Figure 8.21 A deep-seat socket wrench of a size that fits the spark plug is needed to replace an old plug with a new one. Using any other tool may cause the spark plug to snap off.

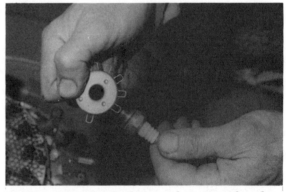

Figure 8.22 Check the gap between the electrodes of the new spark plug with a spark plug feeler. Use the size feeler that is specified in the owner's manual for your engine.

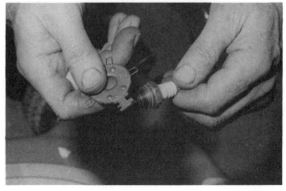

Figure 8.23 If the gap of the new plug is not set to specification, bend the outer electrode to set the gap. Use only the type of tool illustrated here, which is attached to the spark feeler gauge.

Figure 8.24 Inspect the spark plug cable. Replace the cable if it is cracked.

5.   Inspect the spark plug cable, which should be securely attached to the spark plug (Figure 8.24). Replace the cable if it is cracked, which may involve replacing the ignition coil assembly and removing the flywheel (see the following repair).

6.   Make sure the carburetor choke is opening fully, that there is no obstruction in the fuel line, and that the carburetor is adjusted in accordance with the manufacturer's specifications.

7.   If the ignition system uses magneto breaker points, these points and the condenser may have to be replaced. This involves removing the flywheel. It will also be necessary to remove the flywheel to find out if the flywheel key is broken (see the following repair).

8.   Have the carburetor overhauled by a professional.

9.   Have the engine overhauled by a professional.

REPAIR · 5

REMOVING THE ENGINE FLYWHEEL

PROBLEM: You need to work on the ignition system of your gas engine, or you have to install a new flywheel pin or do an engine overhaul.

Removing the flywheel of a two- or four-cycle gasoline engine is easy to do if you use a flywheel holder and flywheel puller. Both of these tools are available from any facility that sells and services small engines. You may also

need a clutch remover. The total cost should be less than $25 for all three tools.

1.   Remove the engine cover.

2.   Remove the screen over the wheel. If there is a clutch over the flywheel, you need a clutch remover (Figure 8.25).

3.   Press the clutch remover down on the clutch, attach the flywheel holder to the flywheel, and engage the clutch remover with a deep-socket wrench (Figure 8.26). The flywheel holder prevents the flywheel from rotating as you turn the wrench to remove the clutch.

Figure 8.25 If there is a clutch over the flywheel, you will need a clutch remover. If there isn't a clutch, the flywheel will be secured by a large nut.

Figure 8.26 The flywheel holder keeps the flywheel steady as the clutch is removed. If your flywheel doesn't have a clutch, but is held by a nut, also use the flywheel holder to remove the nut.

4. Remove the clutch remover and flywheel holder.

5. Set the flywheel puller onto the flywheel. The flywheel puller sits in the crevice left by the clutch remover. (If your engine doesn't have a clutch, the flywheel is held by a nut that can be removed with an ordinary open-end wrench. The flywheel puller occupies the space left by the nut.) You will notice that the flywheel has two indentations. Set the screws of the flywheel puller in these indentations.

6. Alternately tighten the screws of the fly-wheel puller with an open-end wrench—tighten one screw two turns, and then tighten the other screw two turns. Repeat the procedure until the flywheel pops up and you can lift it off the engine.

7. A problem sometimes arises if rust has developed between the flywheel and crank-shaft, and the flywheel sticks. If this should happen, do *not* bang the flywheel with a hammer to try to free it, or you will crack the flywheel. Instead, ignite a propane torch and apply the flame around the flywheel near where the crankshaft protrudes through the flywheel. Hold the flame at this point for 15 seconds. Place pressure on the flywheel with the flywheel puller. If the flywheel still doesn't pop loose, repeat the heating procedure until it does.

Figure 8.27 Note the important flywheel key. If the machine is operated without replacing a fractured key, the crankshaft can be bent, and the machine irreparably damaged.

to snap and stop any damage to the crankshaft. If an inspection reveals that the flywheel key is broken, installing a new key will eliminate the vibration and prevent further engine damage.

3. The engine crankshaft is bent. Usually this won't occur as long as the flywheel key is intact. However, if an impact does damage the crankshaft, the engine will have to be disassembled and the shaft replaced.

REPAIR · 7

PREVENTING THE ENGINE FROM OVERHEATING

PROBLEM: Your gas engine is overheating.

Overheating can cause extensive damage to the small engines of outdoor power equipment. Take the following preventive steps:

1. If yours is a two-cycle engine, be sure you are using a fuel mixture recommended by the manufacturer in the owner's manual. If the amount of oil in the mixture is not sufficient, excessive friction is created as parts of the engine rub together. This can result in higher-than-normal heat and premature engine failure.

2. If yours is a four-cycle engine, consult the owner's manual to make sure you are filling the oil sump with the type and viscosity of motor oil recommended by the manufacturer.

REPAIR · 6

DECREASING ENGINE VIBRATION

PROBLEM: The working end of your power lawn mower hits a rock or some other hard object, causing it to develop a noticeable vibration.

The impact may have resulted in one or more of the following types of damage:

1. The working end, such as a power mower blade, is damaged and has to be replaced.

2. The engine flywheel key is broken. The key is installed in a groove of the crankshaft as a fail-safe device (Figure 8.27). When the equipment strikes an object with sufficient force to bend the crankshaft, the impact is absorbed by the flywheel key, which is supposed

Figure 8.28 Keeping a small engine clean, especially the fins of the cylinder head, prevents the engine from overheating.

Check to see that the level of oil in the sump is at the Full mark as indicated by the oil dipstick. Change the oil at the interval recommended in the owner's manual, because contaminated oil interferes with the cooling process.

3.   Use a paintbrush to clean grass and debris from between the cooling fins of the cylinder head (Figure 8.28). The engines of outdoor power equipment are cooled by air, so if debris falls between the cooling fins and keeps air from reaching the cylinder head, the engine will overheat.

4.   Don't overburden the engine. For example, avoid cutting thick weeds with a power mower, or using a snow thrower to clear more snow than it is capable of handling. An engine that is worked beyond its capacity will overheat.

REPAIR · 8

TROUBLESHOOTING A TWO-CYCLE ENGINE THAT IS HARD TO START

PROBLEM: Your two-cycle gas engine is increasingly hard to start.

Two-cycle engines run on a fuel mixture consisting of fixed percentages of gasoline and oil. When a two-cycle engine is hard to start, the cause often lies with one of the following conditions:

1.   *An improperly mixed or stale fuel mixture.* Drain the fuel tank. If you don't want to bother removing the tank itself, use a syringe to get out every drop (see Safety Precautions, pages 90–91).

Prepare a fresh fuel mixture according to the instructions in the owner's manual. If you have misplaced the manual, call a dealer who sells the particular make of equipment and ask for the correct gasoline/oil ratio.

Pour half of the required amount of gasoline into a clean receptacle. Add all the oil and then the remainder of the gasoline. Screw the cap tightly onto the receptacle and shake it vigorously for at least one minute to make sure the gasoline and oil blend together thoroughly. Then pour the fuel mixture into the fuel tank.

Start the engine. If it still won't start promptly, proceed to the next step.

2.   *A worn or incorrect type of spark plug.* Consult the owner's manual, or ask a dealer which type and designation of spark plug is recommended for the engine. Also, find out the width of the gap at which spark plug electrodes should be set (see box, page 90).

3.   *A dirty air filter.* Remove the air filter and wash it in a solution of liquid detergent and water. Place the wet filter on paper towels and press it down several times to squeeze out excess water. Don't twist it or you may tear it apart. Spread a light layer of SAE 30 motor oil over the filter and put it back on the engine.

Note: If the filter is damaged, buy a replacement.

4.   *Sticking carburetor control parts.* To clean, spray carburetor cleaner over the cable and throttle valve lever located at the carburetor.

REPAIR · 9

TROUBLESHOOTING A FOUR-CYCLE ENGINE THAT IS HARD TO START

PROBLEM: Your four-cycle gasoline engine is difficult to start.

The following steps will help you find out whether the cause of hard starting with your four-cycle engine lies in the fuel or ignition system or results from a lack of engine compression:

1. Disconnect the spark plug cable from the spark plug. Ground the engine by extending jumper wire from the cable terminal to a metal part of the engine.

2. Crank the engine a few times.

3. Remove the spark plug and examine the electrodes. If the electrodes are dry, the reason for hard starting may lie in the fuel system. If the electrodes are wet, the cause of hard starting is a malfunctioning ignition system or a loss of engine compression.

4. To verify a fuel system malfunction, pour 1 ounce of gasoline into the engine through the spark plug hole, install the spark plug, connect the cable, and try to start the engine. If the engine starts, the cause of the trouble is a restricted fuel filter, an improper fuel mixture, a bad fuel pump, or a damaged carburetor.

5. If the spark plug electrodes are wet, install a new spark plug. A worn spark plug is the number-one cause of hard starting. If the engine is hard to start even with a new spark plug, the ignition system and engine compression will have to be tested (see the following repairs).

REPAIR · 10

TROUBLESHOOTING THE IGNITION SYSTEM OF AN ENGINE THAT DOESN'T START

PROBLEM: The engine is hard to start or doesn't start at all.

To find out if hard starting is being caused by a malfunction in the ignition system, do the following:

1. Remove the spark plug from the engine and reconnect it to its cable.

2. Using a pair of insulated pliers, hold the spark plug close to a metal part of the engine.

3. As you observe the electrode end of the spark plug, have an assistant pull the recoil starter rope. If a bright blue spark jumps be-

tween the electrodes and engine, it confirms that the ignition system is in good condition. If the spark is yellow, the cause of hard starting is in the ignition system.

REPAIR · 11

TESTING ENGINE COMPRESSION

PROBLEM: The engine is hard to start.

If a small gasoline engine loses compression, the engine will be hard to start. To test compression, you need a compression gauge, which you can purchase from a dealer of outdoor power equipment parts and supplies.

To test for compression:

1. Remove the spark plug.

2. Screw the compression gauge into the spark plug port of the engine (Figure 8.29), or, if necessary, hold it in place. The gauge must be held or screwed in as tightly as possible.

3. Pull the recoil starter rope three or four times as you note the maximum reading attained by the compression gauge. Repeat this step twice more to verify the reading.

4. Call a dealer who sells your make of equipment and ask what the compression specification is for that particular engine. Compare the reading you got with the specification. If

Figure 8.29 To perform a compression test, screw the compression gauge into the spark plug port of the engine, or hold it there as tightly as possible.

Figure 8.30 Bolts that come loose are a common cause of compression loss from around the cylinder head. Tighten the cylinder head bolts and do another compression test.

the reading is more than 10 percent below the specification, one of the following problems exists:

- A *loose cylinder head.* Tighten cylinder head bolts (Figure 8.30). Then retest compression to see if it has improved.

- A *buildup of carbon on valves and pistons.* Ask the service department of a dealer who sells your particular make of equipment to recommend a solvent that you can add to the engine to eliminate the carbon.

- A *blown cylinder head gasket, damaged valves, or worn piston rings.* In any of these cases, the engine needs to be overhauled.

HELPFUL HINT

Preventing a Fuel System Problem in a Four-Cycle Gas Engine

Never leave gasoline in the fuel system of a four-cycle engine for any length of time without adding a fuel stabilizer. Gas will gum up and clog the fuel delivery system, making a complete overhaul necessary.

If you can't run the fuel tank dry before storing the equipment for longer than a month, do the following:

1. Go to a small-engine or automotive parts store and buy fuel stabilizer.

2. Carefully read the directions on the container concerning how much of the stabilizer to use for the amount of gasoline still in the fuel tank. Pour the liquid into the tank.

3. Start the engine. Run it at idling speed for a minute to distribute the stabilizer throughout the fuel system.

4. Turn the engine off.

REPAIR · 12

TROUBLESHOOTING A GAS ENGINE THAT RUNS TOO FAST

PROBLEM: The gas engine of your power equipment races.

Don't take your outdoor power equipment to a repair shop just because the engine runs too fast. The cause of the problem may be located in the throttle cable that extends from the engine speed-control lever to the throttle lever on the carburetor.

Here is how to find and correct the problem:

1. Dirt could be preventing the throttle valve in the carburetor from closing properly, with the result that the engine can't throttle down. Turn off the engine. Dampen a rag with carburetor solvent, a product available at au-

tomotive parts stores. Read label instructions carefully first. Then wipe down the throttle cable. Wipe any remaining dirt off with a clean rag.

Start the engine to determine whether the cleaning procedure has solved the problem. If it hasn't, turn off the engine and proceed to the next step.

2. Check to see if the throttle cable is held to the engine cover by a bracket. If so, loosen the screw holding the bracket to the cover.

Start the engine. If the engine now runs at a normal speed, loosening the bracket has removed the pressure that was restricting the cable's movements within its sheath. Turn off the engine and tighten the screw holding the bracket to the engine cover just enough to secure the bracket.

3. If loosening the bracket doesn't affect engine speed, the throttle cable is probably defective. Examine how the cable is attached to the throttle lever on the carburetor and to the speed-control lever. Unhook the cable. Take the cable to a dealer who sells your make of equipment, and buy a new one.

4. Install the new throttle cable. Adjust it by placing the speed-control lever on Fast, and moving the throttle cable back and forth until the throttle lever just comes into contact with the boss on the carburetor that controls the lever. Secure the cable bracket to the engine cover.

REPAIR · 13

RESTORING A FROZEN GAS ENGINE

PROBLEM: The engine of your outdoor power equipment has been kept in storage for a long time and won't operate at all.

A "frozen" engine, as it is called, is apparent when you can't pull the recoil starter rope far enough out to get the engine to crank.

To restore, do the following:

1. Remove the spark plug.
2. Take off the engine cover to reveal the flywheel (see Repair 5, above).
3. Attach a socket of the proper size to the flywheel nut or a clutch remover to a clutch, and attach a breaker bar to the socket.
4. Give the breaker bar a quick, strong jerk in a counterclockwise direction.
5. Pull the recoil starter rope. If it is still restricted, give the socket another strong pull, and squirt a couple of drops of SAE 30 engine oil into the cylinder. Pull the recoil starter rope all the way out of its housing several times to circulate the oil through the cylinder.
6. Install the spark plug, attach the spark plug cable to the plug, put on the engine cover, and start the engine.

9

LARGE OUTDOOR POWER EQUIPMENT

*T*he equipment covered in this section includes walk-behind and riding lawn mowers and snow throwers. The tips and repairs described here involve non-engine areas; engine repairs have been covered in the previous chapter.

Safety Precautions

Certain safety procedures must be adhered to when attempting to repair power equipment. Be sure to follow these rules:

• To avoid serious injury, never place your hands near the working end of a piece of outdoor power equipment or near a revolving belt.

• Always turn off the engine and set any braking device before doing a repair or leaving the equipment.

• If draining of the fuel tank is called for, be sure to work outdoors. *Don't smoke.* Don't bring anything near the area where you're working that may produce a spark or a flame. If fuel is going to be poured back into the fuel tank and reused, be sure to use a clean receptacle to catch the fuel. To avoid engine damage, discard any contaminated fuel, but do so in an environmentally safe manner.

• REPAIRS TO LARGE OUTDOOR POWER EQUIPMENT •

Following is a list of repairs presented in this chapter, and the tools and materials needed to make them:

REPAIRS	TOOLS AND MATERIALS
1. Cleaning the blade housing of a riding mower	Garden hose, circular lawn sprinkler
2. Avoiding drive belt failure in a riding lawn mower	None
3. Replacing worn snow-thrower paddles	Syringe, gasoline container, open-end or socket wrench
4. Avoiding the breakdown of a snow thrower's drive belt	Jumper wire, open-end or socket wrenches, pliers

• RIDING MOWERS •

REPAIR · 1

CLEANING THE BLADE HOUSING

PROBLEM: *Grass clippings and dirt are clogging the blade housing of your riding mower.*

Here's an easy and efficient way to clean the blade housing of a riding mower:

1. Turn off the engine. Set the hand brake.
2. Connect a garden hose to a large-size circular grass sprinkler.
3. Slide the sprinkler under the blade housing.
4. Turn on the water.
5. After a few minutes, shift the position of the sprinkler to wash another part of the housing, repeating the process until the entire undersurface has been cleaned.

Use the above method after every cutting. Frequent treatment prevents grass and dirt from compacting and becoming difficult to remove.

REPAIR · 2

AVOIDING DRIVE BELT FAILURE

PROBLEM: *Your riding mower suddenly stops working.*

To prevent drive belt failure in your riding mower, do the following:

1. Adjust belts properly. A drive belt of a riding mower should deflect no less than ¼ inch and no more than ½ inch when you press the belt at a spot about midway between the pulleys.
2. Inspect pulleys for damage. A sharp edge, rough spot, or gouge in the groove of a pulley will cut into and weaken the belt. Replace a damaged pulley.
3. Buy the correct belt for the equipment from a dealer who sells the particular make and model. Different models take different sizes.
4. Do not put unnecessary stress on belts. Avoid going over obstructions such as tree roots and edges of sidewalks. To identify spots that could put extreme stress on belts, first walk over the area where you want to mow. Mark any potentially damaging obstacles so you can steer around them.

Using Power Mowers Safely

The most mechanically efficient power lawn mower will not protect the operator or bystanders if the equipment isn't used properly. The following procedures are recommended by the Outdoor Power Equipment Institute:

- Review the owner's manual periodically to reacquaint yourself with the manufacturer's operating recommendations and to review the location and purpose of all the functional and safety controls on the mower.

- Don't disable or remove any safety device or protective guard installed on the equipment by the manufacturer.

- Dress for safety. Wear heavy shoes, long pants, and form-fitting clothing that will not get snarled in the equipment if you get too close.

- Wear safety goggles to protect your eyes against any object flung by the equipment as it operates.

- Wear ear protection. The loud noise emitted by a large power mower can damage hearing.

- If you smoke, leave smoking materials and matches in the house.

- Fill the fuel tank outdoors when the engine is cold.

- Store leftover fuel in a container made expressly for the purpose, and place that container in a location away from the house—*not* in an attached garage.

- Clear the lawn area to get rid of rocks and other objects that may be flung about by the mower.

- Do not operate the mower if anyone is within 25 yards of where you are working.

- Keep hands and feet away from the rotating parts of the equipment. If you have to get near the mower to clear away debris that might impede its operation, or to empty a grass catcher, shut off the engine.

- Don't leave the mower running if you have to leave the area.

- Don't cut grass when it is wet. You could slip.

- Never push a walk-behind power mower up or down a slope. Instead, go across the slope.

- Mow up and down slopes with a riding mower—never across. The machine may turn over.

- Don't trot or run as you mow the lawn.

- Push a walk-behind power mower —don't pull it. If you happen to slip, you may pull the blade over your foot.

- Don't let anyone sit on a riding mower with you when the machine is running.

- Before shifting a riding mower into reverse, look behind you to make certain no one is standing there.

- If your riding mower is equipped with a grass catcher, turn off the engine before removing the bag to empty it.

• SNOW THROWERS •

REPAIR • 3

REPLACING WORN SNOW-THROWER PADDLES

PROBLEM: The snow thrower fails to remove snow.

The rubber paddles on the snow thrower may be worn. To replace them, do the following:

1. If the fuel tank contains fuel that could spill when you tip the snow thrower, use a syringe to draw fuel from the tank. Empty it into a clean container.
2. Tip the snow thrower back onto the upper part of the handle. Loosen the screws holding the worn paddles, and slide them from the retainer.
3. Slip the new paddles into place and tighten the screws.
4. Pour the fuel from the container back into the fuel tank.

REPAIR • 4

AVOIDING THE BREAKDOWN OF A SNOW THROWER'S DRIVE BELT

PROBLEM: You want to prevent the snow thrower's drive belt from suddenly breaking when the machine is in operation.

Inspect the drive belt of your snow thrower at the start of every season to prevent breakage when you are using the equipment. Do the following:

1. Disconnect the spark plug cable from the spark plug.
2. Remove the cover over the drive belt housing.

3. Examine the top of the belt for cracks and frayed edges. Then twist the belt and inspect the bottom for cracks, worn areas, and glaze (shiny surface). The presence of any of these conditions is reason to replace the belt.
4. Every snow thrower has a motor pulley and a driven pulley. The motor pulley drives the belt, which causes the driven pulley to turn and move the paddles or blades. Some snow throwers have a third pulley, called an idler. It provides support for a longer belt. Determine if the belt on your unit extends around two or three pulleys.
5. If your equipment has an idler pulley, slide the belt off this pulley first and then off the other two pulleys. If your snow thrower doesn't have an idler pulley, look for a spring on the driven pulley or motor pulley. Release the spring to loosen the belt so you can slide it off the pulleys.
6. Take the belt to a dealer who sells your make of snow thrower. Make sure that you get a new belt of the correct size.
7. Install the new belt. If an idler pulley is used, loop the belt around the motor pulley, beneath the idler pulley, and around the driven pulley. If you have difficulty getting the belt around the driven pulley, rest the belt on the edges of the pulley and press it onto the pulley with one hand as you turn the pulley counterclockwise with the other. To install the new belt on a snow thrower that doesn't have an idler pulley, extend the new belt around the motor and driven pulleys and reattach the spring.

HELPFUL HINT
How to Store a Snow Thrower Properly

To protect your snow thrower while it is in storage for the summer and to have it ready for next year, do the following:

1.   Remove the spark plug.

2.   Unbolt the fuel tank and pour off all fuel, or use a long-stemmed syringe to remove all fuel from the tank. Fuel left in the tank can turn gummy. *Use caution around fuel,* and always dispose of leftover fuel properly (see page 91).

3.   If yours is a four-cycle engine, drain oil from the engine and pour fresh oil into the crankcase. Be sure the oil is of the viscosity recommended in the owner's manual.

4.   Inspect drive belts. Replace any that are cracked or frayed.

5.   If the snow thrower uses a chain to drive the auger, clean the chain with a rag and then spray it with silicone lubricant.

6.   Install a new fuel filter and air filter as directed in the owner's manual for your unit.

7.   If the snow thrower uses rubber paddles, measure their thickness. If paddles are less than $\frac{1}{16}$ inch thick, replace them.

8.   Spread a coating of auto body wax on the auger and on the inside of the discharge chute.

9.   Lubricate the control linkage, using only the lubricant called for by the manufacturer in the owner's manual.

10.   Squirt some two-cycle engine oil into the combustion chamber of a two-cycle engine through the spark plug port. Squirt some SAE 30 engine oil into the combustion chamber of a four-cycle engine through the spark plug port.

11.   Install a new spark plug.

12.   Clean the body of the snow thrower and apply a coating of auto body wax.

10

SMALL OUTDOOR
POWER EQUIPMENT
and GARDENING TOOLS

*T*his chapter covers engine and component repairs on gasoline-powered grass trimmers and chain saws, as well as repairs on electric grass shears, hedge trimmers, and ordinary lawn sprinklers.

Although the general engine repair procedures for large outdoor gasoline-powered equipment (see chapters 8 and 9) apply to all two-cycle engines, including the ones described here, the extra steps pointed out in this chapter are necessary for the safe and efficient operation of these smaller pieces of equipment.

Keep in mind, too, that the motors of electrically powered tools are the same, except for variations in size. They are constructed the same way, with the same parts: an armature, a commutator on the end of the armature, and two brushes located one on each side of the commutator. It follows, then, that the repair procedures described here can be used as a guide for troubleshooting and repairing any electric garden and lawn tools, including walk-behind electric lawn mowers.

• GASOLINE-POWERED GRASS TRIMMERS •
AND CHAIN SAWS

Safety Precautions

• Wear eye and ear protection whenever you operate a grass trimmer or chain saw.

• Never put your hand anywhere near the working end of a grass trimmer or chain saw, or proceed with any repair, unless the equipment is turned off and grounded as described below.

• When you handle gasoline, observe the following precautions:

1. To ensure that you do not accidentally start the engine by inadvertently cranking the engine shaft while working, disconnect the spark plug cable from the spark plug.
2. To ensure that the spark plug cable plug does not accidentally come back into contact with the spark plug and complete the ignition circuit, short-circuit the ignition system by grounding the cable to the engine (see page 91).
3. If a procedure directs that you handle gasoline, take the equipment you're working on outdoors for ventilation.
4. Do not allow any object near the gasoline that may create a spark or flame.
5. If the procedure directs you to drain fuel from the fuel tank and discard it, take the precautions noted above. Do not pour the fuel on the ground, down a drain, or down a toilet, or do anything else with it that is environmentally unsafe.

• REPAIRS TO SMALL OUTDOOR POWER EQUIPMENT •

Following is a list of repairs presented in this chapter, and the tools and materials needed to make them:

REPAIR	TOOLS AND MATERIALS
1. Preventing a breakdown in a grass trimmer	Jumper wire, open-end or socket wrenches, wooden or plastic implement, can of compressed air, air cleaner
2. Replacing a grass trimmer's starter rope	Jumper wire, screwdriver, open-end or socket wrench, knife, nylon rope
3. Troubleshooting incessant starter rope failure in chain saws	None
4. Sharpening the cutters of a chain saw	File holder, raker depth gauge, flat metal-cutting file, round metal-cutting file
5. Replacing the nose sprocket of a chain saw	Jumper wire, bench grinder or metal-cutting file, punch, conventional hammer, nose sprocket, rivets, ball-peen hammer
6. Repairing electric garden and lawn tools that run erratically	Power cord, screwdriver, on-off switch, motor brushes
7. Restoring full action to lawn sprinklers	Thin wire, pliers

• GRASS TRIMMERS •

REPAIR · 1

PREVENTING A BREAKDOWN IN A GRASS TRIMMER

PROBLEM: The engine is backfiring.

To prevent a problem with your gasoline-powered grass trimmer, inspect the air cleaner after each use. If it is black and singed, the engine is backfiring. If the cause of the backfire isn't corrected, the engine could be damaged.

One reason for engine backfire is unnecessary engine revving, so avoid this practice. Another cause is a muffler and exhaust port that clog with built-up carbon.

To clean the muffler and exhaust ports, do the following:

1. Disconnect the spark plug cable from the spark plug. Ground the engine by attaching one clip of a jumper wire to the spark plug cable terminal. Attach the other clip of the jumper wire to a metal part of the trimmer, such as an engine bolt.
2. Take off the engine cover to reveal the muffler and exhaust port housing.
3. Remove the bolt holding the cover over the housing. Take off the cover and gasket. (Handle the gasket carefully, because it has to be reused.)
4. Pull the starter rope all the way out of the recoil starter housing. Tie a knot in the starter rope at the recoil starter housing. Then ease the rope back until the knot catches on the housing. This action moves the piston to the top of the combustion chamber. Here it closes the exhaust port to prevent any carbon dislodged during the cleaning procedure from falling into the combustion chamber and possibly damaging the engine.
5. Use a wooden or plastic implement to loosen carbon lodged in the exhaust port. Then scrape loose the carbon clinging to the inside of the muffler.
6. Using a can of compressed air (obtainable from photographic supply stores), blow out carbon particles from the exhaust port and muffler.
7. When the exhaust port and muffler are clean, release the knot in the starter cord and let the cord wind itself back into the recoil starter housing.
8. Reinstall the cover over the muffler and exhaust port housing. If the gasket has been damaged, buy another from a dealer who sells your particular make of grass trimmer.
9. Install a new air cleaner, reattach the engine cover, and connect the spark plug cable to the spark plug.

REPAIR · 2

REPLACING A GRASS TRIMMER'S STARTER ROPE

PROBLEM: The starter rope of your grass trimmer is snarled or snaps.

If your grass trimmer is similar to most models, you can replace the starter rope in the following way:

1. After grounding the ignition system according to the instructions on page 112, undo the screws holding the recoil starter housing to the engine. Take off the housing.
2. Remove the screw and washer holding the rope reel to the recoil starter housing. Lift the reel out of the housing. Do this carefully; if you pull the reel off sharply, the recoil spring can be dislodged. You will then have to rewind and reinsert the spring.
3. Cut the handle off the old rope. Notice that the rope is secured to the handle by a metal retainer. Lay the handle and metal retainer aside for use with the new rope.
4. Note carefully how the rope is held to the reel. Unwind the rope from the reel. (Slight variations may exist between your type of trimmer and the one described here.)
5. Buy a length of nylon rope from a dealer who sells your make of grass trimmer. Be sure

the new rope is the same diameter and length as the old rope.

6. To keep the ends of the rope from unraveling, hold a lit match to the ends of the new rope until they char. When the end of the rope turns black, use a wet rag to cool it. *Caution:* Perform this action safely away from the trimmer, and watch your hands. The rope can get very hot.

7. Tie a knot ¾ inch or less from one end of the rope.

8. Pass the unknotted end of the rope through the hole in the reel and pull the rope through the reel until the knot you just made presses up against the hole. To lock this end of the rope to the reel, press it into a slot in one of the ribs of the reel.

9. Hold the reel in your hand with the knot facing you, and wind the rope tightly around the reel in a clockwise direction. Leave about 6 inches of rope free of the reel.

10. Line up the backside of the reel with the inside of the recoil starter housing. Place the reel into the housing, moving it back and forth until it drops into the housing.

11. Secure the reel to the housing with the screw and washer removed in step 2, above.

12. Turn the reel counterclockwise until you are able to thread the 6 inches of remaining rope through the eyelet in the recoil starter housing. Then pull out about 12 inches of rope and tie a temporary knot so that the rope won't recoil all the way back inside the housing.

13. Insert the end of the rope into the handle and tie the metal retainer onto the rope.

14. Place the recoil starter housing on the engine and tighten the mounting screws.

15. Untie the temporary knot and allow the rope to wind itself fully into the recoil starter housing.

• CHAIN SAWS •

REPAIR • 3

TROUBLESHOOTING INCESSANT STARTER ROPE FAILURE IN CHAIN SAWS

PROBLEM: *Your chain saw starter rope keeps snapping.*

There are three main reasons that a starter rope may keep breaking:

- *You are pulling the rope at an angle, so it rubs against the side of the recoil starter housing.* The correct way to pull the starter rope is to draw it straight out of the recoil starter housing.

- *You are buying replacement ropes that are too short.* If the rope isn't of a size specified by the manufacturer, it won't stand up to the stress of pulling for long. Ask the dealer to check manufacturer's specifications for the particular model of chain saw, to be certain that the rope is the required length.

- *The engine has a malfunction that is causing hard starting.* An engine that doesn't start promptly requires more pulling on the starter rope per start, which causes the rope to wear out sooner than it should. If this is the case, look for a worn spark plug, dirty air filter, or damaged ignition coil.

REPAIR • 4

SHARPENING THE CUTTER OF A CHAIN SAW

PROBLEM: *Your chain saw has increasing difficulty in cutting through wood.*

A dull cutter (chain) makes it harder to slice through wood and creates more wear and tear than normal on the engine.

To sharpen the cutter, you need the following tools, all available from a dealer who sells your make of chain saw:

- A file holder, to maintain the teeth at the correct angle for sharpening. The teeth are those parts of the cutter that slice the wood.

- A depth gauge, to even out the height of the rakers (those parts of the cutter that establish the depth of the cut made by the teeth). Each tooth has a raker.

- A *flat* metal-cutting file and a *round* metal-cutting file. The round file has to fit the rounded groove of the tooth.

To sharpen a cutter, do the following:

1. Tighten the chain-tension screw. This will prevent the chain from wobbling while the sharpening is done.
2. Place the round file into the file holder.
3. Position a tooth on the file holder and give it three firm strokes with the file, *going in one direction only* from the inside of the tooth toward the outside. Apply pressure as you push the file away from you.
4. After you have sharpened a tooth, even out the height of its raker by placing the depth gauge over the raker and filing it with the flat file until the height of the raker becomes even with the surface of the depth gauge. Using the flat file, round off the corner of the raker, if the adjustment for height has caused the corner to become pointed. *Note:* As you finish filing each tooth and raker, place a mark on that assembly with a piece of chalk to identify the tooth and raker units you have treated; this will prevent you from mistakenly repeating the operation.
5. When all teeth and rakers in the midsection of the chain have been treated, loosen the tension screw and move the next section of chain into position.

HELPFUL HINT
How to Mix Fuel for a Chain Saw

The two-cycle engine of a chain saw runs on fuel consisting of gasoline and two-cycle engine oil. Both are mixed together before being poured into the fuel tank. If the mixing is done haphazardly, however, the engine can sustain major damage.

To begin with, check the owner's manual to determine the manufacturer's recommendation concerning the amount of oil to mix with gasoline. If the owner's manual has been misplaced, call a dealer who sells your make of chain saw.

Here is how mixing should be done:

1. Fill a *clean* gas can halfway with gasoline.
2. Pour the required amount of two-cycle engine oil into the can. *Caution:* Use a brand of oil manufactured specifically for two-cycle engines—any other type may cause engine damage. You can buy a suitable product from a dealer who sells chain saws.
3. Add enough additional gasoline to the gas can to bring the ratio of the mixture to that recommended by the manufacturer.
4. Screw the cap tightly onto the can and shake it vigorously for at least one minute *just before* filling the fuel tank of the chain saw.
5. Fill the fuel tank.
6. To store leftover fuel, screw the cap tightly on the gas can and place the can in a location away from the house, such as a storage shed or a detached garage. When you use the stored fuel, be sure to shake the can for at least one minute before pouring it into the fuel tank of the chain saw.

REPAIR · 5

REPLACING THE NOSE SPROCKET OF A CHAIN SAW

PROBLEM: The nose sprocket of your chain saw is damaged, impeding its proper operation.

Replacing a damaged nose sprocket may seem at first to be a formidable task, because the nose sprocket is riveted onto the chain bar. If you follow these steps, however, you may be able to do the job yourself:

1.   Remove the guide bar from the saw, and the chain from the guide bar, following the instructions provided in the owner's manual.
2.   Use an electric or a metal-cutting file to grind down the heads of the rivets that are holding the nose sprocket to the guide bar.
3.   Using a hammer and punch, drive out the rivets and free the damaged nose sprocket.

4.   Buy a new nose sprocket for your model from a dealer who sells your make of chain saw. You will also need new rivets. *Caution:* The new nose sprocket may come in a case— do *not* remove the part from the case, which is designed to make sure the nose sprocket is installed properly without disrupting the bearings.
5.   Place the designated end of the case against the guide bar and carefully slide the nose sprocket onto the guide bar.
6.   Put rivets into the holes. Then place the nose sprocket on a flat metal plate, such as the anvil part of a bench vise, and flatten the rivets with the peen (round) end of a ball-peen hammer.
7.   Put the chain back on the guide bar, and the guide bar on the motor housing. Adjust the chain. (Instructions for adjusting the chain should be in the owner's manual.)

· ELECTRIC GARDEN AND LAWN TOOLS ·

Safety Precautions

•   Keep your fingers away from the working end of an electric tool as long as the power cord is plugged into an electric outlet.

•   Before proceeding with a repair, always check to make sure the power cord plug is disconnected from the electric outlet.

•   Make sure you reattach wires to their respective terminals. If you cross wires, you may create a short circuit that could lead to a deadly electric shock. Use a labeling system to mark the wire and its terminal. First, write "#1" in red crayon on two self-adhering labels or strips of masking tape. Place one of the labels on a wire; put the other on the terminal that holds the wire. Do the same for the second wire (#2), but use a blue crayon. With this method, you can keep track of where to reconnect each wire.

•   Before reassembling a tool, make sure that no part of the wires touches the housing.

•   Never operate or try to repair an electric tool if the ground you are standing on is damp or wet, or if water is present on the workbench.

REPAIR · 6

REPAIRING ELECTRIC GARDEN AND LAWN TOOLS THAT RUN ERRATICALLY

PROBLEM: An electric garden and lawn tool doesn't start or runs only intermittently.

The first of the following repairs is not within the tool itself; the rest require opening the motor housing.

1.   If the tool is usually plugged into an extension cord, the extension cord and not the tool may be at fault. Plug the power cord of the tool into a wall outlet and turn it on. If the tool now works, you need a new extension cord. *Caution:* Make sure an extension cord used with electric garden and lawn tools is

approved for outdoor conditions by the Underwriters Laboratories, and always make sure that any extension cord is at least as heavy in gauge as the cord attached to the tool or appliance.

2. With the power cord of the tool plugged into a wall outlet, place the tool on a flat surface with the blade pointing up or to a side. Keep your hands away from the blade. Flip the on/off switch to On. Now flex the power cord back and forth over every inch of the cord from the plug end to where the cord enters the housing. If the tool springs to life, even momentarily, the reason for the problem lies with a damaged power cord. Pull the power cord plug from the wall outlet. Open the tool housing. Replace the power cord by disconnecting it from the switch (see page 141).

3. To determine if the cause of the problem is a damaged on/off switch, flip the switch between On and Off a few times. A worn-out switch will be loose and won't click. Replace the switch (see page 142).

4. If the power cord and switch aren't damaged, the motor brushes are probably worn. These brushes are made of carbon and transmit electricity to the motor. When brushes wear out, the motor won't run or will run erratically.

An electric tool has two brushes. Before opening the housing, look for slotted caps on the sides of the tool. These are the brush access caps. With the power cord disconnected from the wall outlet, unscrew the brush caps. The brushes should pop partially out of the holes.

Pull them out all the way, but don't put any stress on the wires.

Brushes should be at least ¼ inch long. If either brush measures less, you'll need to replace both brushes. Buy them at any store that deals in power tools. Slip the brushes out of their holders and insert new brushes in their place.

5. The tool may not have brush access caps. In that case, you can open the housing. Make sure the power cord is disconnected from the wall outlet. Look for a brush housing on each side of the motor commutator.

R E P A I R · 7

RESTORING FULL ACTION TO LAWN SPRINKLERS

PROBLEM: The supply of water emitted by your oscillating lawn sprinkler is severely reduced.

If some of the jets of your sprinkler are clogged, do the following:

1. Using a thin strand of wire, ream any deposits from each nozzle.

2. Attach the sprinkler to a garden hose and turn on the water full force.

3. If full sprinkling action hasn't been restored, use pliers to unscrew the nozzles from the sprinkler. Now clean the holes again, from the rear as well as the front.

11

SMALL ELECTRIC APPLIANCES

*O*f all the equipment discussed in this book, small electric appliances are the most difficult to repair. There are two reasons.

First, manufacturers discourage repairs by making it difficult to open the appliances and even more difficult to get replacement parts. Moreover, the fasteners that hold together the housings of a small electric appliance are usually hidden or are tamperproof and require a special tool not generally available to do-it-yourselfers.

Second, even if you manage to disassemble the appliance, inside you will find a confusing array of small components all crammed together. Separating the parts without damaging them is a tedious and complicated task. Toasters and food mixers/blenders are prime examples.

In light of these severe setbacks, we recommend that you replace a small electric ap-

pliance if you can't fix it. The retail prices of these small units are relatively low, making it more economical and less frustrating to buy a new one.

Safety Precautions

The safety precautions to keep in mind when working on small electric appliances are the same as those to be observed when working on electric lawn and garden tools. To summarize:

• Always check to make sure the power cord is withdrawn from the electric outlet before you try to disassemble the appliance.

• Make sure you reattach a wire to its correct terminal. If you cross wires, you may create a short circuit that could lead to a deadly electric shock. Use a labeling system to mark the wires and terminals (see page 116).

• Before reassembling an appliance, make certain that a wire won't come into contact with the housing when the appliance is in operation.

• Never operate or work on an electric appliance if the ground is damp or wet, or water is present on the workbench.

• REPAIRS TO SMALL ELECTRIC APPLIANCES •

Following is a list of repairs present in this chapter, and the tools and materials needed to make them.

REPAIR	TOOLS AND MATERIALS
1. Removing frozen assembly screws	Knife, screwdriver, hammer
2. Restoring retention in an electric can opener	Toothbrush
3. Repairing a drip-style coffee maker that steams excessively	Vinegar, screwdriver, nut driver, thin wire
4. Repairing a percolator coffee maker	Drip tube
5. Restoring power to a cordless electric toothbrush	Mouthwash
6. Troubleshooting a nonwarming electric blanket	None
7. Overcoming double-cutting with an electric knife	Typing paper
8. Determining when new electric knife blades are needed	Ruler
9. Restoring full power to a food blender or mixer	Screwdriver, nut driver, pliers, motor brushes and springs, fine-grade (no. 00) sandpaper, self-adhering labels
10. Fixing a loose handle on a food blender or mixer	Hand grinder, cyanoacrylate adhesive
11. Restoring the variable speed feature to a food blender or mixer	Screwdriver, nut driver, self-adhering labels, variable speed (governor) switch
12. Repairing a food processor that won't run	Power cord, screwdriver, nut driver, self-adhering labels, electrician's tape, jumper wire, on-off switch, safety switch
13. Replacing the drive belt of a food processor	Screwdriver, nut driver, drive belt
14. Resealing a leaky steam iron	Screwdriver, nut driver, putty knife, liquid silicone sealer, hard rubber roller

REPAIR	TOOLS AND MATERIALS
15. Testing and replacing a toaster power cord	Screwdriver, nut driver, pencil eraser, ohmmeter, power cord
16. Restoring pickup power to an upright vacuum cleaner	Drive belt
17. Troubleshooting a sluggish vacuum cleaner motor	Adjustable pliers, adjustable wrench, screwdriver, motor brushes and springs
18. Repairing a short circuit in a small appliance	Power cord, pliers, electrician's tape, insulators, neon tester

---

H E L P F U L   H I N T

When Not to Attempt to Repair Your Small Electric Appliances

Many small electric appliances are manufactured with tamper-resistant screws or fasteners to discourage do-it-yourself repair. Furthermore, some manufacturers will not provide replacement parts to companies that cater to the do-it-yourself market.

Before you proceed to make a repair, therefore, do the following:

1. Inspect the appliance to determine whether you are able to disassemble it.
2. Call the companies listed in the appendix or in the yellow pages of the telephone book under the heading "Appliances, Household, Small" to determine whether parts are available for your particular unit.

R E P A I R · 1

REMOVING FROZEN ASSEMBLY SCREWS

PROBLEM: The screws refuse to budge when you attempt to disassemble the housing of a small appliance.

First, make sure the appliance is disconnected from the wall outlet. Then do the following:

1. Using the blade of a knife, scrape off any dirt from the slot of the screw.
2. Using a screwdriver, twist with one hand as you use your other hand to tap the handle of the screwdriver with a hammer.

R E P A I R · 2

RESTORING RETENTION IN AN ELECTRIC CAN OPENER

PROBLEM: Your electric can opener no longer holds cans securely to the cutting assembly.

The gear that rotates the can may be dirty. Use a toothbrush to scrub it clean. Test the unit to see if this treatment has helped. If it hasn't, the gear is worn and you will have to replace the can opener.

REPAIR · 3

REPAIRING A DRIP-STYLE COFFEE MAKER THAT STEAMS EXCESSIVELY

PROBLEM: Your drip-style electric coffee maker steams and sputters as it operates.

Steaming and sputtering from a drip-style coffee maker indicates that mineral deposits left by tap water have clogged the drip tube. The drip tube is a vertical tube through which heated water rises into the coffee basket. Usually, a cleaning with vinegar and water will get rid of deposits.

Pour plain vinegar into the tank. Turn on the coffee maker to allow the vinegar to rise up through the drip tube to clear the deposits. Do the same with plain water. Repeat the process, if necessary.

If this treatment doesn't work, do the following:

1. Disconnect the power cord from the wall outlet.
2. Turn the coffee maker upside down and remove the screws from the base plate. Take off the base plate. If it doesn't come free, there may be a screw hidden inside one of the legs or under a label, or one or more of the legs may be holding the base plate. See if you can find and remove all screws.
3. With the base plate removed, you will see the drip tube extending from the base of the coffee maker toward the coffee basket. Insert a length of narrow wire into the drip tube to break up deposits.
4. Reinstall the base plate. Plug the power cord into the electric outlet, and give the coffee maker another cleaning with vinegar and then water to flush out all the deposits that have come free.

REPAIR · 4

REPAIRING A PERCOLATOR COFFEE MAKER

PROBLEM: Your electric percolator makes hot water instead of coffee.

If a coffee percolator gives you hot water rather than coffee, make sure you are placing the bottom of the vertical tube assembly, called the drip tube, fully into the well in the base of the percolator. If you are placing it correctly, the problem lies elsewhere—you may have to replace the tube.

In the bottom of the tube is a washer that acts as a pump and pushes hot water up the tube so it overflows into the coffee basket (Figure 11.1). When this washer wears out or loses resiliency, the water gets hot, but stays in one place and doesn't reach the coffee. Replace the tube, if possible.

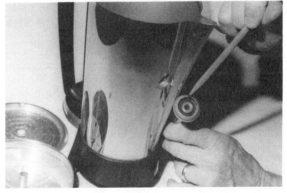

Figure 11.1 Deterioration of this small washer at the end of the drip tube of a percolator may be the reason the percolator is not brewing coffee.

REPAIR · 5

RESTORING POWER TO A CORDLESS ELECTRIC TOOTHBRUSH

PROBLEM: Your cordless toothbrush is operating sluggishly.

The following procedure may restore full power:

1. Make sure that you have the charging base plugged into a *live* wall outlet. If power to the

outlet has been turned off, the appliance has been losing power rather than having power maintained at maximum level.

2.   After the toothbrush holder has been in the charging unit for 12 hours, remove the holder and put your hand on its base. If it doesn't feel warm, the self-charging battery pack is faulty. Don't attempt to make this repair yourself—you could ruin the unit. Instead, mail back both the charging unit and the toothbrush holder to the manufacturer.

3.   If the base of the toothbrush holder is warm, the charging unit is performing properly and the self-charging battery pack is in good condition. The fault, therefore, may lie with a worn toothbrush stem. Insert a new brush in the holder to find out if it performs with more power than the old one.

4.   If you have reached this point in the repair procedure without positive results, fault may lie with a toothbrush holder that is clogged with toothpaste. Failure to clean the instrument properly after each use allows the toothpaste to work its way down into the head of the holder and clog the reciprocating gears. These gears move the brush. To clean congealed toothpaste from the head, remove the brush and pour mouthwash into the head of the holder. Turn the on-off switch to On for 10 seconds. Repeat this procedure five times. Then place the holder back into the charging unit for 12 hours before testing it again. If power hasn't been restored, you need a new toothbrush holder. To prevent further clogging of the toothbrush holder's reciprocating gears, treat the holder with mouthwash once a week.

REPAIR · 6

TROUBLESHOOTING A NONWARMING ELECTRIC BLANKET

PROBLEM: Your electric blanket doesn't get as warm as you would like.

The following simple procedures can help you pinpoint whether there is a defect in the blanket:

1.   Unplug the power cord from the wall outlet. Plug a lamp in the outlet. Turn the lamp on to confirm that the wall outlet is live.

2.   If the blanket is plugged into an extension cord, unplug the blanket from the cord. Connect a lamp to the extension cord to confirm that the extension cord is not defective.

3.   Fold the blanket as if you were going to repack it into its original box or plastic bag. Connect the folded blanket to a wall outlet and turn it on. Set the temperature control dial on High. Wait 15 minutes. Then place your hand between the folds. If the blanket feels hot to the touch, it is performing normally.

Note: There aren't any do-it-yourself repairs to be made to an electric blanket. If your blanket isn't adequate as far as you're concerned, return it to the manufacturer for evaluation.

HELPFUL HINT

Keep Your Cordless Electric Shaver Working When You Travel

Do you take along a cordless electric shaver when traveling? Keep in mind that even a fully charged cordless shaver starts to lose power as soon as the power cord of the charging base is disconnected from a wall outlet.

If you keep the charging base unplugged for 24 hours, the shaver will lose about 2 percent of its power. If it operates sluggishly, the batteries are probably past their prime. You can nurse them along by plugging the charging base into a wall outlet as soon as you reach your hotel.

R E P A I R · 7

OVERCOMING DOUBLE-CUTTING IN AN ELECTRIC KNIFE

PROBLEM: Thin slivers of meat or poultry issue from between the twin blades of an electric knife as the main slices fall on the platter.

There are two reasons for double-cutting: either too much pressure is being put on the knife, or the space between the blades is excessive.

To determine if there is too much of a gap between the blades, do the following:

1. Fold and refold a strip of typing paper until you get a thickness of ¼ inch.

2. *Unplug the power cord from the wall outlet.* Insert the test strip between the blades at the handle and draw the strip down the length of the two blades. If the test strip passes along easily without encountering resistance, you will need to replace the blades. However, if you have to exert an effort to push the test strip along, the blades are adequate. The problem of double-cutting, therefore, is a result of putting too much pressure on the knife as you cut. Ease up and let the blades do the work.

R E P A I R · 8

DETERMINING WHEN NEW ELECTRIC KNIFE BLADES ARE NEEDED

PROBLEM: Your electric knife is not cutting as well as it once did.

To find out if the cutters are worn, do the following:

1. Detach the power cord from the wall outlet. Check to make sure the blades are seated firmly in the handle.

2. Replug the power cord into the wall outlet. Alternately turn the knife on and off until you get the blades to stop so that the points of one blade fall in the hollows between the points of the other blade.

3. Pull the power cord from the wall outlet.

4. Measure the relative heights of the cutter points. If the points of one blade aren't higher than the points of the other blade, the cutters are worn. Replace the blades.

R E P A I R · 9

RESTORING FULL POWER TO A FOOD BLENDER OR MIXER

PROBLEM: Your food blender or food mixer, which has given satisfactory performance for many years, has begun to run erratically.

The cause of the trouble usually is worn motor brushes.

If you are able to disassemble the appliance, replace the brushes by doing the following:

1. Unplug the power cord from the wall outlet.

2. Detach all removable items, such as the food container and blade.

3. Turn the motor housing over and remove the assembly screws to open the housing.

4. If necessary, jiggle the motor out of the housing so you can reach the brush holders. There is one on each side of the commutator. Be careful not to pull on wires.

5. When the brush holders are fully accessible, undo the screws holding them to the motor. Remove the brush and spring from each holder.

6. Buy new brushes (preferably precured brushes that fit the arc of the commutator) and springs from a dealer in small appliance parts.

7. Examine the commutator. If it is pitted or has black tracks around it, clean it by rubbing it lightly with a piece of fine-grit (no. 00) sandpaper.

8. If you weren't able to obtain precured brushes, put an arc into the brushes by placing a piece of sandpaper on the motor commutator with the grit side facing up. As you hold the brush firmly against the sandpaper, have an assistant rotate the motor until the end of the brush has an arc to match the curvature of the commutator.

FIXING A LOOSE HANDLE ON A FOOD BLENDER OR MIXER

PROBLEM: The handle of your blender or mixer has come off the housing.

If the handle of your food mixer is attached to the housing by screws projecting through the housing, the threaded parts of the screws can strip.

Before discarding the appliance, do the following:

1. Disconnect the unit from the wall outlet.
2. If the handle can't be set firmly down onto the screws, use a hand-held grinder to shave down the screws until they fit the holes in the handle.
3. Following the safety directions on a package of cyanoacrylate adhesive, spread a small amount of the adhesive onto the screws.
4. Press the handle into place on the screws. Don't disturb the repair for 12 hours.

If the above repair is successful and the handle stays in place, refrain from ever immersing the handle in water. Water can affect the bond made by the cyanoacrylate adhesive. Instead, use a damp cloth or sponge to clean the appliance.

RESTORING THE VARIABLE SPEED FEATURE IN A FOOD BLENDER OR MIXER

PROBLEM: Your food mixer, which originally offered low, medium, and high speeds, now provides only one speed.

The part involved in a speed feature is called the governor switch. In this case, the switch is defective and must be replaced.

Here is how to do this job:

1. Unplug the power cord from the wall outlet.
2. Pry off the end cap and unscrew the control knob. The governor switch is right behind the control knob.

3. Remove the handle and the top half of the housing.
4. Disconnect the wires at the governor switch and unscrew the switch. If possible, try to purchase a new switch of the same make from a store that handles appliances from that particular manufacturer. Make sure you get the right one for your unit.
5. Install the new governor switch and reassemble the mixer.

REPAIRING A FOOD PROCESSOR THAT WON'T RUN

PROBLEM: Your food processor won't operate at all.

If a professional service technician repairs a food processor, the cost often equals the price of a new appliance. So most people prefer to buy a new unit. An alternative solution is to try to make the repair yourself. *Note:* Keep in mind that a food processor has *two* on-off switches you must deal with. One is a safety switch that allows the processor to be turned on only when the bowl and lid are properly mounted and aligned; the other is the regular on-off switch.

Here is how to proceed:

1. With the power cord plugged into a wall outlet, tighten the bowl on the housing. This activates the safety switch beneath the bowl.
2. Turn on the on-off switch.
3. Starting at the plug, flex the power cord back and forth. Work each part of the cord a little at a time, all the way up to where it enters the appliance.

If the food processor springs to life even momentarily, you have identified the cause of the problem as a defective power cord, which can be replaced inexpensively by a service technician. If you can disassemble the appliance, you can replace the power cord yourself (see page 141).

4. If a faulty power cord doesn't seem to be the reason for the problem, try to disassemble the food processor. To remove tamperproof screws, you may need a special screwdriver (called a tamperproof screwdriver) that you might be able to get in a hardware store or small appliance parts store.

After removing the bowl, turn off the regular on-off switch. Unplug the power cord from the wall outlet and turn the appliance upside down. Take out the screws or fasteners to open the housing, which should uncover the two switches.

5. Tighten each wire connection just in case a loose wire is the reason for the problem. Also inspect wires carefully to determine whether a bare spot is causing a short circuit; if so, wrap electrician's tape securely around that area of the wire.

6. To test the regular on-off switch and safety switch:

    a. Make sure the power cord is disconnected from the wall outlet.

    b. Pull off the wires from the safety switch.

    c. Connect a jumper wire between the ends of the two disconnected wires.

    d. Press down the safety switch, if it's accessible. Stick tape on it to keep the switch in the On position.

    e. Turn the on-off switch to the On position.

    f. Keeping your hands away from the food processor to avoid getting a shock, plug the power cord into the wall outlet. Does the food processor start? If it does, the safety switch should be replaced.

    g. Pull the power cord from the wall outlet and reconnect wires to the safety switch. Keep the tape in place.

    h. Disconnect the wires from the regular on-off switch and connect a jumper between the two wires.

    i. Keeping your hands away from the food processor, plug in the power cord.

    j. If the appliance comes alive, disconnect the power cord and replace the on-off switch.

REPLACING THE DRIVE BELT OF A FOOD PROCESSOR

PROBLEM: The motor of your food processor starts, but the revolving shaft doesn't rotate.

A nonrevolving shaft means the drive belt has probably snapped.

If you can open the housing, you can install a new belt. Do the following:

1. Disconnect the power cord from the wall outlet. Remove the bowl and implements from the food processor.

2. Lay the appliance on its side. Take out the screws holding the bottom and top housings together. Open the housing.

3. If the housing doesn't come apart easily, don't use force. There is probably a hidden screw somewhere. If one of the legs has a hole through its center, the screw may be embedded deep in this hole. If not, the legs themselves may be holding the two housings together. Turn the legs to determine if they unscrew. A screw also may be hidden beneath a name plate; pry off the plate to check.

4. Once you have opened the housing, the drive belt should be accessible. Remove the belt and see if you can get a replacement.

5. Attach the new belt between the motor and drive pulleys on the bottom of the drive shaft.

6. Reassemble the unit.

RESEALING A LEAKY STEAM IRON

PROBLEM: Steam and moisture leak from the housing of your iron when you press the steam button.

First inspect the steam chamber cover. If it is cracked, the iron is no longer usable. If there is no visible damage, a new seal is probably needed between the steam chamber cover and housing.

To make this repair, do the following:

1. Disconnect the power cord from the wall outlet.

2. Remove the screws holding the steam chamber and housing together. (If there are no screws, you won't be able to do this job.)

3. Scrape any particles from the steam chamber and housing. They must be clean for the iron to operate efficiently.

4. Buy a container of liquid silicone sealer from an automotive parts dealer or hardware store. You also need a hard rubber roller, which you can get at an office supply store.

5. Apply a thin coating of the silicone sealer to the raised area of the steam chamber, rolling it on with the rubber roller. Don't leave any gaps.

6. Let the silicone sealer dry for 15 minutes.

7. Reassemble and test the iron. If it still leaks, repeat the procedure. If you still aren't successful, you'll have to replace the iron. When you go to buy your next iron, examine it carefully to see if it can be opened and repaired.

HELPFUL HINT

How to Maintain a Toaster

Crumbs that drop inside pop-up toasters hamper the operation of the cradle latch. To clean out a toaster and prevent potential trouble, do the following:

1. Disconnect the power cord.

2. Open the clean-out trap.

3. Brush out crumbs with a clean one-inch paintbrush. *Caution:* Do not use a knife, as it may damage delicate wire connections.

4. Using a can of compressed air, blow crumbs and other food matter, such as raisins, from parts you can't reach with a brush. (Compressed air can be purchased in a photographic supply store.) Use only short bursts of air, and don't aim the nozzle directly at thin wire elements.

REPAIR · 15

TESTING AND REPLACING A TOASTER POWER CORD

PROBLEM: Your toaster doesn't toast.

To troubleshoot the cause of toaster failure, test the power cord with an ohmmeter, as follows:

1. Pull the power cord plug from the wall outlet.

2. Turn the toaster over and remove the screws holding the cover in place. Take off the cover.

3. Inspect the power cord terminals to see if they are loose. If so, tighten them.

4. Disconnect the power cord terminals. Clean them by rubbing them with a pencil eraser.

5. Reconnect one of the terminals.

6. Attach one lead of the ohmmeter to the loose terminal. Connect the other ohmmeter lead to one of the prongs of the power cord plug. With the ohmmeter set on the Rxl scale, the meter needle will settle on zero, slightly above zero, or infinity (∞). Make a note of the reading.

7. Remove the ohmmeter lead from the terminal. Reconnect the terminal. Then disconnect the other terminal and attach the ohmmeter lead to it. This time the meter needle should swing to the opposite end of the scale. In other words, if the needle was on zero or slightly above zero, it should now be on infinity. If it was on infinity, it should now be on zero or slightly above zero. But if the needle stays where it was in step 6, the power cord is defective.

8. To replace the power cord, release the strain-relief device and disconnect both terminals.

9. Be sure the new power cord you purchase is recommended for toasters. Connect the terminals of the new power cord to the toaster and slide the strain-relief device back into place.

Note: Follow the above procedure to test the power cords of other appliances and tools.

REPAIR · 16

RESTORING PICKUP POWER TO AN UPRIGHT VACUUM CLEANER

PROBLEM: Your upright vacuum cleaner fails to clean, although the motor runs and suction is adequate.

Spotty pickup usually indicates that the belt that drives the brush is worn or has failed. Do the following:

1. Unplug the power cord from the wall outlet.
2. Position the unit so that the underside is accessible.
3. Snap open the housing cover and see if the belt is still attached to the brush.
4. If the belt is not in the correct position, or has stretched or looks worn and cut, unhook the brush roller and remove the belt.
5. Buy a new belt of the correct size from a dealer who sells the same make of vacuum, or from a hardware store.
6. Attach the new belt from the drive pulley to the groove in the brush. Install the brush and close the cover.

REPAIR · 17

TROUBLESHOOTING A SLUGGISH VACUUM CLEANER MOTOR

PROBLEM: Your vacuum cleaner motor runs slowly or not at all.

Sluggish performance indicates worn motor brushes. You may be able to repair the unit by replacing the brushes.
Follow this procedure:

1. Disconnect the power cord from the wall outlet.
2. Open the motor housing to uncover the motor.
3. Find and loosen the clamps or screws that secure the motor to the case. Remove the motor.
4. Find the brush housings on both sides of the motor. Open them.

5. Ease the brushes and springs from the housings. Note how the brushes and springs are placed.
6. Purchase new brushes and springs from a dealer who sells your make of vacuum cleaner.
7. Install the new brushes and springs.
8. Reassemble the unit.

H E L P F U L   H I N T

Maintaining the Hose of Your Canister-type Vacuum Cleaner

If you own a canister-type vacuum cleaner, be aware of the following facts about the accordion-type hose used with most of these units:

• The life expectancy of an accordion hose is approximately five years. After that, the hose can become porous and develop air leaks. A leaking or porous hose causes a reduction in the suction power of the vacuum cleaner, affecting its ability to pick up dirt. If this happens to your unit, purchase a new hose from a dealer who sells your particular make of machine.

• If the end of the hose (where the hose and metal or plastic connector join) is damaged, you probably won't be able to make the repair yourself. In most cases, the hose is press-fit into the fitting, and a special tool is needed. Take the hose to the dealer and let him or her judge whether the hose is worth saving or whether the purchase of a new one is more practical. If the hose can be repaired, the dealer should send it back to the manufacturer.

REPAIR · 18

REPAIRING A SHORT CIRCUIT IN A SMALL APPLIANCE

PROBLEM: You feel a tickle whenever you touch one of your small appliances.

The tickle is a warning that your appliance has a short circuit. This is a very serious problem, one capable of injuring you severely. Do not use the appliance any further until the short circuit is corrected.

A short circuit is created when a bare or worn wire, or part of a heating element, comes into contact with the outer case of an appliance. The tickle you feel is electrical current being transmitted to your hand.

The following steps describe finding and repairing a short circuit in a waffle iron, an appliance in which shorts often occur. However, you can use the information to repair a short circuit in any small electrical appliance:

1.   Unplug the power cord from the wall outlet.

2.   Inspect the power cord. Is its insulation frayed? If so, replace the power cord (see page 126).

3.   Lift out the grids to uncover the heating elements and insulators. The covers over them may be held in place by metal tangs. Using a pair of pliers, straighten the tangs and remove the covers.

4.   Examine the wires passing from the power cord terminals to the heating elements, paying particular attention to where the wires pass through openings close to metal edges. Wires at these points are susceptible to damage. Wrap burned or frayed wires with electrician's tape.

5.   Examine the ceramic insulators. If an insulator has broken apart and is allowing the element to touch the metal case, you have identified the area of danger.

6.   Release the element and remove the insulator. Buy a new insulator from an electrical supply store and install the element.

7.   Reassemble the appliance and plug it into a wall outlet. Hold one probe of a neon tester (you can buy this tool in any hardware store) to the metal shell of the appliance. Hold the other probe to an unpainted metal surface, such as the cover plate of a wall switch. The neon bulb should not glow. Now, reverse the appliance plug in the socket, if you can. If the neon bulb glows in either position, have a service technician inspect and fix the appliance. Or discard the appliance and buy a replacement.

12

VIDEO
and AUDIO EQUIPMENT

This chapter gives you information on how to prevent damage and perform small maintenance and repair tasks on television sets, telephones, videocassette recorders, compact disks, record players, tape recorders, cassette tapes, and personal computers. We do not recommend disassembling TV sets, VCRs, tape recorders, or PCs, since special training and tools are needed. Also, external factors are much more often the cause of problems than internal failures.

Safety Precautions

There is one main precaution: Turn the equipment off and make sure its power cord is unplugged from an electric wall outlet before you perform any repair that involves the interior of the unit.

Do not remove the cover of a television set. Any repair involving the interior of a TV should be done by a professional.

• VIDEO AND AUDIO EQUIPMENT REPAIRS •

Following is a list of the repairs presented in this chapter, and the tools and materials needed to make them:

REPAIR	TOOLS AND MATERIALS
1. Tracking down the cause of noisy TV reception	None
2. Getting rid of TV static	Tuner cleaner
3. Eliminating poor TV picture quality that is VCR-induced	VCR head-cleaning cartridge
4. Repairing muffled telephone reception	Screwdriver, no. 000 sandpaper or emery cloth, modular line cord, ear syringe or can of compressed air
5. Repairing a telephone that transmits your voice poorly	No. 000 sandpaper or emery cloth, screwdriver, modular line cord, ear syringe or can of compressed air, transmitter
6. Fixing dial-tone problems	Screwdriver, ear syringe or can of compressed air, modular line cord
7. Taking the buzz out of a cordless telephone	None
8. Repairing a record player turntable that doesn't revolve	Screwdriver, awl
9. Repairing a broken cassette tape	Cassette tape splicing kit, screwdriver, empty cassette case

REPAIR • 1

TRACKING DOWN THE CAUSE OF NOISY TV RECEPTION

PROBLEM: You are experiencing interference on your TV in the form of "noise" (streaks and dots).

The interference is caused by one of three things: an electric tool or small appliance inside the house; a malfunction of electric company equipment outside the house; or the TV set itself. To find out, do the following:

1. Turn on the TV. Wait for noise to appear. Check to make sure that all electric appliances and tools in the house are turned off. If noise continues, the source of interference is either the set itself or external conditions outside the house.

2. If, on the other hand, the noise disappears when appliances and tools are off, have a member of the family watch the TV as you turn on each appliance and tool to determine which one causes the poor quality. That appliance or tool is on the same circuit as the TV, so move it to another circuit.

3. If testing to this point fails to turn up the cause of noise, keep the TV set on. As an assistant watches the screen, turn off all but one circuit breaker or loosen all but one fuse in the home's main electric service panel. Then turn on each appliance and tool on that circuit

to determine if one produces the poor quality. If so, that particular appliance or tool has a malfunction and should be repaired or replaced.

4.   If the distortion continues, turn your attention to the doorbell or door chime system in your home. This signaling unit uses a transformer that might be the source of the interference. Most transformers contain sensors that automatically deactivate them if the ambient temperature in the area reaches a level that might cause them to overheat.

Is the transformer in the attic, and does TV noise appear only in hot weather? Conditions in the attic can cause temperature variations that make the transformer sensor cycle on and off. It's this cycling that can interfere with TV reception.

To find out if this is happening, wait for the interference to occur. Then disconnect the wires at the transformer. If the noise disappears, the transformer is the cause. Move it to a cooler part of the house, such as the basement or a closet.

5.   An effective way to determine whether you are dealing with an external interference source is to ask your neighbors if they are experiencing the same problem with their TVs. If they are, call the customer service department of the electric company and report the condition.

6.   Finally, if the cause of the interference seems to be within the TV set itself, consult a service technician. If you have cable service, call the cable company. It may be necessary to install a filter or modify the antenna system.

REPAIR · 2

GETTING RID OF TV STATIC

PROBLEM: Electrical interference in the form of a multitude of white dots appears on your TV screen.

Dirt on the tuner of a TV set can cause this type of static. If the set has a channel control knob, you can verify that the interference is the result of a dirty tuner. Turn on the set.

Keep your eye on the screen as you tap the channel control knob with your knuckles. If the interference disappears for a few seconds, the tuner needs a cleaning. Do the following:

1.   Buy a spray can of tuner cleaner from an electronic parts and supply store.
2.   With the TV turned off, pull the channel control knob off the tuner shaft.
3.   Insert the nozzle of the tuner cleaner into the cavity around the shaft and spray a small amount on the tuner.
4.   Attach the channel control knob. Turn on the set, and slowly rotate the knob clockwise from channel to channel until you have made one complete revolution.
5.   Turn off the set. Pull off the channel control knob, and give the tuner a second treatment with the cleaner.
6.   Reattach the channel control knob. Again, slowly rotate the knob, but this time counterclockwise, from channel to channel until you have made a complete revolution.

HELPFUL HINT
Installing a Satellite Dish

As of this writing, there are no federal laws governing the installation of a TV satellite dish by a homeowner. Nor is it a requirement to obtain a license from the Federal Communications Commission (FCC).

Before you buy and install a satellite dish, however, it's prudent to call your municipal offices to determine whether there are local requirements concerning the type, size, and appearance of the dish. There is a pamphlet that provides valuable tips about buying and installing a dish. Titled *Home Satellite Dish Installation*, it is published by the FCC, and can be obtained at no charge by writing that agency at 1919 M Street, N.W., Washington, DC 20554.

HELPFUL HINT
Wavy-Line Interference in a TV Set

If wavy lines appear on a TV screen, it's usually because someone in the house is operating an electric tool or a small electric appliance. The problem lies with the tool or appliance—not with the TV. The interference is a result of electricity arcing between the brushes and commutator of the electric motor. An arc is actually a band of sparks that occurs when electric current leaps the gap between two components. This energy is transmitted to the TV through the home's electrical system.

Arcing is often caused by worn brushes in an appliance. Therefore, once you have identified the faulty tool or appliance, you can replace the brushes to eliminate the problem. But what if the brushes aren't worn? The only solution then is to modify the tool or appliance, which means having a technician solder a 0.001 microfarad (mfd) disk capacitor having a rating of 1,000 volts between the brushes and the frame.

Caution: Do not attempt this modification yourself. Incorrect wiring could divert AC line voltage to the frame of the tool or appliance, resulting in serious injury to someone using it.

Sometimes wavy lines appear on a TV screen that are not traceable to the use of an electric tool or a small appliance in the home. This type of interference is probably caused by a transmitter outside the house, such as a CB radio, amateur radio unit, or FM radio station. The interference lasts only as long as the transmitter is sending.

To verify that the disturbance is coming from this source, switch your TV to a UHF channel the next time wavy lines appear. If the lines disappear, the cause is the nearby transmitter.

Installing a high-pass filter between the antenna connection terminals on the TV and the antenna lead may help alleviate the problem. To do this, connect the wires of the filter to the TV, and attach the antenna lead to the other side of the filter. When you purchase a high-pass filter from an electronics parts store, specify whether the antenna wire is round coaxial cable or flat twin-lead wire.

If the high-pass filter fails to eliminate all the interference, inserting a filter inside the TV set will probably do the job. If you have cable TV, call their service department for help and advice; otherwise, contact a TV service center.

REPAIR · 3

ELIMINATING POOR TV PICTURE QUALITY THAT IS VCR-INDUCED

PROBLEM: A fuzzy picture appears on your set only when a videocassette recorder is in use.

A fuzzy picture is probably not the fault of the TV, but is more likely caused by dirt that has settled on the heads of the VCR. To resolve this problem, clean the heads with a cleaning cartridge that is available in stores that sell VCRs or rent videocassette tapes.

To clean the heads, do the following:

1. Turn on the VCR.
2. Insert the cleaning cartridge.
3. Allow the cartridge to rotate in the VCR for the amount of time indicated in the directions on the cleaning cartridge package.

REPAIR · 4

REPAIRING MUFFLED TELEPHONE RECEPTION

PROBLEM: Voices are hard to distinguish on your telephone.

While this repair procedure applies primarily to telephone models 500 and 2500, you might be able to apply the instructions to other models as well. The model 500 is an older-style desk telephone with a rotary dial. The model 2500 is also a desk telephone, but has a touch-tone dial. To identify your phone, look for the model number on the bottom plate.

To trace the problem, do the following:

1. Plug the phone into a jack in another room. Make a call. If the reception is adequate, the cause of the transmission problem lies with the wiring in the room where the phone is normally used. You may want to call a technician to make any wiring repairs. (Trouble with wiring is a relatively rare occurrence, however.)

2. Continue troubleshooting. Disconnect the phone from the jack and unscrew the earpiece cover from the handset. Let the receiver drop into your hand.

3. Tighten the screws holding the two wires to the receiver. Then test reception.

4. If reception is still poor, undo the screws from the receiver. Using a piece of very fine sandpaper (000 grit) or emery cloth, gently rub each of the contacts and wire terminals. Reconnect and test the phone.

5. If reception continues to be muffled, test the cord that is plugged into the wall jack, but only if there is a modular-type jack so that the cord can be disconnected from the phone and the jack without tools. Substitute a cord from one of the other phones in the house for the one that has been in use. If the reception problem clears up, buy a new cord. (Testing a cord that is wired directly into the phone or into the wall should probably be done by a telephone repair technician. Check the yellow pages under "Telephone, Equipment and Systems.")

6. If the reception problem has not been eliminated, the cause of the trouble probably lies with the switch-hook assembly. This consists of a series of contacts located inside the phone. The assembly is protected by a transparent plastic cover. To service it, do the following:

   a. Disconnect the phone from the modular cord and turn the phone upside down.

   b. Loosen the two screws that hold the bottom plate to the phone housing (Figures 12.1 and 12.2).

Figure 12.1 Start to make repairs to an older telephone (one that does not use electronic circuit boards) by unscrewing the cover.

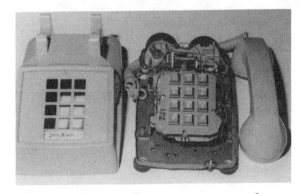

Figure 12.2 Once the cover is removed, you can reach the switch-hook assembly. First, though, remove the touchpad or rotary dial.

c. The switch-hook contacts are behind the rotary dial or the touchpad. Remove the dial or pad by loosening the screw on each side (Figure 12.3).

d. Remove the plastic cover that protects the switch-hook contacts (Figure 12.4). To do this, press in the tab on top of the cover while squeezing its sides, and lift up to free the cover.

e. Use an ear syringe or can of compressed air (sold at photographic supply stores) to blow out dust and dirt from between the contacts (Figure 12.5).

Figure 12.3 To release the dial, undo the screw on each side.

Figure 12.4 Once the dial is removed, you can reach the switch-hook assembly, which has a plastic cover over it.

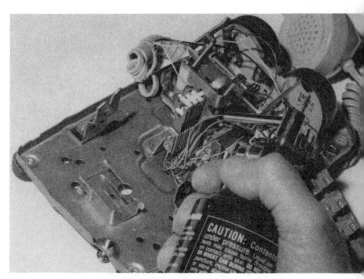

Figure 12.5 Using a can of compressed air, blow away any dirt that may be causing switch-hook contacts to stick.

f. Press down the switch-hook and release it slowly to open and close the contacts. If you see that some contacts are still sticking together, more cleaning is necessary.

g. Reassemble the telephone. Test reception.

7. The only other malfunction that can affect reception is a faulty receiver in the handset. Buy and install a new one, but make sure it matches the style of the one you're replacing.

R E P A I R · 5

REPAIRING A TELEPHONE THAT TRANSMITS YOUR VOICE POORLY

PROBLEM: People on the other end of the line complain that they have trouble hearing you.

This repair procedure applies to telephone models 500 and 2500. Check the model number of the telephone by looking at the bottom plate.

1. Unplug the phone from the jack. Unscrew the mouthpiece cover of the handset and remove the transmitter, a small disk.

2. Inside the handset are two metal contacts. Clean the contacts and the metal surface on the back of the transmitter with very fine emery cloth or sandpaper. Then bend each contact upward slightly to ensure that it touches the transmitter.

3. Tap the transmitter on a hard surface to loosen granules of dust or dirt.

4. Replace the transmitter and mouthpiece. Test the phone.

5. If transmission quality isn't improved, test the modular cord and clean the switch-hook contact assembly (see Repair 4, above). If necessary, purchase a new transmitter, but make sure it matches the style of the old one.

REPAIR · 6

FIXING DIAL-TONE PROBLEMS

PROBLEM: Dial tone is intermittent or absent, or continues throughout dialing, and outgoing calls don't connect.

The *external* repair procedures outlined here apply to all telephones that are connected to wall jacks. The *internal* repair procedures apply to telephone models 500 (desk phones with rotary dials) and 2500 (desk phones with touch-tone dials).

Dial-tone problems can be fixed by following these procedures:

1. *Constant dial tone.* If you dial a number and instead get a constant tone, disconnect the line cord from the wall jack and unscrew the bottom plate of the phone to expose the interior. Examine the network, which is the panel to which the tangle of interior wires is connected. Depending on the type of phone, the wires will be connected either with push-on/pull-off spade connectors or with screws. If your model uses spade connectors, push down on each wire to make sure it is attached securely. If the wires are fastened with screws, tighten each screw. Now test the phone.

If the dial tone is still constant, switch the positions of the red and green wires on the network one at a time. Make a sketch of their original positions so that you can put the wires back where they were, if necessary. Test the phone.

Finally, clean the switch-hook contact assembly as described in Repair 5 above.

2. *Intermittent dial tone.* If you don't get a dial tone every time, the problem is probably caused by a defective modular cord. Replace the cord with a cord from a properly operating phone. If the substitute cord doesn't solve the problem, service the switch-hook contact assembly (see Repair 4, step 6, above).

3. *No dial tone.* When you don't get a dial tone at all, check that the modular cord is connected securely to the phone and wall jack. Then test the cord for damage by substituting another one.

If the modular cord isn't at fault, open the phone and check to make sure the switch-hook spring hasn't come loose. See whether the spring is connected to the upper and lower arms of the switch-hook. Also, since the switch-hook contacts may be at fault, you may have to clean the assembly as described in Repair 5, above.

REPAIR · 7

TAKING THE BUZZ OUT OF A CORDLESS PHONE

PROBLEM: You get a loud buzzing noise when you use your cordless telephone.

There are three reasons why a cordless phone may emit a buzzing sound.

1. Someone in the house is using an appliance or electric tool. The interference will cease as soon as the appliance or tool is turned off.

2. The battery in the phone is overcharged, and the excessive buildup of electricity is creating the interference. To fix this, leave the phone off the charging cradle until the battery discharges. Then flip the switch on the phone

to Off or Standby, and put the handset back onto the charging cradle. Let the battery charge. The complete process will take about 12 hours.

3. An amateur radio operator in the house or one living nearby is using a radio transmitter at the same time you are using the phone. This happens because cordless telephones operate on radio frequencies, and your phone may be calibrated to the same frequency as the radio transmitter. If this is the case, take the phone to a dealer who sells your particular make, and have the phone recalibrated to a different frequency.

H E L P F U L   H I N T

Preventing Damage to Your VCR

Heat given off by a television set may damage a VCR that is sitting on top of the TV. If it's not convenient to move the VCR to another location, raise it to provide an air space of at least ¼ inch between the two units.

Here's how:

1. Cut four spacer blocks from a piece of ¼-inch plywood.
2. Paint the spacer blocks the same color as the TV or VCR.
3. Put one spacer block under each corner of the VCR.

R E P A I R · 8

REPAIRING A RECORD PLAYER TURNTABLE THAT DOESN'T REVOLVE

PROBLEM: Your record player turntable has stopped turning, or turns only fitfully.

To determine whether a broken belt is preventing the turntable of your record player from revolving, do the following:

1. Lift off the rubber cover lying over the turntable (Figure 12.6). If there are slots in

the turntable, you will be able to inspect the mechanism underneath. If not, you have to remove the turntable as described below.

Figure 12.6 To inspect the drive belt of a record player, remove the cover.

2. Rotate the turntable by hand as you look through the slots. You may see a thin, flat rubber belt stretched between the underside of the turntable and a thin vertical stem (Figure 12.7).

Figure 12.7 Look through the slot to see if the belt is in position and extends around the turntable and the stem.

If the belt is correctly in position and moves smoothly, the problem is probably a burned-out motor. To make sure, take the turntable to an audio equipment parts store and have the dealer test the motor.

3. If you don't see the belt in the position described above, proceed with the repair. Remove the turntable. With most units, this is done by prying off a small clip and washer from around the base of the record spindle (Figure 12.8) and lifting the turntable from the base of the record player.

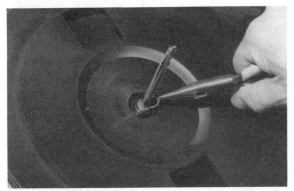

Figure 12.8 If the belt has to be replaced, remove the small C-clip at the base of the record spindle and lift off the turntable.

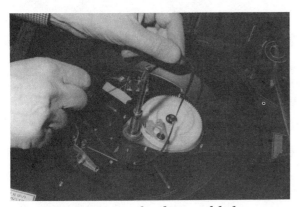

Figure 12.9 Remove the damaged belt.

4. Remove the damaged belt (Figure 12.9). Take it to an audio equipment parts store and get a new one.

5. Place the new belt around the underside of the turntable. Holding the belt in place with an awl or small screwdriver, lower the turntable toward the deck. As you do so, extend the belt around the stem.

6. Place the turntable back on the deck and insert the clip on the record spindle.

HELPFUL HINT

Getting Rid of a Hissing Sound in a Tape Recorder

A faulty tape should be the first thing you think of if a tape recorder you've just had repaired makes a hissing noise. If the noise is still present with another tape, however, there's a chance that the repair facility may have failed to demagnetize the heads of the recorder after making the repair. Take the equipment back to the shop and ask them to do so.

HELPFUL HINT

Repairing a Scratched Compact Disk

You may not have to discard a scratched compact disk. Help is available in the form of a restoration kit containing an ultrafine abrasive material that polishes out deep scratches. The kit also includes a cleaning fluid that eliminates dirt and particles from the surface. The amount of material in the kit allows you to treat approximately 24 CDs.

To find a store that sells the kit, turn to the "Records, Tapes, and Compact Disks—Retail" section in the yellow pages of your telephone book.

REPAIR·9

REPAIRING A BROKEN CASSETTE TAPE

PROBLEM: One of your cassette tapes has broken.

You don't have to discard a split cassette tape. You can buy a splicing kit at an audio equipment parts store, which contains a trimmer, splicing tape, and instructions on how to make a splice if the ends of the broken tape are outside the case.

If the ends of the broken tape are trapped inside the case, however, do the following:

1.　Cut off a strip of the sticky splicing tape supplied in the kit.

2.　Slide the strip inside the cassette to snare the ends of the broken tape.

3.　Slowly fish the ends of the tape out of the cassette and make the splice according to the instructions in the kit.

4.　If you find that this procedure is too difficult to do, you will have to open the cassette. Some cassettes are held together with screws. Remove the screws (Figure 12.10). Slowly lift off the top half of the cassette (Figure 12.11). Bring the two broken ends of the tape to each other, making sure the tape goes around the routing wheels and passes in front of the pressure pad. After completing the splice with the repair tape in the splicing kit, screw the two halves of the case back together.

5.　If the two halves of a cassette case are crimped together, pry them apart with a screwdriver. This procedure will destroy the case, so have an empty case ready. You can buy one in an audio equipment parts store.

6.　When you have split open the old cassette, lay the half that contains the tape alongside the half of the new cassette that has the routing wheels and pressure pad. Transfer the two parts of the broken tape into the new cassette. Then pass the tape around the routing wheels and in front of the pressure pad (Figure 12.12), and splice the two ends together with the adhesive tape found in the repair kit. Align the top half of the new cassette with the lower half and either screw or snap the two together.

Figure 12.10 Remove the small screws. (If the two parts of the case are crimped together, you'll have to pry open the cassette.)

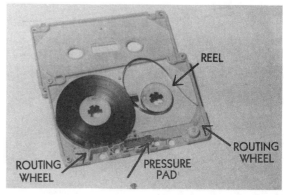

Figure 12.11 This is what you will find inside a cassette: two routing wheels, a pressure pad, broken tape, and reels.

Figure 12.12 Bring the tape around the routing wheels and in front of the pressure pad.

HELPFUL HINT
Batteries in Personal Computers

A 6-volt battery provides a computer with the energy to keep date-and-time boards current when power to the computer is off. (To find out if you have such a battery in your unit, refer to the owner's manual or call the dealer from whom you purchased the equipment.)

When a battery wears out, the date and time are lost when the computer is switched off. Therefore, if your PC is equipped with a battery, keep in mind that the expected life of that battery is only two years.

Manufacturers often equip their per-sonal computers with so-called permanent batteries that are soldered right into the unit. If your batteries wear out, and your owner's manual doesn't tell you how to replace them, take your computer to a service center. Ask the serviceperson to install a user-replaceable battery pack—either a four-pack of AA batteries, or some other easily available 1.5-volt dry cells. Then, simply by removing a few screws in the back of your computer and sliding the outer casing off the unit, you will be able to replace the batteries yourself.

13

WORKSHOP
POWER TOOLS

The maintenance and repair advice in this chapter refers to portable and stationary power tools. The troubleshooting and repair procedures outlined here apply to all portable power tools, including drills, circular saws, jigsaws, routers, and sanders.

Safety Precautions

It's helpful that the electric motors that run power tools are the same on all such tools; this simplifies repairs. It also means, however, that disassembling any of these tools can pose a danger if you don't take a number of precautions, as follows:

• Never work on a power tool without first checking to make certain that the power cord plug is disconnected from the electric outlet.

• If you have to disconnect wires, be sure to mark each wire and its terminal with self-adhering labels or strips of masking tape. For example, mark one wire and its terminal with the number "1" in red crayon. Then mark another wire and its terminal with "2" in blue crayon. Make sure you reconnect each wire to its respective terminal, or you can create a short circuit that may cause a severe shock when you use the tool.

• Before reassembling a tool, make sure that none of the interior wires can come into contact with the metal housing.

• Never operate or work on an electric portable or stationary power tool while standing on a damp or wet floor, or if water is present on the workbench.

• WORKSHOP POWER TOOL REPAIRS •

Following is a list of repairs presented in this chapter, and the tools and materials needed to make them.

REPAIR	TOOLS AND MATERIALS
1. Repairing a portable power tool that runs sluggishly or not at all	Self-adhering labels, vise, screwdriver, power cord, paper clip, on-off switch, ruler, motor brushes and springs
2. Replacing the chuck of a portable electric drill	Screwdriver, chuck key, hammer
3. Restoring power to a cordless electric portable tool	Screwdriver, paintbrush, can of compressed air, paper clip
4. Repairing hard-to-turn table saw handwheels	Grease-cutting solvent, silicone lubricant or lightweight household oil, screwdriver, adjustable wrench
5. Removing rust from the table of a stationary power tool	Rust remover, coarse grade of aluminum oxide sandpaper, paste wax

REPAIR • 1

REPAIRING A PORTABLE POWER TOOL THAT RUNS SLUGGISHLY OR NOT AT ALL

PROBLEM: A portable power tool won't run, or runs poorly.

There are three reasons that a power tool doesn't operate correctly: a faulty power cord, a malfunctioning on-off switch, or worn motor brushes. To troubleshoot the cause, do the following:

Test and replace the power cord. Mount the tool in a vise. Lock the switch in the On position, and plug the power cord into a wall outlet. Keep your fingers away from the working end of the tool.

Beginning at the plug end of the power cord and working toward the housing, flex the power cord over its entire length. If the tool comes alive, even momentarily, the trouble is caused by a faulty power cord.

To make the repair:

1. Unplug the power cord.

2. If the tool has a clamshell housing, remove the screws holding the two halves together and take them apart. If the tool has a solid case, remove the screws that hold together the two parts of the handle and lift off the top part of the handle (Figure 13.1).

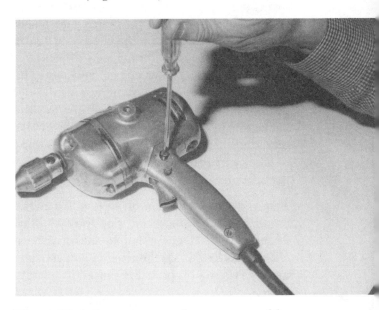

Figure 13.1 Gain access to the power cord by unscrewing the handle.

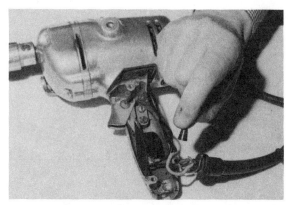

Figure 13.2 Inside the handle, release the wires that are attached to the power cord. Identify each wire with a self-adhering label.

3. If the power cord is connected to wires with wire nuts or screws, remove the wire nuts or loosen the screws to disconnect the power cord (Figure 13.2). Attach a new cord. You can buy one from a dealer of workshop power tools.

If the wires that make up the power cord are inserted in the on-off switch, slip the end of a straightened paper clip into the holes of the switch. Pressing the spring clips in the holes with the end of the paper clip will allow you to free the wires.

Connect the wires of the new power cord by pressing down on the spring clips with the paper clip as you push the wires into place. Then release pressure on the clips. Tug gently on the wires to make sure they are secure.

Important: The new power cord must be connected in exactly the same way as the old power cord. Therefore, when you remove the damaged power cord, make a sketch or use self-adhering labels or strips of masking tape to label wires so you can tell where to reconnect them.

Test and replace the on-off switch. Does the on-off switch feel loose and sloppy as you flick it on and off? Does it fail to make a sharp clicking sound? If so, the trouble you are having with the tool is probably caused by a faulty switch.

To replace a faulty switch, disconnect the wires attached to it. Remove the switch. Install

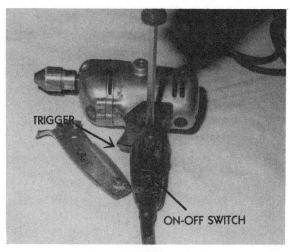

Figure 13.3 The on-off switch is attached to the triggering device that you push to operate the tool. Unscrew the assembly from the drill housing.

a new switch, and reconnect the wires (Figures 13.3–13.5).

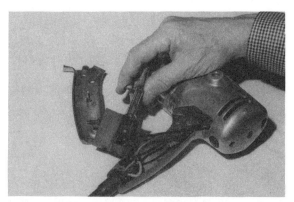

Figure 13.4 To replace a defective switch, release it from the handle, and disconnect the trigger and wires.

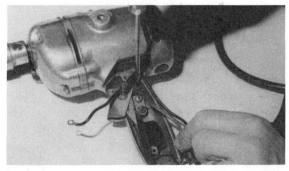

Figure 13.5 This is the ground wire, which is usually green or bare copper. After making repairs to the cord or switch of an electric tool, make certain this wire is tightly attached at both ends to clean terminals.

Replace motor brushes. Brushes are the carbon elements on each side of the motor. They transfer electric power from the power cord to the motor. When the motor falters, it often means the brushes are worn and should be replaced.

To replace brushes, do the following:

1. Make sure the power cord is disconnected from the wall outlet.
2. If brush caps are in place on each side of the case, one directly opposite the other, unscrew them (Figures 13.6 and 13.7). The brushes and brush springs will pop out.
3. Measure the brushes. If either is ¼ inch or less in length, replace both brushes and their springs (Figure 13.8).

Figure 13.6 To inspect and, if necessary, replace motor brushes, unscrew the caps over the brush housings.

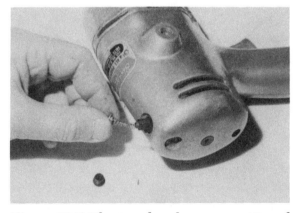

Figure 13.7 The two brushes are positioned opposite each other. If there isn't a brush housing cap, or if there is only one, you must disassemble the tool to reach the other brush.

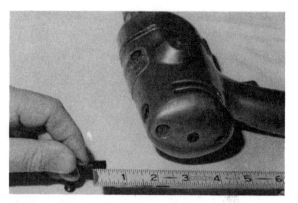

Figure 13.8 If brushes are over ¼ inch in length, they are still usable.

4. If the tool has a clamshell housing, there may not be brush caps on the sides of the housing. In that case, open the housing and locate the brush retainers on each side of the motor commutator to make this repair.

REPAIR · 2

REPLACING THE CHUCK OF A PORTABLE ELECTRIC DRILL

PROBLEM: The bit of the electric drill isn't secure and wobbles as you drill a hole.

The chuck of a portable electric drill—the part that holds the bit—may wear out in time. This will result in irregularly shaped holes or snapped bits.

To install a new chuck, do the following:

1. First check to make sure the drill has a switch that allows you to reverse the direction of rotation. Open the jaws of the chuck. Insert a screwdriver to engage the screw that secures the chuck to the drill. Remove the screw by turning it clockwise (Figure 13.9). *Note:* A nonreversible drill, which turns only in a clockwise direction, doesn't have this screw; if you are repairing a nonreversible drill, begin with step 2.
2. Put the chuck key in the hole of the chuck. Strike the key sharply with a hammer so that the chuck loosens in a counterclockwise direction (Figure 13.10). Unscrew the chuck by

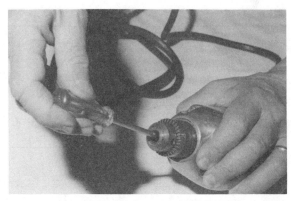

Figure 13.9 To remove the chuck of a reversible drill, first take out the screw inside the chuck.

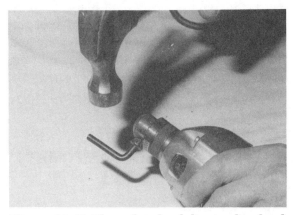

Figure 13.10 Place the chuck key in the chuck and strike the key with a hammer.

hand. Buy a new chuck at any store that sells power tools of the same make as yours.

3.   Thread the new chuck onto the drill. To be sure you don't cross-thread it and damage threads, screw it on by hand for several turns. When you can't tighten the chuck any farther by hand, place the chuck key into the hole in the new chuck. Using a hammer, give the chuck key one sharp tap to secure the chuck to the drill. This tap should be made so that the chuck tightens in a clockwise direction.

4.   If the drill is a reversible model, insert and tighten the screw that holds the chuck to the drill.

RESTORING POWER TO A CORDLESS ELECTRIC PORTABLE TOOL

PROBLEM: A cordless electric portable tool is not as lively as it once was.

The reason for the sluggishness may be either an accumulation of dirt or worn brushes (Figure 13.11).

Figure 13.11 Dirt can impede the action of the motor and clog ventilation slots. Clean out dirt from these slots on a regular basis.

To find out, examine the housing. Is the tool held together with screws? If it is, follow the procedure outlined here. But if it isn't, you will have to seek out the services of a trained technician with the necessary tools for doing the job.

Note: As you do this job, make a sketch of the location of parts as you remove them, and use the sketch as a guide in reassembling the tool.

1.   Detach the battery pack by releasing the clip or screws holding it to the main assembly.

2.   Remove the screws and open the tool.

3.   Using a clean paintbrush, sweep away any dirt from inside the tool. Also use a can of compressed air (available from a photographic supply store) to blow dirt from crevices you can't reach with the brush. Treat the unit gently so you don't damage fragile wires.

4.   Carefully examine the two brush assemblies. The brushes lie 180 degrees apart and

are in contact with the commutator of the electric motor. They will have wires attached to them that connect to the on-off switch.

5. Take out the on-off switch so you can release the brush wires. Do this by sliding a straightened paper clip into the slots in the switch that hold the wires and pressing the spring clips as you pull wires free.

6. Undo the screws holding the cover over the motor. Once that is done, the brush retainer on each side of the motor commutator will be accessible.

7. Open the retainer to release the brush hold-down spring. *Caution:* The spring is under tension and could fly out, so do this with care; wear eye protection.

8. Remove the brush and wire.

9. Install new brushes and brush springs. Put on the motor cover. Attach the brush wires to the on-off switch, reinstall the on-off switch, and finish reassembling the tool.

H E L P F U L   H I N T

Preventing Blade Failure in Jigsaws

Before using a jigsaw to cut soft metal, such as aluminum or brass, apply a thin layer of lightweight household oil along the cutting line. This prevents the blade from getting clogged with metal filings, and makes it easier for it to cut through the metal. It also reduces vibration that can cause a blade to snap, and it will keep the blade from overheating and failing prematurely.

R E P A I R · 4

REPAIRING HARD-TO-TURN TABLE SAW HANDWHEELS

PROBLEM: The handwheels of your table saw have jammed.

A table saw has one handwheel for adjusting the elevation of the blade, and another, called the tilt wheel, for adjusting the angle. Accumulated sawdust can eventually make the wheels difficult to turn.

Here is how to clean the shafts:

1. Disconnect the power cord plug of the table saw from the wall outlet.

2. Working underneath the table, clean sawdust off the threads of the handwheel shafts. If sawdust is thick, apply a grease-cutting solvent that makes it easier to eliminate.

3. When the shafts are clean, lubricate them with a thin coating of household oil or silicone lubricant.

If cleaning and lubrication don't make the tilt wheel any easier to turn, the wheel needs adjustment:

1. Remove the screw that holds the wheel to the shaft. Take off the wheel. If your table saw is like most models, this will reveal a screw above the shaft and a screw under the shaft.

2. Reach behind one of the screws with a wrench to engage the nut that holds the screw. Turn the screw one-quarter turn counterclockwise with a screwdriver. Do the same to the other screw.

3. Place the wheel back on the shaft and turn it to see if it moves more freely. If it doesn't, turn both screws another one-quarter turn counterclockwise.

4. If this adjustment procedure doesn't seem to help, locate the bolts holding the table to the base of the saw. (There are probably four.) Loosen them and shift the table on the base. Turn the tilt wheel as you do this to determine at which spot the wheel becomes easier to turn. When you have found the best position, tighten the bolts.

R E P A I R · 5

REMOVING RUST FROM THE TABLE OF A STATIONARY POWER TOOL

PROBLEM: You have bought a used drill press, lathe, table saw, or other stationary home workshop power tool that is in good condition, except that the table is rusted.

To remove the rust, do the following:

1. Apply a liquid rust remover of the kind that can be bought in any hardware store. Carefully follow the directions on the label, especially those concerning safety. The manufacturer may suggest wearing rubber gloves and some form of eye protection.

2. If treatment with the rust remover doesn't help, sand the table with a coarse grade of aluminum oxide sandpaper. Don't press down too hard.

3. Hand sanding should do the job. If you decide to use a power grinder or power sander, take care. If you use a heavy hand, the power tool will leave an uneven surface on the table, making it unusable.

4. Once the rust has been removed (or to prevent rust to begin with), apply a coat of automotive paste wax to the table every six months.

14

POWER CORDS,
WATER HEATERS,
OUTBOARD MOTORS,
PUMPS, *and* WINDOW FANS

*H*ere we provide tips and repair information about a group of miscellaneous equipment, including power cords, electric and gas water heaters, pumps, electric fans, outboard motors, and other tools and appliances that don't fit into other chapters.

Because of the diversity of items, there are cautions that apply to each particular piece of equipment and repair.

Safety Precautions

• When replacing the plug of a power cord, notice whether the wires of the power cord have different colors to identify the *hot* wire (usually black), the *neutral* wire (white or some color other than black), and the *ground* wire (green or bare copper). Before releasing the power cord from the damaged plug, also note the color of the terminal screw to which each

wire is attached. Terminal screw colors are usually brass or gold to designate the hot terminal, silver to designate the neutral terminal, and green on a six-sided screw to designate the ground terminal. Be sure to connect each wire to its proper terminal when installing the new plug.

• When draining water from a water heater, wear heavy gloves and adequate protective clothing to prevent burns from scalding hot water.

• When replacing elements of an electric water heater, turn off the circuit breaker or remove from the home's main electric service panel the fuse that serves the water heater. If you do not know which circuit breaker or fuse controls power to the unit, do *not* make repairs. Instead, consult a professional technician.

• If you have to replace the switch of an electric window fan, first make sure the fan's power cord is disconnected from the electric outlet.

• Remember that your outboard motor probably uses a fuel that contains gasoline. Therefore, take all precautions necessary to protect yourself from this volatile fuel. Do not smoke, or bring anything that may produce a spark or flame near the work zone. Make repairs in an open, well-ventilated area, and try not to inhale fumes.

• MISCELLANEOUS REPAIRS •

Following is a list of repairs presented in this chapter, and the tools and materials needed to make them.

REPAIR	TOOLS AND MATERIALS
1. Replacing the plug of a power cord	Knife, screwdriver, self-adhering labels
2. Reducing the noise level of a gas water heater	Pail or garden hose
3. Eliminating a sulfur odor from hot water	Adjustable pliers or wrench, aluminum anode rod
4. Restoring hot water in an electric water heater	Heavy work gloves, pail or garden hose, screwdriver or nut driver, masking tape or self-adhering labels, pipe wrench, small brush
5. Repairing the pilot of a gas water heater	Brush, copper wire, adjustable wrench
6. Troubleshooting a submersible pump that cycles too frequently	None
7. Replacing the three-speed switch of an electric window fan	Pliers, screwdriver or nut driver, Allen wrench, adjustable wrench, paper clip
8. Preventing corrosion on an outboard motor	Masking tape
9. Resolving an intermittent loss of outboard motor power	Screwdriver, high-speed carburetor jet recommended for high-altitude performance
10. Troubleshooting a stalling outboard motor	Screwdriver, fuel pump rebuild kit

• POWER CORDS •

REPAIR • 1

REPLACING THE PLUG OF A POWER CORD

PROBLEM: You want to replace a damaged plug on the cord of a power tool.

The power cords of appliances and home workshop tools use flat-cord plugs, round-cord plugs, three-prong plugs, or polarized plugs. Although replacing a damaged plug is easy enough, you have to be careful that the replacement plug is the correct one, and that the wires of the power cord are connected correctly to the terminals of the plug. If an incorrect plug is put on a power cord, or the plug is not attached properly, you could injure yourself when you use the equipment, or you may create a fire hazard.

The replacement plug should match the size, shape, and blade configuration of the old plug. For example, if the old plug is a two-prong flat plug that's been attached to a no. 18 power cord, purchase a two-prong flat plug rated for a no. 18 power cord. The rating should be stamped on the plug package or on the plug itself.

Another way to make sure of getting the correct replacement plug is to cut the damaged plug off the power cord and take it with you to a hardware or home supply store. There you can match the old plug to the new plug.

Attach the various types of plugs in the following manner:

1. *Two-wire flat-cord plugs* come in several styles, but there is one that doesn't require stripping insulation from the two wires that make up the power cord. This easy-to-use replacement plug is equipped with a slot and a lever. To put it on your power cord, cut off the damaged plug from the power cord so the ends of the wires are square. Pull apart the two wires to a distance of about ¼ inch. It is not necessary to strip the individual wires.

Open the lever of the new plug, insert the ends of the wires into the slot in the plug, and press the lever down. The metal terminals pushed into place by this action will pierce the insulation to establish contact between the power cord and plug.

2. *Two-wire round-cord plugs* are replaced by cutting off the old plug and pulling apart about 1½ inches of the two wires that make up the power cord. Strip off about ½ inch of insulation from each wire. Insert the two wires through the rear of the replacement plug and tie them in what is called an Underwriters knot (Figure 14.1). This type of knot relieves any strain that may be put on the wires of the power cord. Place the bare ends of the wires around the terminal screws of the plug. It doesn't matter which wire attaches to which screw; however, before you tighten the screws, make sure that no strands stick out from either side.

Figure 14.1 How to make an Underwriters knot.

3. *Three-prong plugs* are called *grounded* plugs. Here, it is very important to know which wire goes to each terminal. To acquaint yourself with the replacement plug before attaching it to a power cord, identify the screw to which the ground wire of the power cord has to be connected. This ground screw may be painted green. If it isn't, it will have a six-sided screw head. Be sure to attach the ground wire of the power cord to this screw so any stray current that reaches the appliance's case will be diverted back to the house ground, and not cause a shock to someone using the appliance.

The ground wire of the power cord is usually wrapped in green insulation or is a bare copper wire. One of the other two wires of a three-wire power cord will be black. This is the hot wire; it is connected to the brass or gold terminal screw of the replacement plug. (An easy way to remember this is to associate the *b* in *brass* with the *b* in *black*.) The other wire of a three-wire power cord will be white or some light color other than black or green. This is the neutral wire; it should be connected to the silver terminal screw of the replacement plug.

To attach a three-wire power cord to a new three-prong plug, cut off the damaged plug. Make the cut carefully so the ends of the wire are even.

Strip off about ½ inch of insulation from each wire. Wrap the bare ends of the wires around their respective terminal screws. Make sure that no strands are left sticking out before tightening the screws.

Note: You may come across a power cord in which the wires are not color-coded to identify them as hot, neutral, and ground. In that case, use self-adhering labels to clearly identify which wire goes to each terminal screw. Do this before removing the damaged plug so you can attach the new plug in the same way.

4. *Polarized plugs* have one wide prong and one narrow prong. The wide prong is inserted into the wide slot of the wall outlet; the narrow prong is inserted into the narrow slot of the wall outlet.

Caution: Never shave down the wide prong to get it to fit a narrow slot of a wall outlet. This will defeat the purpose of the polarized plug, which is to make sure that the terminals within the appliance are connected to the hot and neutral sides of the line, as intended. If polarization is reversed, the appliance may pose a shock hazard and could be damaged.

Replace a damaged polarized plug in the same way you replace a round two-prong plug, but with one exception. You must attach the wires of the power cord to the correct terminal screws of the plug.

The screw of the narrow blade is connected to the hot (black) wire of the power cord. The screw of the wide blade is attached to the neutral (white) wire of the power cord.

HELPFUL HINT

How to Select a Safe Extension Cord

Before buying an extension cord to use with an electric appliance or power tool, consider the following:

• The extension cord must be able to handle the amount of current that will be surging through it. If it is not, you risk a fire. To get an extension cord that can handle the load, compare the amperage rating of the cord (printed on the package) to the amperage rating of the appliance or tool. The extension cord rating should equal or exceed the rating of the appliance or tool. Amperage rating (also called the current draw) is usually noted on the specification plate attached to the appliance or tool.

• If you are going to use the appliance or tool outdoors, make certain the extension cord you buy is built to withstand outdoor use. This information will be printed on the cord package or on the cord itself.

• Never buy an extension cord that doesn't carry the Underwriters Laboratories (UL) mark on the product or on the cord package.

• WATER HEATERS •

R E P A I R · 2

REDUCING THE NOISE LEVEL OF A GAS WATER HEATER

PROBLEM: Your gas water heater starts to make rumbling and popping sounds.

Noise is not a sign that the heater is about to start leaking. Actually, a noisy unit can last for many years. But it is annoying.

Noise is made by sediment that has accumulated in the bottom of the tank. Sediment expands as it gets hot, and begins to vibrate against the floor of the tank. The noise it makes is amplified and causes the problem to sound worse than it is.

The quickest way to reduce the noise level is to drain a few pails of water from the drain faucet on the lower part of the tank. If that doesn't work, you can flush the tank, as follows:

1. Turn the burner control to Off.
2. Turn off the main gas valve on the pipe going to the burner.
3. Close the shut-off valve on the cold-water pipe leading into the tank.
4. Drain the tank. Do this by drawing off one pail of water after another, or attach a hose to the drain faucet and extend the hose to a proper draining site. This site has to be below the level of the drain faucet, in a sump-pump pit for example. Patience is necessary, because it can take several hours for the tank to empty. *Caution:* If you haven't allowed the water in the tank to cool all the way down before you start the draining step, be careful—the water may be hot enough to scald you.
5. When no more water comes from the drain faucet, connect a hose to the faucet (if you haven't already done so) and run it to a draining site. In this case the site, such as a sink, can be above the level of the drain faucet.
6. Open the cold-water feed valve. Water flowing into the tank will strike the bottom of the tank with sufficient force to stir the sediment, which will then pour out of the tank through the open drain faucet with the water. Allow this drainage to continue for about a half hour.
7. Close the drain faucet and open a couple of hot-water faucets in the house. Let the tank fill.
8. When water pours from the faucets, indicating that the tank is full, shut off the faucets and turn on the gas valve. Light the pilot according to the instructions on the plate attached to the water heater, and set the gas burner control dial at the desired temperature.

R E P A I R · 3

ELIMINATING A SULFUR ODOR IN YOUR HOT WATER

PROBLEM: There is a bad odor coming from the hot-water faucets in your home.

One way to eliminate a hot-water sulfur odor is to replace the anode rod in the water heater. The anode rod (also called the sacrificial rod) is in the heater to retard corrosion.

Water heaters are usually equipped with anode rods made of magnesium. The odor of sulfur may be the result of the magnesium reacting with chemicals in the water. Therefore, replacing the magnesium anode rod with an aluminum anode rod may help.

Here is how to do the job:

1. Turn off the main gas valve or electricity. Allow the water in the tank to cool.
2. Place adjustable pliers or a wrench on the knob and unscrew the rod from the tank by turning it counterclockwise. *Caution:* Be careful; the rod may still be hot.
3. After lifting out the old rod, insert the new aluminum rod in the tank and screw it into place. Tighten the rod just enough to secure it to the tank.

Contrary to popular belief, draining a pail or two of water from a water heater periodically will not prolong the life of the unit. Only a water heater that uses gas as the source of heat requires draining, and the reason is to increase its operating efficiency, not to extend its life. The reason is that sediment that settles on the bottom of the storage tank can insulate water from the gas burner, which is under the tank. This insulating effect requires a gas burner to stay on longer to heat the water, which adds to the cost of operating the unit.

Electric water heaters, on the other hand, have the bottom heating element approximately 12 inches above the floor of the tank. Therefore, draining water from an electric water heater to clean out sediment will not have the same salutary effect on energy use.

How often should a gas water heater be drained? The authority on the subject is the manufacturer of the water heater, so consult the instruction manual that accompanied the heater when it was installed. If the manual has been misplaced, draining one pail of water every three months is ample.

R E P A I R · 4

RESTORING HOT WATER IN AN ELECTRIC WATER HEATER

PROBLEM: Suddenly you don't have enough hot water for a shower or bath.

This is a common complaint. Another is that the water isn't hot enough.

If the capacity of an electric water heater has been sufficient to meet the needs of the family to this point, the reason for a sudden state of insufficient hot water is a burned-out *bottom* electric element.

If an electric water heater suddenly delivers only lukewarm water, this usually points to a burned-out *top* electric element.

To replace an electric element, do the following:

1. First turn off the circuit breaker or remove the fuse that controls current to the water heater. If you aren't certain which circuit breaker or fuse to deactivate, turn off the main switch in the home's electric service panel. Since an electric water heater receives 240 volts of current, failure to turn off the electricity can cause you serious or fatal injury.

2. Close the valve on the cold-water pipe coming into the water heater. If you are replacing the bottom element, drain practically all the water in the tank. If you are replacing the top element, you have to drain about half of the water.

3. Remove the access cover over the appropriate element.

4. Put on a pair of work gloves to protect your hands. Spread apart the insulation that covers the particular element you are replacing.

5. If there is a cover over the element, take that off.

6. Two wires are connected to the element. Using self-adhering labels or strips of masking tape, label each one, and the terminal to which it attaches, and then disconnect the wires.

7. Using a pipe wrench, grasp the flat surfaces of the element and turn counterclockwise to unscrew the element from the tank.

8. Buy a new heating element from a dealer who sells your particular make of water heater. Also get a new gasket to fit around the threaded part of the element.

9. Before installing the new element, brush and wipe clean the threads in the element seat in the tank.

10. Place the new gasket on the element. Insert the element into the tank.

11. Being careful not to cross threads (which

HELPFUL HINT
Insulating a Water Heater

If you can lower your home-heating bills by insulating the attic, it's only logical to assume that you can cut your water-heating bills by wrapping an extra layer of insulation around the tank of your water heater. By insulating the tank, you can reduce the amount of heat lost through the walls of the water heater, thus reducing the amount of energy required to keep the water in the tank hot.

A typical insulation kit consists of a fiberglass blanket, about 1½ inches thick, that wraps around the heater and is secured with tape. Any kit will produce a greater saving if installed on an older water heater that has relatively little insulation. The kit also will deliver a greater saving if your water heater is in a cold room or if its thermostat is set higher than 140 degrees. In choosing an insulation kit, be sure it will fit your particular water heater.

It should be possible to install an insulation kit in about an hour. The job is relatively easy, and the only tool needed may be a pair of scissors. Make sure you keep the insulation away from the heater's controls and wiring.

Fiberglass insulation kits should carry a warning concerning the handling of fiberglass, as it is nasty stuff. When handling it, wear a dust mask, gloves, and a long-sleeved shirt. Later, wash your clothes separately so that the fibers are not transferred to other clothing.

We have tested and found satisfactory the following two products; their manufacturers were still in the business of making water-heater insulation kits as of mid-1992:

- *Thermo Saver:* S&S Industries, Inc., P.O. Box 5538, Maryville, TN 37802. Phone (615) 970-3097.

- *Frost King:* Thermwell Products Co., 150 East 7th Street, Paterson, NJ 07524. Phone (201) 684-5000.

Safety precautions. If you decide to insulate your water heater, keep the following in mind:

- Do not cover any labels that the manufacturer has attached to the water heater. They are intended to convey important information that you may have to refer to later.

- If you have a gas water heater, do not cover access openings into the tank, and do not place the insulation over the top of the tank. It can interfere with the performance of the draft hood and may allow carbon monoxide to escape into the house.

- Don't insulate the bottom section of a tank heated by gas; covering the burner compartment can interfere with proper combustion. To be on the safe side, make sure the bottom edge of the insulation falls no lower than just above the drain faucet.

- If your water is heated by electricity, do not cover the electric cable, or it may overheat, creating a fire hazard.

could damage the gasket and cause a leak), turn the element clockwise by hand until you can't turn it any farther. Only then, use the pipe wrench to tighten the element to the tank. *Don't overdo it.* Stop turning when it becomes necessary to use real strength to tighten farther.

12. Open a hot-water faucet or two in the house. Then open the cold-water shut-off valve on the tank.

13. As the tank fills, check around the element for a leak. If a leak appears, tighten the element one-quarter turn more. If the leak won't stop, the gasket was damaged as you installed the element. Turn off the water, drain the tank, remove the element, and install another gasket.

14. Connect the wires to the correct terminals. Wait for water to flow from the open hot-water faucets in the house before turning off the faucets. At this point the tank is full.

15. The thermostat probably has an electric reset button. Press that button.

16. Replace the cover and screw the element access panel back on the tank.

17. Turn on the electricity.

4. Following directions on the instruction plate attached to the water heater, attempt to light the pilot. If it does not light, or if it lights and goes out, continue to the next step.

5. With the burner control knob turned to Pilot, insert a piece of thin copper wire into the orifice of the pilot and gently move the wire up and down once in each direction to dislodge dirt that might be impeding the supply of gas to the pilot. Do not use an instrument made of any material other than copper, or you could damage the orifice.

6. Following directions on the instruction plate, attempt to light the pilot. If it still refuses to work properly, continue to the next step.

7. Be sure the burner control knob is turned to Pilot. Hand-tighten the nuts holding the thermocouple and pilot. Then turn each nut one-quarter turn with a wrench. Try to light the pilot.

8. If none of the above procedures has resolved the problem, call the utility company that supplies gas to your home. In all likelihood, the thermocouple has to be replaced. This is a job for a trained technician.

R E P A I R · 5

REPAIRING THE PILOT OF A GAS WATER HEATER

PROBLEM: The pilot of your gas water heater keeps going out.

Before calling a service technician, do the following:

1. Turn the burner control to Pilot.

2. Take the cover and shield off the burner/pilot housing. Be careful—the shield in particular may be very hot.

3. Using a clean brush, sweep out the air shutter. An unrestricted flow of air through the air shutter is necessary to keep the pilot flame burning.

• SUBMERSIBLE PUMPS •

R E P A I R • 6

TROUBLESHOOTING A SUBMERSIBLE PUMP THAT CYCLES TOO FREQUENTLY

PROBLEM: The pump bringing water into your home from a well seems to cycle on and off too often.

This malfunction does not usually mean the pump is about to fail. Chances are the condition is being caused by one of the following problems:

1. *A leak in the home's plumbing.* Find and repair a leaky faucet, shut-off valve, toilet tank, or water pipe.

2. *A waterlogged water holding tank.* Prepare a soapy water solution and spread suds on the vent on the top of the holding tank. If suds bubble, the rubber vibrator inside the tank has cracked.

The vibrator drives water into and through the pipes in the home. If the vibrator has a hole in it, water will leak through the vibrator into the air reservoir on the other side. The air space is needed to give the vibrator room to pulsate as it drives water out of the tank into the pipes. The leaking of water out of the water-holding section of the tank is detected by the submersible pump, which cycles on to keep the tank full. Because the tank can't be opened to install a new vibrator, the tank itself has to be replaced.

3. *A leaking check valve.* This one-way valve is attached to the base of the pump and allows water to flow forward to the house. It also blocks backflow to the well. If this valve fails, water will flow back into the well, causing the pump to keep cycling to make up the loss. A damaged check valve can be replaced, but to do the job, the pump has to be taken out of the well.

• ELECTRIC FANS •

R E P A I R • 7

REPLACING THE THREE-SPEED SWITCH OF AN ELECTRIC FAN

PROBLEM: The three-speed switch of your window box fan doesn't allow the fan to run at a full range of speeds.

To replace the faulty switch, do the following:

1. Make sure the switch control knob isn't loose and sliding past the speed setting. To find out, pull off the knob. With the fan plugged into a wall outlet, use pliers to turn the switch. Does the switch engage at all speeds? If it does, the knob is at fault. Try to tighten it on the switch stem. If that doesn't work, replace the knob.

2. Assuming that the switch is bad, jot down the make and model number of the fan. Call a dealer of small appliances to see if you can locate a replacement three-speed switch for the fan.

3. To replace the switch, first disconnect the fan power cord from the wall outlet.

4. Remove the screws holding the front grille to the fan housing. Take off the grille.

5. If the fan blade blocks access to the switch, take the assembly off the motor shaft. It is probably secured to the shaft by a C-clip or an Allen screw. If the fastener is a C-clip, hold the tip of a screwdriver behind the clip and pry it off. Be sure to retrieve all washers lying behind the clip. If the blade assembly is secured to the motor shaft by an Allen screw, loosen the screw with an Allen wrench and slide the blade unit off the shaft.

6. After removing the switch control knob, remove the nut holding the switch to the fan housing. Press the switch out of its seat in the housing.

7. Slip the end of a straightened paper clip down alongside the wires attached to the switch. Press down on the clips holding the wires as you pull them from the faulty switch.

8. Line the new switch up with the old switch to note the similar characteristics. In-

sert the wires into the terminals of the new switch. To seat the wires, slip the paper clip into the terminal of each one, and press down on the clip as you push the wire into place. Tug both wires gently to make sure they are secure.

9. When wires have been transferred, insert the new switch into the fan housing. Tighten it to the housing using the washer and nut. Place the fan blade assembly on the motor shaft. Secure it with the C-clip and washers or the Allen screw. Reattach the front grille.

• OUTBOARD MOTORS •

R E P A I R • 8

PREVENTING CORROSION ON AN OUTBOARD MOTOR

PROBLEM: The lower unit or gear housing of your outboard motor keeps rusting, even though it's been given a fresh coat of corrosion-inhibiting paint.

Recurring lower-unit corrosion could result because of the following:

1. *The housing wasn't prepared properly to accept the paint.* All corrosion must be removed by sanding down to bare metal. You should then apply a corrosion-resistant primer to the bare metal. After the primer dries, paint the housing.

2. *The zinc anode plug installed by most manufacturers in the lower unit to retard corrosion is no longer effective.* Perhaps you inadvertently coated the plug with paint. To prevent this, remember to cover the anode with masking tape before painting the lower unit. It's usually located under the plane.

3. *The zinc anode plug has been eaten away and can no longer provide protection.* Unscrew the old plug and install a new one, which you can purchase from a dealer of outboard motors.

R E P A I R • 9

RESOLVING AN INTERMITTENT LOSS OF OUTBOARD MOTOR POWER

PROBLEM: Your outboard motor puts out normal power at times, but lacks power at other times.

Consider the circumstances of the power failure. An outboard motor that performs perfectly in waterways located at lower altitudes can falter when you take it to a location that is 4,000 feet or more above sea level.

If the motor is equipped with the propeller recommended by the manufacturer, there may be an inexpensive solution to this altitude problem. You can, for example, install a high-altitude, high-speed jet in the carburetor when you take the motor to the higher altitudes.

The high-speed jet regulates the amount of gasoline that mixes with air in the carburetor before the fuel mixture is delivered to the engine. The jet that is presently in the carburetor may be perfectly suited to the demands of the outboard as long as the motor is used at lower altitudes. At an altitude above 4,000 feet, however, the jet is delivering too much gasoline. Consequently, the fuel mixture is overly rich. An overly rich mixture is a primary reason that an outboard motor loses power.

Generally, the aperture of a high-speed jet should be decreased from low-altitude size by 0.002 inch at 4,000 feet and by an additional 0.002 inch for every 3,000 feet of elevation above 4,000 feet where the motor is used. Check with the service department of a dealer who sells your make of outboard motor to determine what size jet the manufacturer of the equipment recommends for high altitude use. Then buy that jet.

To install the new jet, do the following:

1. Take off the motor housing to gain access to the carburetor.
2. Check the diagram in your owner's manual to find the location of the high-speed jet.
3. Unscrew the present jet and put the new one in its place. Do not overtighten the jet.
4. Store the jet you have removed in a safe place so you can put it back in the carburetor when you return the outboard motor to a lower altitude.

REPAIR · 10

TROUBLESHOOTING A STALLING OUTBOARD MOTOR

PROBLEM: Your outboard motor stalls at idle and slow speeds, while high-speed performance remains normal.

To find the cause of the roughness and stalling at lower speeds, do the following:

1. After the motor has been running at idle speed for a few minutes, turn it off. Remove the spark plug. Is the end wet with gasoline? If so, continue with the next step.
2. Locate the fuel pump housing. Take off the cover. Inside you will probably find a rubberized diaphragm. The diaphragm, which pulsates to drive gasoline from the fuel tank to the engine, may have cracked. The result is that too much gas can pass through the crack and into the engine, where it drowns the spark plug. At higher speeds, the engine is able to absorb this excess, but not at idle or slow speeds.
3. Purchase a fuel pump rebuild kit for your make of outboard. As you remove the damaged diaphragm, notice how it is sandwiched between two gaskets.

Appendixes

Appendix A

*T*ROUBLESHOOTING *I*NSTRUMENTS and *T*OOLS

Your refrigerator or washing machine breaks down. The first step is to diagnose the problem. You may depend on nothing more than your senses at this stage: If the appliance makes strange noises, it's a fairly clear indication that the trouble is mechanical. A quiet reluctance to run suggests an electrical problem, especially if smoke or a burning odor was apparent at the time of failure. In that case, check first for a tripped circuit breaker or blown fuse before calling in a serviceperson or attempting further repairs. If the circuit has tripped or the fuse has blown (and either one is not overloaded with too many competing items), reset the breaker or replace the fuse and see if it happens again. If it does, it means the appliance has probably developed a short circuit, and the breaker or fuse is doing its job in protecting the house wiring from overheating—and possibly causing a fire.

The motors of air conditioners, refrigerator/freezers, clothes dryers, and washing machines also generally contain an internal protector that interrupts the motor circuit when it senses excessive temperature or load current. When things cool down, these devices reset themselves and resume operation—but only temporarily in the face of a persistent overload. Overload may be caused in a washing machine, for example, by nothing more than too many clothes circulating in too little water. Or an air conditioner's refusal to start on a particularly hot day may be the result of the low voltage supplied during a brownout. On the other hand, if an appliance cuts out regularly for no apparent reason, you may assume that something serious is going on, namely in the electrical circuits of the unit.

To correct the problem, it helps to understand the behavior of electricity. It can be compared to the flow of water in a swimming pool filter system, in which a pump sucks up water from the pool through a hose and drives it through the filter, whereupon a return hose conducts the water back to the pool. A generator can be thought of as a pump of electricity; it develops the pressure (voltage) to drive the current (amperage) through a wire to an appliance. The appliance, like the filter, does its job while offering some resistance (ohms) to the flow of the current. A return wire completes the circuit back to the generator (which is why a line cord has to have at least two conductors).

To find the source of an electrical problem, it may be necessary to check various components with an ohmmeter.

• THE OHMMETER •

The instrument of preference for do-it-yourself electrical troubleshooting is the ohmmeter. You can purchase an ohmmeter separately, or in combination with a voltmeter. When the two instruments are combined into one case, the device is referred to as a VOM (volt/ohmmeter) or multitester. If you buy a VOM rather than a plain ohmmeter, it is important to recognize that the VOM is actually two separate instruments.

An ohmmeter measures *ohms* (resistance) in a circuit. A voltmeter measures *voltage* in a circuit. In this book, we do *not* advocate using a voltmeter for two reasons. First, voltage tests using a VOM have to be made with the electricity on and flowing through the circuit you're testing. This is a dangerous procedure—and can even prove fatal if you get careless and make a mistake. This cannot happen with an ohmmeter since tests using an ohmmeter are made with the electricity off.

Second, with a voltmeter you need the manufacturer's specifications to determine the specific voltage requirements of the equipment. This is not the case with an ohmmeter, since the requirements for this instrument's implementation are simpler and more universal.

TYPES OF OHMMETERS. Outlets such as Radio Shack carry a selection of ohmmeters and VOMs. They range in price from about $10 to $25 for an ohmmeter and from about $15 to $100 for a VOM. If you decide you want a VOM rather than a plain, ordinary ohmmeter, an instrument in the $20–$40 range will suffice

for the tests described in this book.

Two basic types of ohmmeters are available in the lower price range: the traditional analog (moving-needle) meter, and the more contemporary, digital variety equipped with a liquid crystal display. The latter is generally easier to read, offers more precise measurement, and is less sensitive to rough handling. The display of a liquid crystal meter, however, may go dead if subjected to elevated temperatures—as can happen if, for example, you leave one in a parked car on a hot summer day.

An ohmmeter, or the ohmmeter section of a VOM, is powered by an internal battery and needs no line cord. Ohmmeters come with one or more sets of wire leads, for connection to the circuit or the component to be checked. One type of lead has an alligator clip on its end; this is a spring clamp with teeth that can be clipped onto bare wires, electrical terminals, lugs, etc. Clip-on leads are available in other sizes and shapes for a few dollars a pair. You might need a set with miniature clips for access to the confines of some small appliances. The other common type of lead is equipped with a probe—a plastic rod with a metal tip.

HOW TO USE AN OHMMETER. The easiest way to describe the use of an ohmmeter is to cite some practical applications. For example, let's say you find that dishes come out wet from your dishwasher. At the next use, you open the machine during the drying cycle and notice that the heating element isn't glowing as usual.

The first thing to do is to kill the power to the appliance by turning off the appropriate circuit breaker on your home's main electric service panel. Next, remove the machine panel below the door. Note where the ends of the heating element project through the tub bottom into the machinery compartment. You'll find wires attached to the pair of terminals at the element ends. Set the meter selector knob of the VOM to read the ohms (resistance) and clamp an alligator clip on the bare part of each terminal. A reading in the neighborhood of 5 to 30 ohms says the element is in good working order. Anything much above this, or a reading of infinity (∞), indicates that the element has burned out.

Here's another example: Switch failures are not uncommon in appliances. To troubleshoot, first unplug the appliance's power cord or turn off the circuit. Clip one of the two ohmmeter leads to each of the switch terminals. If the switch is working properly, resistance should be zero when the switch is on, and infinity (∞) when the switch is off.

Looking for electrical problems via resistance measurements with an ohmmeter is safe. You should know what to expect when taking a reading, of course, so you can recognize an abnormal one—but you don't have to know exactly. In the absence of a repair manual or a circuit diagram with listed values, use the following numbers as a general guide:

- Appliance (drive) motor: 2–5 ohms
- Heating element: 5–30 ohms
- Water inlet valve: 500–1,000 ohms
- Timer motor: 500–1,000 ohms

Much of the time, component failures will be obvious from the reading; that is, the item is burned out and shows an infinitely high resistance. Or it may be shorted and read less than an ohm or two.

• TOOLS FOR APPLIANCE REPAIR •

Hand tools are designed not to sever or distort the materials of fabrication, but to serve the connecting hardware, i.e., to secure or unfasten the various bits and pieces that hold the main components of a main assembly together.

Most connecting hardware discussed in this book consists primarily of threaded fasteners. The wrench, therefore, is one of the most widely used tools, although the nut driver has gained major prominence and has become even more widely used than the wrench. Size requirements differ, of course, but for the repair and maintenance of appliances and other consumer hard goods, you will need most of the common hand tools that are virtually universal in application. This rule of thumb means that the assortment of tools that are needed to address a washing machine repair, for example, also can be found in an auto mechanic's tool box. Bear this in mind when you are confronted with the substantial cash outlay required to purchase a comprehensive set of tools. You can spread out the cost over possible future applications, including those jobs you wouldn't otherwise tackle if you didn't have the tools on hand.

The following list describes those hand tools that are needed to make many of the repairs found in this book:

Wrenches

The function of a wrench is to exert torque, or turning force, on nuts and bolt heads. Most wrenches are intended to engage the flat surfaces on such hardware, but some special types are designed to grip the round profile of studs and pipes. Wrenches made from chrome vanadium and similar alloys are best; cheap varieties are sometimes seen in cast iron, or made from steel stampings (rather than forgings). Don't be misled by the heft of a wrench;

cheapies are often of apparently heavy construction to compensate for a weaker alloy. Anyone who has ever struggled with crude wrenches in tight quarters will appreciate the way slender, high-quality tools can be manipulated.

OPEN-END WRENCH. The most familiar pattern has open jaws, configured like the letter C. They are not as strong as some other types, since the open jaws tend to "spring" wider under maximum loads. But they can be used from the side, when there is an obstruction that prevents a wrench from being slipped over a nut endwise. Open-end wrenches can be fitted to both square and hexagonal nuts. These tools are usually double-ended, differing in size at either end, so unless you have a fancy set with duplicate sizes, you'll need extra wrenches to get the same-size grip on both ends of a bolt-nut connection.

BOX WRENCH. The British call this a ring spanner, which is more descriptive of its business end—an enclosing hoop. Since a box wrench must be slipped over the end of the fastener, it cannot be used on pipe fittings and the like. Stronger than an open-end wrench, the box wrench is preferable, whenever possible. It's less likely to slip and round off a nut under heavy effort than is an open-end wrench, since every corner of the nut is contacted. It's also better suited to close-quarters work, since less clearance is needed around the nut for fitting and manipulation.

SOCKET WRENCH. A short cylinder of steel, with an opening at each end—one to engage the nut, the other to accept the necessary drive handle, or an extension. Its advantages are similar to those of a box wrench, but it's even more flexible in fit and manipulation. A great advantage is that various handles are available: a ratchet-drive handle is useful where clearance to swing a wrench is limited; a flex handle allows drive at an angle, as does a universal-joint accessory. Extensions come in various lengths, and permit driving nuts from more remote locations. Socket wrenches are useful for removing spark plugs and for other small-engine repairs.

ADJUSTABLE WRENCH. Numerous designs are available, but this tool is essentially an open-end wrench with a movable jaw. "One size fits all," up to the jaws' maximum opening. It offers economical backup to duplicate sizes in conjunction with a proper set of wrenches, and is a make-do substitute for the occasional encounter with odd-size hardware. Such wrenches are relatively bulky, however, and some examples tend to "spring" under heavy effort.

ALLEN WRENCH (OR KEY). An L-shaped tool made in a wide range of sizes from bar stock of a hexagonal cross-section, this tool is used to drive a screw with a matching recess in its head (such as those commonly used as set screws in appliance control knobs).

Pliers

General-purpose gripping tools, pliers are used to pull and twist components into position, or restrain them should that prove necessary. They are also used to cut and bend wire. (Ordinary pliers should not be used as a substitute for a wrench or a nut driver; slippage is likely, which will mar or distort the hardware.)

SLIP-JOINT PLIER. Perhaps the most familiar plier type, its jaws have both flat and round areas for gripping items of various configurations. The slip joint allows you to adjust the size of the jaw opening for the best grip. The jaws usually have a sharp-edged area for cutting wire.

LONG-NOSED PLIER. Available with various jaw shapes—flat, round, or bent—this tool is not intended for heavy effort, but is used more like tweezers in tight spots.

PUMP PLIER. A tool with offset jaws and long

handles, a pump plier is used for gripping large components; it has a slip joint with multiple positions allowing for jaw openings up to several inches wide.

DIAGONAL CUTTING PLIER. Has pincer jaws for cutting wire, brads, etc. Not for gripping.

LOCKING PLIER. Commonly called by a trade name, "Vise-Grip." A locking plier that can be adjusted to provide great clamping force. Used on pipe or irregular objects; often the tool of last resort for a nut or bolt head that has been stripped round.

Screwdrivers

The name of this familiar tool is self-explanatory. It comes in a variety of sizes, shapes, and lengths. Originally, screwdrivers had wooden handles, but they are more commonly fitted nowadays with fluted plastic handles that are more durable and provide a better grip. (In spite of appearances, a screwdriver is not meant to be used as a chisel or pry bar.)

STANDARD (FLAT-BLADED) SCREWDRIVER. Common blade widths range from ⅛ to 5⁄16 inch; blade lengths (not including handle) are generally proportional to width and typically range from 3 to 8 inches. An example of a size designation is 3⁄16 × 4. For best performance, select a screwdriver whose blade width matches the width of the screw slot. "Stubby" screwdrivers have blade lengths of only an inch or two, even in larger widths, and are intended for work in close quarters.

PHILLIPS SCREWDRIVER. This screwdriver has a pointed, four-fluted end; a Phillips screw has a matching cross-shaped recess in its head. Phillips screws are commonly used on finished surfaces since the driver is less likely to slip off the screw head than is the flat-bladed type. Size designations are nominal, the common ones being #0, #1, #2, and #3. Various shank lengths are available, including stubby models. (Don't attempt to drive Phillips screws with a standard screwdriver.)

MISCELLANEOUS SCREWDRIVERS. Other unique screw hardware systems requiring special drivers include Pozidriv, Torx, and clutch-head designs. These systems offer production advantages to a manufacturer, but are a nuisance to deal with in an isolated encounter when you're unprepared to work on them.

Nut Drivers

A nut driver resembles a screwdriver, with a handle and shank, but has a socket wrench on the shank end. A necessary tool for working on appliances and small engines, among other equipment, it's also used to extract the six-sided screw-type fasteners that manufacturers use to assemble components. The two most common sizes needed for making the repairs described in this book are ¼ and 5⁄8 inch.

LIST of DEALERS for OLD and NEW APPLIANCE PARTS

Obtaining replacement parts is one of the most troublesome problems you will face in trying to repair a major household appliance that is more than 10 years old. Major appliance manufacturers generally stop producing parts for a particular model a decade after terminating the production of that model. Luckily for the do-it-yourselfer, however, so-called after-market parts dealers buy up huge quantities of these "obsolete" components. This means parts are still available for appliances that are as much as 25 years old, if you know where to find them.

• LOOK LOCALLY FIRST •

When you need a part, look first in the yellow pages of your phone book under the heading "Appliances—Major—Supplies & Parts" for a local source. A local dealer is better because it helps to be able to take a damaged part to a store to match it with a new one. In addition, you can make the repair without having to wait a number of weeks for a part to come in the mail.

If a local source can't supply the part, you'll have to look further. Don't give up too quickly. Just because one or more of the nationwide suppliers listed in the following pages doesn't have the component you want, that doesn't mean some of the others don't.

• HOW TO USE THIS LIST •

You'll notice that many of the companies have toll-free (800) numbers and more than one location. Only one toll-free number is supplied here for each company. If you call the first location and the part is not available, inquire about toll-free numbers for the other locations of the company as well, or call information, 1-800-555-1212.

Although this list gives a state-by-state breakdown, you don't have to confine yourself to the companies in your state. Most parts dealers on this list provide a mail-order service. Before ordering, however, make sure you can return a part for credit or for a refund in case of a shipping error or a mistake on your part, such as the incorrect name or model number.

ALABAMA

AAA Appliance Parts, Inc.
705 Graymont Ave., North
P.O. Box 10671
Birmingham, AL 35202
(205) 328-2142; (800) 627-2604

Appliance Parts, Inc.
412 20th Ave.
Tuscaloosa, AL 35401
(205) 345-2828; (800) 452-5973

Washer & Refrigeration Supply Co., Inc.
716 Second Ave., North
Birmingham, AL 35201
(205) 322-8693

ALASKA

Appliance Parts Supermarket
(2 locations)
(1) 12000 Industry Way, No. 3
    Anchorage, AK 99515
    (907) 345-0219
(2) 360 Boniface Rd., No. A31
    Anchorage, AK 99504
    (907) 337-3914

ARIZONA

Appliance Dealer Supply Co., Inc. (2 locations)
(1) 740 West Grant St.
    Phoenix, AZ 85007
    (602) 252-7506; (800) 821-8195
(2) 4620 East Speedway Rd.
    Tucson, AZ 85712
    (602) 881-7855; (800) 468-6551

Appliance Parts Co. (2 locations)
(1) Bell and 43rd Ave.
    Glendale, AZ 85308
    (602) 938-0446
(2) 2333 North 35th Ave.
    Phoenix, AZ 85009
    (602) 269-6385

G&N Appliance Parts Co.
1537 South 4th Ave.
Tucson, AZ 85713
(602) 624-2102

ARKANSAS

Mid-South Appliance Parts Co.
(5 locations)
(1) 720 North 11th St.
    Fort Smith, AR 72901
    (501) 785-4267
(2) 1020 West 14th St.
    Little Rock, AR 72201
    (501) 376-8351
(3) 8635 Chico Rd.
    Little Rock, AR 72209
    (501) 565-4144
(4) 2300 Pike Ave.
    North Little Rock, AR 72114
    (501) 753-9052
(5) 918 Young St.
    Springdale, AR 72764
    (501) 756-9540

CALIFORNIA

API Appliance Parts, Inc.
(2 locations)
(1) 1645 Old County Rd.
    San Carlos, CA 94070
    (415) 591-4467; (800) 950-7278
(2) 1545 South Van Ness Ave.
    San Francisco, CA 94110
    (415) 826-2223

Cal Sales Corp. (4 locations)
(1) 641 Monterey Pass Rd.
    Monterey Park, CA 91754
    (213) 283-7741
(2) 2945 West 5th St.
    Oxnard, CA 93030
    (805) 984-1143
(3) 7060 Gerald Ave.
    Van Nuys, CA 91406
    (818) 781-3320
(4) 7345 Radford Ave.
    North Hollywood, CA 91605
    (818) 503-4495

Coast Appliance Parts Co.
(10 locations)
(1) 948 Colton Ave.
    Colton, CA 92324
    (714) 781-9400
(2) 9817 Inglewood Ave.
    Inglewood, CA 90301
    (213) 679-9208
(3) 6250 Cherry Ave.
    Long Beach, CA 90805 5
    (213) 423-8688
(4) 4692 Cardin St.
    San Diego, CA 92111
    (619) 576-9696

(5) 1702 South Lyon St.
    Santa Ana, CA 92705
    (714) 542-9944
(6) 2606 Lee Ave.
    South El Monte, CA 91733
    (818) 579-1500
(7) 5915 Kester Ave.
    Van Nuys, CA 91411
    (818) 782-5770
(8) 220 Eureka St.
    Bakersfield, CA 93305
    (805) 324-9891
(9) 312 East Tulare St.
    Visalia, CA 93277
    (209) 625-5177
(10) 3260 East McKinley
     Fresno, CA 93703
     (209) 485-4444

Electrical Appliance Parts Co.
(5 locations)
(1) 820 East Shields Ave.
    Fresno, CA 93704
    (209) 225-5880
(2) 1116 F St.
    Sacramento, CA 95814
    (916) 446-5241
(3) 290 Townsend St.
    San Francisco, CA 94107
    (415) 777-1900
(4) 1140 Lincoln Ave.
    San Jose, CA 95125
    (408) 998-5322
(5) 1728 Gilbreth Rd.
    Burlingame, CA 94010
    (415) 259-9401

Hughes Appliance Parts Co.
(2 locations)
(1) 240 Iowa Ave.
    Riverside, CA 92507
    (714) 686-8641
(2) 12513 Venice Blvd.
    Los Angeles, CA 90066
    (310) 643-9211

Pacific Coast Parts Distributors, Inc.
15024 Staff Ct.
Gardena, CA 90248
(213) 515-0207; (800) 421-5080

R&B Appliance Parts Co.
5070 Lindsay Ct.
Chino, CA 91710
(714) 591-9405; (800) 421-2189

COLORADO

Akrit Appliance Supply Co.
402 Arrawanna St.
Colorado Springs, CO 80909
(719) 635-3569

CONNECTICUT

All-Appliance Parts, Inc.
(2 locations)
(1) 223 Brainard Rd.
    Hartford, CT 06114
    (203) 247-4212
(2) 474 Frontage Rd.
    West Haven, CT 06516
    (203) 932-3090

American Appliance Parts, Inc.
2516 Whitney Ave.
Hamden, CT 06518
(203) 248-4444

DELAWARE

Appliance Parts Co., Inc.
111 South Lincoln St.
Wilmington, DE 19805
(302) 652-3701

Coastline Parts Co.
Rte. 1
Fenwick Island, DE 19944
(302) 539-2119; (800) 892-1525

Jacoby Appliance Parts, Inc.
228 West Market St.
Newport, DE 19804
(302) 999-9981

FLORIDA

All-Appliance Parts (5 locations)
(1) 4419-1 Del Prado Blvd.
    Cape Coral, FL 33904
    (813) 542-3800
(2) 2309 Fowler St.
    Fort Myers, FL 33901
    (813) 334-1061

(3) 108 10th St., North
    Naples, FL 33940
    (813) 262-3343
(4) 2691 Tamiami Trail
    Port Charlotte, FL 33952
    (813) 625-1818
(5) 14508 Tamiami Trail
    Fort Myers, FL 33912
    (813) 481-8711

Appliance Components
(2 locations)
(1) 511 Airport Rd.
    Panama City, FL 32405
    (904) 769-0379
(2) 3109 North T St.
    Pensacola, FL 32505
    (904) 432-0730

Appliance Parts Headquarters
(2 locations)
(1) 6110-2 Power Ave.
    Jacksonville, FL 32217
    (904) 731-9115
(2) 6460 126th Ave., North
    Largo, FL 33543
    (813) 536-0421; (800) 282-0109

Marcone Appliance Parts Center
(11 locations)
(1) 6301 Metro Plantation Rd.
    Fort Meyers, FL 33912
    (813) 278-5802
(2) 812 Rosselle St.
    Jacksonville, FL 32204
    (904) 354-3398;
    (800) 999-3459
(3) 8347 N.W. 36th St.
    Miami, FL 33166
    (305) 594-0203
(4) 777 N.W. 79th St.
    Miami, FL 33150
    (305) 693-4335
(5) 2108 West Central Blvd.
    Orlando, FL 32805
    (407) 841-8582;
    (800) 521-5513
(6) 3706 North Pace Blvd.
    Pensacola, FL 32505
    (904) 432-2448;
    (800) 624-6035
(7) 1800 North Powerline Rd.

Pompano Beach, FL 33069
(305) 960-0180
(8) 12965 S.W. 85th Ave.
South Miami, FL 33156
(305) 255-4333
(9) 1440 Capital Circle, N.W.
Tallahassee, FL 32303
(904) 575-0696;
(800) 342-2825
(10) 4410 Adamo Rd.
Tampa, FL 33605
(813) 247-4410;
(800) 282-6636
(11) 1300 North Florida Mango
Rd.
West Palm Beach, FL 33409
(407) 683-0077

GEORGIA

Appliance Parts Warehouse, Inc.
765 South Marietta Parkway
Marietta, GA 30060
(404) 428-7948

Brackett Supply
5864 New Peachtree Rd.
Atlanta, GA 30340
(404) 458-8191; (800) 241-0801

Fox Appliance Parts (4 locations)
(1) 3503 Wrightsboro Rd.
Augusta, GA 30909
(404) 737-3400
(2) 2508 Cussetta Rd.
Columbus, GA 31903
(404) 687-2267
(3) 5375 North Parkway
Lake City, GA 30252
(404) 363-3313; (800) 342-5369
(4) 6357 Hawkinsville Rd.
Macon, GA 31205
(912) 788-1793

HAWAII

Appliance Parts Co., Inc.
1550 Kalani St.
Honolulu, HI 96817
(808) 847-3271

ILLINOIS

A&J Appliance Parts, Inc.
2237 West 63rd St.
Chicago, IL 60636
(312) 476-7545

Appliance Parts Distributors
3900 West 127th St.
Aslip, IL 60658
(708) 371-4477

Automatic Appliance Parts Corp.
(6 locations)
(1) 1506 East Algonquin Rd.
Arlington Heights, IL 60005
(708) 439-4095
(2) 1598 North Farnsworth Ave.
Aurora, IL 60505
(708) 851-6300
(3) 7757 West Lawrence Ave.
Norridge, IL 60656
(708) 453-8384
(4) 14728 South Campbell Rd.
Posen, IL 60469
(708) 371-1700
(5) 926 22nd St.
Rockford, IL 61108
(815) 398-0650
(6) 2222 Burlington Ave.
Downers Grove, IL 60515
(708) 960-2266

C.E. Sundberg Co. (6 locations)
(1) 8233 South Princeton Ave.
Chicago, IL 60620
(312) 723-2700; (800) 621-9190
(2) 3037 West 111th St.
Chicago, IL 60655
(312) 445-5511
(3) 4906 West Cermak Rd.
Cicero, IL 60650
(708) 863-4100
(4) 4811 West 159th St.
Oak Forest, IL 60452
(708) 535-3200
(5) 2225 West Jefferson St.
Joliet, IL 60435
(815) 725-4311; (800) 522-4134
(6) 125 West State St.
South Elgin, IL 60177
(708) 697-3640

Garrons, Inc.
1650 North Mannheim Rd.
Stone Park, IL 60165
(708) 344-2340

Marcone Appliance Parts Co.
8306 North University St.
Peoria, IL 61615
(309) 691-7050

Midwest Appliance Parts Co.
(2 locations)
(1) 2600 West Diversey
Chicago, IL 60647
(312) 278-1300; (800) 621-1932
(2) 2507 East Oakland Ave.
Bloomington, IL
(309) 662-7643

INDIANA

Appliance Parts Supply Co.
1241 Wells St.
Fort Wayne, IN 46808
(219) 424-5327

Bell Parts Supply, Inc.
(4 locations)
(1) 4730 Hohman Ave.
Hammond, IN 46327
(219) 932-5960; (800) 235-5243
(2) 2609 45th St.
Highland, IN 46322
(219) 924-1200
(3) 2007 Kossuth St.
Lafayette, IN 47905
(317) 448-4619
(4) 210 West Monroe Ave.
South Bend, IN 46601
(219) 232-3088

Evansville Appliance Parts Co.
900 East Diamond Ave.
Evansville, IN 47711
(812) 423-8867

Hagan Parts Corp.
807 Oak Hill Rd.
Evansville, IN 47711
(812) 423-4254

IOWA

Dey Appliance Parts Co.
320 LaPorte Rd.
Waterloo, IA 50704
(319) 232-8998

Garrons Iowa Parts Supply Co.
801 S.E. 14th St.
Des Moines, IA 50316
(515) 244-7236

Major Appliance Parts, Inc.
2800 Delaware Ave.
Des Moines, IA 50317
(515) 266-0107

Tri Cities Sales Co., Inc.
5311 Tremont
Davenport, IA 52809
(319) 386-3693; (800) 397-3693

KANSAS

Arrow-Cold Central Appliance Parts
28 North 10th St.
Kansas City, KS 66102
(913) 371-4677

Marcone Appliance Parts Co.
(2 locations)
(1) 9130 Flint Ave.
    Overland Park, KS 66214
    (913) 492-0600; (800) 821-3298
(2) 909 E. Waterman
    Wichita, KS 67202
    (316) 263-4230; (800) 678-8188

KENTUCKY

Brown Appliance Parts Co.
933 Liberty Rd.
Lexington, KY 40508
(606) 254-4051

Dayton Appliance Parts Co.
7133 Turfway Rd.
Florence, KY 41011
(606) 282-7100

Duvall Appliance Parts Co., Inc.
(2 locations)
(1) 213 South Main St.
    Elizabethtown, KY 42701
    (502) 765-2936
(2) 2079 South Dixie Highway
    Radcliffe, KY 40160
    (502) 351-3581

Marcone Appliance Parts Co.
4422 Kiln Ct.
Louisville, KY 40218
(502) 456-4422; (800) 626-2441

NAPCO, Inc. (2 locations)
(1) 1424 Sanita Rd.
    Louisville, KY 40213
    (502) 459-3114
(2) 1300 New Circle Rd. Unit 115
    Lexington, KY 40505
    (606) 233-3474

LOUISIANA

Action Appliance Parts, Inc.
(3 locations)
(1) 1545 North Foster Dr.
    Baton Rouge, LA 70806
    (504) 924-2176
(2) 1129 Tamari Dr.
    Baton Rouge, LA 70815
    (504) 275-8258
(3) 111 East Ascension
    Gonzales, LA 70737
    (504) 644-8140

Bruce's Distributing Co.
550 East 70th St.
Shreveport, LA 71106
(318) 861-7662

Sunseri's
4500 South I-10 Service Rd.
Metairie, LA 70001
(504) 888-3773

Superior Appliance Parts, Inc.
3738 Plank Rd.
Baton Rouge, LA 70805
(504) 356-2472

Veazey Suppliers, Inc.
(2 locations)
(1) 214 Edwards Ave.
    Harahan, LA 70123
    (504) 733-5234
(2) 2136 Dallas Dr.
    Baton Rouge, LA 70806
    (504) 928-2988

MAINE

Appliance Parts Co.
255 Danforth St.
Portland, ME 04102
(207) 774-6381

Twin City Supply Co.
105 St. James St.
Portland, ME 04102
(207) 774-4444

United Refrigeration
22 Thomas Dr.
Westbrook, ME 04092
(207) 774-5764

MARYLAND

Appalachian Appliance Parts
14508 McMullen Highway
Cresaptown, MD 21502
(301) 722-7278

Appliance Parts City, Inc.
2907 Greenmount Ave.
Baltimore, MD 21218
(410) 243-0056

Coastline Parts Co.
818 Snow Hill Rd.
Salisbury, MD 21801
(301) 742-8634; (800) 892-1525

Trible's, Inc. (4 locations)
(1) 901 Southern Ave.
    Oxon Hill, MD 20745
    (301) 894-6161; (800) 874-2537
(2) 771 Hungerford Dr.
    Rockville, MD 20850
    (301) 251-9611
(3) 2624 Lower Baltimore Dr.
    Suite A

Baltimore, MD 21244
(410) 265-6655
(4) 10731 Baltimore Ave.
Beltsville, MD 20705
(301) 937-7440

MASSACHUSETTS

AAA Appliance Parts, Inc.
37–39 Park St.
Dorchester, MA 02122
(617) 288-2928

All Appliance Parts
298 Medford St.
Malden, MA 02148
(617) 324-3344

Appliance Parts Co., Inc.
(2 locations)
(1) 5204 Washington St.
West Roxbury, MA 02132
(617) 327-7481
(2) 253 Millbury St.
Worcester, MA 01610
(508) 755-4795

Gene's Appliance Parts Co.
(2 locations)
(1) 788 Gorham St.
Lowell, MA 01852
(508) 453-2896
(2) 106 East Haverhill Rd.
Lawrence, MA 01841
(508) 683-7890

Hall Electric Supply Co., Inc.
315 Salem St.
Medford, MA 02155
(617) 391-4300

Mass Appliance Parts, Inc.
404 Main St.
Brockton, MA 02401
(508) 587-7100

MICHIGAN

Apco, Inc. (5 locations)
(1) G-3437 Miller Rd.
Flint, MI 48507
(313) 732-8933
(2) 3520 Jefferson, S.E.
Grand Rapids, MI 49508
(616) 452-8741

(3) 411 West Milhan
Kalamazoo, MI 49006
(616) 329-2676
(4) 3305 South Pennsylvania
Lansing, MI 48910
(517) 882-5745
(5) 3100 Enterprise
Saginaw, MI 48603
(517) 790-2244

Bussard Appliance Parts
454 Orchard Lake Ave.
Pontiac, MI 48341
(313) 332-6445

E&G Appliance Service Co., Inc.
1435 Lawndale
Detroit, MI 48209
(313) 842-2252

Electric Appliance Parts
5824 South Cedar St.
Lansing, MI 48910
(517) 393-0700

Servall Co. (11 locations)
(1) 13545 Northline
Southgate, MI 48195
(313) 282-2666
(2) 6619 Schaefer Hwy.
Dearborn, MI 48126
(313) 582-7900
(3) 228 East Baltimore St.
Detroit, MI 48202
(313) 872-3655;
(800) 989-7378
(4) 25755 Grand River Ave.
Detroit, MI 48240
(313) 538-0150;
(800) 899-7270
(5) 24312 Gratiot Ave.
East Detroit, MI 48021
(313) 778-1600
(6) 630 West Kearsley St.
Flint, MI 48503
(313) 238-5678;
(800) 899-5677
(7) 440 Lake Michigan Drive,
N.W.
Grand Rapids, MI 49504
(616) 451-2691; (800) 899-
2691
(8) 5111 East Miller St.

Suite 5
Kalamazoo, MI 49001
(616) 344-6980; (800) 899-
6980
(9) 25211 Dequindre
Madison Heights, MI 48030
(313) 541-8848
(10) 2501 South Cedar
Lansing, MI 48912
(517) 487-9550
(11) 1124 South Water St.
Saginaw, MI 48601
(517) 754-0497

MINNESOTA

Allied Appliance Parts, Inc.
(2 locations)
(1) 4419 Nichollet Ave. South
Minneapolis, MN 55409
(612) 822-0134
(2) 2440 North Charles St.
North St. Paul, MN 55109
(612) 777-4002

Appliance Parts, Inc. (2 locations)
(1) 1251 Washington Ave., North
Minneapolis, MN 55401
(612) 333-0931
(2) 964 Rice St.
St. Paul, MN 55117
(612) 489-8004

Dey Appliance Parts (4 locations)
(1) 3431 East Highway 13
Burnsville, MN 55337
(612) 890-9358
(2) 328 East Central Entrance
Duluth, MN 55811
(218) 723-1626
(3) 525 North Snelling Ave.
St. Paul, MN 55104
(612) 647-0171
(4) 1401 Wolters Blvd.
Vadnais Heights, MN 55110
(612) 490-9191; (800) 397-1339

MISSISSIPPI

Appliance Parts Co., Inc.
(3 locations)
(1) 1236 Pass Rd.
Gulfport, MS 39501
(601) 863-2996

(2) 1009 Timothy Lane
    Hattiesburg, MS 39401
    (601) 583-3391
(3) 727 South Gallatin St.
    Jackson, MS 39204
    (601) 948-4680

May & Co., Inc.
838 West Capitol St.
Jackson, MS 39203
(601) 354-5781

MISSOURI

Aberdeen Appliance Parts, Inc.
3425 Bridgeland Dr.
Bridgeton, MO 63044
(314) 291-8788; (800) 234-4554

Carroll Appliance Parts
3150 Mercier
Suite 526
Kansas City, MO 64111
(816) 753-3545; (800) 875-3545

Citytronics, Co., Inc.
1641 Dielman Rd.
St. Louis, MO 63132
(314) 427-3420

Marcone Appliance Parts Center
(3 locations)
(1) 3113 Main St.
    Kansas City, MO 64111
    (816) 756-3131
(2) 4012 North Service Rd.
    St. Peters, MO 63301
    (314) 928-1123
(3) 2300 Clark Ave.
    St. Louis, MO 63103
    (314) 231-7225; (800) 325-7588

Schepker Parts Supply Co.
1 North Service Rd.
St. Peters, MO 63376
(314) 278-4600

Washer Equipment Co., Inc.
1715 Main St.
Kansas City, MO 64108
(816) 842-3911; (800) 892-5846

NEBRASKA

All Makes Appliance Parts Co.
4040 Hamilton St.
Omaha, NE 68131
(402) 551-4668

Appliance Parts Supply Co., Inc.
(2 locations)
(1) 14647 Industrial Rd.
    Omaha, NE 68144
    (402) 334-1555
(2) 6710 Grover St.
    Omaha, NE 68106
    (402) 393-7100

Lincoln Appliance Parts Supply
728 South 27th St.
Lincoln, NE 68510
(402) 476-6908

NEVADA

Appliance Parts Co. of Arizona
2001 South Western Ave.
Las Vegas, NV 89102
(702) 382-6532

Electrical Appliance Parts Co.
611 Kuenzli St.
Reno, NV 89502
(702) 786-0210

NEW HAMPSHIRE

Gene's Appliance Parts
62 Kinsley St.
Nashua, NH 03060
(603) 889-5331

United Refrigeration
60 Buckley Circle
Manchester, NH 03109
(603) 669-2896

NEW JERSEY

Abbott Appliance Parts Co.
(2 locations)
(1) 1753 Rte. 88 West
    Bricktown, NJ 08723
    (908) 899-2828

(2) 809 Main St.
    Toms River, NJ 08753
    (908) 244-2040

All-Appliance Parts, Inc.
470 U.S. Highway 46
Teterboro, NJ 07608
(201) 641-3444

All-Brand Appliance Parts, Inc.
(2 locations)
(1) 170 North Blackhorse Pike
    Mount Ephraim, NJ 08059
    (609) 933-2300;
    (800) 736-5870
(2) 517 West Main St.
    Pleasantville, NJ 08232
    (609) 641-1036

Alps Appliance Parts, Inc.
135 Monmouth St.
Red Bank, NJ 07701
(908) 842-5091

AWG Appliance Parts, Inc.
Pond Rd. Shopping Center,
  Rte. 9
Freehold, NJ 07728
(908) 431-9100

Jacoby Appliance Parts
(5 locations)
(1) 269 Main St.
    Hackensack, NJ 07601
    (201) 489-6444
(2) 1374 Springfield Ave.
    Irvington, NJ 07111
    (201) 371-8800
(3) 600 Jersey Ave.
    New Brunswick, NJ 08901
    (908) 846-0300
(4) 5051 Rte. 38
    Pennsauken, NJ 08109
    (609) 488-1310
(5) 923 North Olden Ave.
    Trenton, NJ 08636
    (609) 392-6051; (800) 522-6291

Maco Electronic & Appliance Parts
206 Bellevue Ave.
Hammonton, NJ 08037
(609) 561-7270

Valley Appliance Parts Distributors
2222 Hamburg Turnpike
Wayne, NJ 07470
(201) 835-2157; (800) 522-4134

Will's Appliance Parts, Inc.
(2 locations)
(1) 144 Rte. 73 North
Marlton, NJ 08053
(609) 983-8530
(2) 767 Delsey Dr.
Vineland, NJ 08360
(609) 696-1991

NEW MEXICO

Akrit Appliance Supply Co.
3442 Stanford, N.E.
Albuquerque, NM 87107
(505) 884-0166; (800) 388-3442

NEW YORK

Alan Appliance Parts Corp.
184 Old Country Rd.
Hicksville, NY 11801
(516) 681-3535

All Appliance Parts, Inc.
(5 locations)
(1) 40 Austin Blvd.
Commack, NY 11725
(516) 543-4444
(2) 3 Kuhl Ave.
Hicksville, NY 11805
(516) 681-2515
(3) 196 Laurel Ave.
Northport, NY 11768
(516) 261-6086
(4) 113-02 Atlantic Ave.
Richmond Hill, NY 11419
(718) 441-4300
(5) 1034 Yonkers Ave.
Yonkers, NY 10704
(914) 237-0500

**Appliance Parts Distributors,
Inc.** (6 locations)
(1) 1175 William St.
P.O. Box 7106
Buffalo, NY 14240
(716) 856-5005; (800) 888-7013

(2) 1130 Emerson St.
Rochester, NY 14606
(716) 254-2274
(3) 2851 Sheridan Drive
Tonawanda, NY 14150
(716) 834-4125
(4) 238 Ellicott St.
Batavia, NY 14020
(716) 343-2295
(5) 3150 Erie Blvd. East
Syracuse, NY 13214
(315) 446-0800
(6) 625 Main St.
Johnson City, NY 13790
(607) 770-0163

ARDCO Supply Co.
125 West Main St.
Endicott, NY 13760
(607) 754-6706

Automatic Supply Co.
(3 locations)
(1) 1264 St. Nicholas Ave.
New York, NY 10033
(212) 795-3400; (800) 443-0322
(2) 2871 Webster Ave.
Bronx, NY 10458
(718) 733-1112
(3) 76 East Rte. 59
Nanuet, NY 10954
(914) 623-1660

**Brighton Washer & Appliance
Parts, Inc.**
120 Otis St.
West Babylon, NY 11704
(516) 491-6950; (800) 221-0952

Jacoby Appliance Parts
(4 locations)
(1) 1023 Allerton Ave.
Bronx, NY 10469
(718) 547-3573
(2) 214 Rte. 59
Suffern, NY 10901
(914) 357-7110
(3) 1654 Central Ave.
Albany, NY 12205
(518) 869-2283; (800) 343-3636
(4) 96 Genessee St.
Utica, NY 13502
(315) 797-2552

Long Island Appliance Parts, Inc.
(2 locations)
(1) 20-50 Hillside Ave.
New Hyde Park, NY 11040
(516) 488-3153
(2) 585 Merrick Rd.
Lynbrook, NY 11563
(516) 593-4686

**Pago Appliance Parts
Distribution Co.**
700 Broadway
Buffalo, NY 14212
(716) 856-8133; (800) 926-7246

Suffolk Appliance Parts Co.
(2 locations)
(1) 1516 Sunrise Highway
Bay Shore, NY 11706
(516) 665-6445
(2) 3669 Rte. 112
Coram, NY 11727
(516) 732-4680

Yemma Appliance Parts, Inc.
1962 Teall Ave.
Syracuse, NY 13206
(315) 437-1608

NORTH CAROLINA

Brackett Supply (2 locations)
(1) 4 Cloyes St.
Asheville, NC 28806
(704) 258-2223; (800) 452-2859
(2) 1703 Highway 70 S.W.
Hickory, NC 28601
(704) 322-4503; (800) 365-4503

Cashwell Appliance Parts, Inc.
(5 locations)
(1) 344 North Louisiana Ave.
Asheville, NC 28806
(704) 254-5714; (800) 768-3221
(2) 2900 North Graham St.
Charlotte, NC 28206
(704) 342-9634
(3) 3609 Sycamore Dairy Rd.
Fayetteville, NC 28303
(919) 867-1135
(4) 3485 Clinton Rd.
Fayetteville, NC 28302
(919) 323-1111

(5) 5750 Oleander Dr.
    Wilmington, NC 28403
    (919) 799-6533

D&L Appliance Parts Co., Inc.
(8 locations)
(1) 2100 Freedom Drive
    Charlotte, NC 28208
    (704) 374-0400
(2) 2821 North Roxboro Rd.
    Durham, NC 27704
    (919) 688-8075
(3) 3319-F Raeford Rd.
    Fayetteville, NC 28303
    (919) 484-1137
(4) 2811 Firestone Dr.
    Greensboro, NC 27406
    (919) 274-7627
(5) 1207 West 14th St.
    Greenville, NC 27834
    (919) 752-0336
(6) 2324 Atlantic Ave.
    Raleigh, NC 27604
    (919) 828-0975
(7) 1090 Burke St.
    Winston-Salem, NC 27101
    (919) 723-3068
(8) 4412-D Monroe Rd.
    East Charlotte, NC 28205
    (704) 377-5910

NORTH DAKOTA

Appliance Parts, Inc.
20 North University Dr.
Fargo, ND 58102
(701) 235-4291

OHIO

American Electric Washer Co.
(4 locations)
(1) 2086 Romig Rd.
    Akron, OH 44320
    (216) 745-6600; (800) 552-7278
(2) 1834 East 55th St.
    Cleveland, OH 44103
    (216) 431-4400; (800) 362-2406
(3) 16924 Detroit Ave.
    Lakewood, OH 44107
    (216) 226-2400
(4) 5817 Pearl Rd.

Parma Heights, OH 44130
(216) 888-3300

Appliance Parts Supply Co.
(3 locations)
(1) 1331 Conant St.
    Maumee, OH 43537
    (419) 891-0911
(2) 235 Broadway St.
    Toledo, OH 43602
    (419) 244-6741
(3) 2453 Tremainsville Rd.
    Toledo, OH 43613
    (419) 472-0228

Dayton Appliance Parts Co.
(5 locations)
(1) 11273 Grooms Rd.
    Cincinnati, OH 45242
    (513) 489-1980; (800) 521-9201
(2) 620 Weber Rd.
    Columbus, OH 43211
    (614) 262-6446
(3) 122 Sears St.
    Dayton, OH 45402
    (513) 224-3531
(4) 6575 Brandt Pike
    Dayton, OH 45424
    (513) 236-4861
(5) 8941 Kingsridge Drive
    Dayton, OH 45458
    (513) 439-2384

Major's Appliance Parts
(2 locations)
(1) 5785 Ridge Rd.
    Cleveland, OH 44129
    (216) 884-7200
(2) 5845 Turney Rd.
    Cleveland, OH 44125
    (216) 663-4650

Mason Supply Co. (2 locations)
(1) 3929 Apple St.
    Cincinnati, OH 45223
    (513) 591-0020; (800) 772-8083
(2) 985 Joyce Ave.
    Columbus, OH 43203
    (614) 253-8607

Mr. Handy Parts Center
195 East John St.

Springfield, OH 45505
(513) 325-3116

Parts America, Inc.
1834 East 55th St.
Cleveland, OH 44103
(216) 431-4400; (800) 362-2406

Pearsol Appliance Parts Co.
2319 Gilbert Ave.
Cincinnati, OH 45206
(513) 221-1195; (800) 992-7337

Shore Appliance Co. (3 locations)
(1) 22199 Euclid Ave.
    Euclid, OH 44117
    (216) 383-8300
(2) 7580 Mentor Ave.
    Mentor, OH 44060
    (216) 951-0511
(3) 6573 Pearl Rd.
    Parma Heights, OH 44130
    (216) 888-4646

Stone Appliance Parts
38296 Western Parkway
Willoughby, OH 44094
(216) 951-2775

V&V Appliance Parts, Inc.
(4 locations)
(1) 3422 West Tuscarawas
    Canton, OH 44708
    (216) 455-3387; (800) 344-9136
(2) 426 Arch St.
    Salem, OH 44460
    (216) 332-9532
(3) 630 High St., N.E.
    Warren, OH 44481
    (216) 399-3552
(4) 27 West Myrtle Ave.
    Youngstown, OH 44507
    (216) 743-5144

OKLAHOMA

Greer Appliance Parts
1018 South Rockford
Tulsa, OK 74120
(918) 587-3346

Pritchard Electric Co., Inc.
3100 North Santa Fe
Oklahoma City, OK 73118
(405) 528-0592

OREGON

Appliance Parts Co.
1009 S.E. Lincoln St.
Portland, OR 97214
(503) 238-1102

Diversified Parts, Inc.
2104 S.E. 9th Ave.
Portland, OR 97214
(503) 236-6140; (800) 338-6342

Hansberry's Appliance Parts Co.
3103 S.E. Division St.
Portland, OR 97202
(503) 239-6050

Johnson Parts & Supply Co.
1108 Broadway, N.E.
Salem, OR 97301
(503) 364-7611; 363-4960

Universal Appliance Parts Co.
12855 S.W. Beaverdam Rd.
Beaverton, OR 97005
(503) 646-3703

W.L. May Co., Inc. (2 locations)
(1) 3629 Franklin Blvd.
    Eugene, OR 97403
    (503) 726-7696
(2) 1120 S.E. Madison St.
    Portland, OR 97214
    (503) 231-7000; (800) 377-8881

PENNSYLVANIA

All-Appliance Parts Co.
5023 Penn Ave.
Pittsburgh, PA 15224
(412) 362-1500

All-Appliance Parts Distributors Corp.
312 North Easton Rd.
Willow Grove, PA 19090
(215) 657-3777

All-Brand Appliance Parts of PA
(2 locations)
(1) 137 MacDade Blvd.
    Folsom, PA 19033
    (215) 534-0800
(2) 949 East Main St.
    Norristown, PA 19401
    (215) 277-5175

AM Parts Co. (4 locations)
(1) Bon Aire Shopping Center
    Butler, PA 16001
    (412) 283-9100
(2) 1548 Pennsylvania Ave.
    Monaca, PA 15061
    (412) 775-8041
(3) 3337 Babcock Blvd.
    Pittsburgh, PA 15237
    (412) 367-8040
(4) 5407 Progress Blvd.
    Bethel Industrial Park
    Bethel Park, PA 15102
    (412) 831-8188

Appliance Parts Distributors, Inc. (2 locations)
(1) 400 Bristol Pike
    Croydon, PA 19020
    (215) 785-6282
(2) 308 West Main St.
    Landsdale, PA 19446
    (215) 362-2444

Arnold's Appliance Parts
261 East Fayette St.
Uniontown, PA 15401
(412) 437-4701

Best Appliance Parts, Inc.
1100 Western Ave.
Pittsburgh, PA 15233
(412) 323-1700

Collins Appliance Parts, Inc.
(2 locations)
(1) 253 Curry Hollow Rd.
    Pittsburgh, PA 15236
    (412) 655-3090
(2) 1533 Metropolitan St.
    Pittsburgh, PA 15233
    (412) 321-3700

D.J. Hurley Co.
18 West Chester Pike
Haverton, PA 19083
(215) 446-8894

Kohler Appliance Parts Supply
(2 locations)
(1) 201-03 Lexington Ave.
    Altoona, PA 16601
    (814) 943-8137
(2) 1217 West 4th St.
    Williamsport, PA 17701
    (717) 323-6711

McCombs Supply Co.
346 North Marshall St.
Lancaster, PA 17602
(717) 394-6248

National Parts Distributors
4279-83 Frankford Ave.
Philadelphia, PA 19124
(215) 743-8020

Resco, Inc.
815 South 26th St.
Harrisburg, PA 17104
(717) 558-7571

Scranton Appliance Parts
(2 locations)
(1) 340 Union St.
    Luzerne, PA 18709
    (717) 288-8676; (800) 441-7760
(2) 830 Capouse Ave.
    Scranton, PA 18509
    (717) 347-2211; (800) 233-4790

V&V Appliance Parts, Inc.
1137 West 26th St.
Erie, PA 16508
(814) 453-6891; (800) 344-9136

Wagner Appliance Parts, Inc.
(4 locations)
(1) 1814 Tilghman St.
    Allentown, PA 18104
    (215) 439-1564
(2) 515 Richmond St.
    Reading, PA 19605
    (215) 372-2385
(3) 1840 East Race St.

Allentown, PA 18103
(215) 264-0681
(4) 651 Gibson Blvd.
     Harrisburg, PA 17104
     (717) 939-8335

RHODE ISLAND

Andersberg's Appliance Parts Co.
560 Mineral Spring Ave.
Pawtucket, RI 02860
(401) 725-6960

Appliance Parts Co., Inc.
316 Cranston St.
Providence, RI 02907
(401) 421-6142

Twin City Supply Co.
233 Harris Ave.
Providence, RI 02903
(401) 331-5930

SOUTH CAROLINA

Brackett Supply Co., Inc.
(2 locations)
(1) 4545-E Rivers Ave.
     North Charleston, SC 29406
     (803) 554-8816; (800) 968-0468
(2) 911 Seaboard St.
     Myrtle Beach, SC 29577
     (803) 448-1034

Coastline Parts Co.
1033 East Montague Ave.
Charleston, SC 29406
(803) 747-7355

D&L Appliance Parts Co., Inc.
901 South Cashua Drive
Florence, SC 29501
(803) 662-3261

G&E Parts Center, Inc.
(3 locations)
(1) 1212 Bluff Rd.
     Columbia, SC 29202
     (803) 771-4346; (800) 226-6600
(2) 2403 South Pine St.

Spartanburg, SC 29302
(803) 585-6277; (800) 226-8989
(3) 1309 Asheville Highway
     Spartanburg, SC 29303
     (803) 582-0501

Harris Appliance Parts Co.
(4 locations)
(1) 110 Highway 29 Bypass North
     Anderson, SC 29621
     (803) 225-7433; (800) 922-2185
(2) 423 Laurens Rd.
     Greenville, SC 29606
     (803) 233-0211
(3) 1525 Cedar Lane Rd.
     Greenville, SC 29611
     (803) 246-0943
(4) 221 Maxwell Ave.
     Greenwood, SC 29646
     (803) 223-4150

SOUTH DAKOTA

Dey Appliance Parts, Inc.
300 North Phillips St.
Sioux Falls, SD 57102
(605) 338-6300; (800) 397-2339

TENNESSEE

Appliance Parts Warehouse, Inc.
2311 East 23rd St.
Chattanooga, TN 37407
(615) 622-4158; (800) 251-6225

Brown Appliance Parts Co.
(4 locations)
(1) 125 New Kingsport Highway
     Bristol, TN 37620
     (615) 968-3138
(2) 2472 Amnicola Highway
     Chattanooga, TN 37406
     (615) 624-0028
(3) 2227 East 23rd St.
     Chattanooga, TN 37404
     (615) 624-7608
(4) 857 North Central Ave.
     Knoxville, TN 37927
     (615) 525-9363

Curtis Appliance Parts Company
(3 locations)
(1) 731 East Brooks Rd.

Memphis, TN 38116
(901) 332-1414; (800) 332-1945
(2) 3858 Park Ave.
     Memphis, TN 38117
     (901) 452-3996
(3) 3979 Jackson Ave.
     Memphis, TN 38111
     (901) 388-3979

Gibbs Electric Co.
739 Greenwood Ave.
Clarksville, TN 37040
(615) 647-6228

Hamilton Appliance Parts Co.
1832 McCalla Ave.
Knoxville, TN 37915
(615) 525-0418

NAPCO, Inc. (5 locations)
(1) 301 College St.
     Clarksville, TN 37040
     (615) 648-4637; (800) 627-2666
(2) 111 Old Hickory Blvd.
     Madison, TN 37115
     (615) 868-7601
(3) 501 South Second St.
     Nashville, TN 37213
     (615) 256-3646
(4) 5510 Charlotte Ave.
     Nashville, TN 37209
     (615) 352-3295
(5) 403 Allied Drive
     Nashville, TN 37211
     (615) 833-8233

TEXAS

Akrit Appliance Supply Co.
(3 locations)
(1) 1719 South Georgia
     Amarillo, TX 79106
     (806) 373-2292; (800) 477-0474
(2) 1805 Montana
     El Paso, TX 79902
     (915) 544-3350
(3) 5307 50th St.
     Lubbock, TX 79414
     (806) 791-0474

Alltex Appliance Parts Co.
4754 Almond

Dallas, TX 75247
(214) 631-4298; (800) 527-2343

Central Supply Co. (9 locations)
(1) 2335D Kramer Lane
Austin, TX 78758
(512) 832-0666
(2) 5365 College
Beaumont, TX 77707
(409) 842-4132
(3) 2639 Electronics Lane, #107
Dallas, TX 75220
(214) 631-5907
(4) 2612 McKinney
Houston, TX 77003
(713) 686-5400
(5) 514 Blue Bell
Houston, TX 77037
(713) 686-5400
(6) 6400 Westpark
Houston, TX 77057
(713) 686-5400
(7) 8206 Mosley
Houston, TX 77075
(713) 686-5400
(8) 1209 South Saint Marys
San Antonio, TX 78210
(512) 225-2717
(9) 101 East Nakoma
San Antonio, TX 78216
(512) 225-2717

Major Appliance Parts Co.
(3 locations)
(1) 1232 North Hackberry St.
San Antonio, TX 78202
(512) 223-2675
(2) 1109 S.W. Military Drive
San Antonio, TX 78221
(512) 921-1675
(3) 2109 Jackson Keller Rd.
San Antonio, TX 78213
(512) 525-0636

Mid-South Appliance Parts Co.
508 Lelia
Texarkana, TX 75501
(903) 792-0232

Nelson's Specialty Supply Co.
(3 locations)

(1) 919 North Mockingbird
Abilene, TX 79603
(915) 672-3284; (800) 346-1606
(2) 1021 East 7th St.
Austin, TX 78702
(512) 478-6468
(3) 3412 East Rancier
Killeen, TX 76543
(817) 699-9001

Pearsol Appliance Co.
3127 East Main St.
Dallas, TX 75226
(214) 939-0930

Seasonal Comfort
248 Garrotsville
Houston, TX 77022
(713) 692-5151; (800) 932-2700

Standard Distributors
2970 Blystone St.
Dallas, TX 75220
(214) 357-6493; (800) 527-5008

Stove Parts Supply Co.
2120 Solona
Fort Worth, TX 76117
(817) 589-7903;
Fax: (800) 272-7358

Washing Machine Parts Co.
(2 locations)
(1) 3314 Ross
Dallas, TX 75204
(214) 827-1023; (800) 346-3262
(2) 704 North Main
Fort Worth, TX 76106
(817) 332-5343

UTAH

Ray Jones Appliance Parts Co.
(2 locations)
(1) 7050 South State
Midvale, UT 84047
(801) 566-9139
(2) 3336 South 300 East
Salt Lake City, UT 84115
(801) 486-5971; (800) 622-4915

VERMONT

Supply Distributors Corp.
Rambury Road
Rutland, VT 05701
(802) 775-4012; (800) 255-5352

VIRGINIA

**Booth Refrigeration Supply Co.,
Inc.** (8 locations)
(1) 1179 5th St., S.W. Ext.
Charlottesville, VA 22901
(804) 295-2178; (800) 552-2874
(2) 507 Lindall Lane
Fredericksburg, VA 22405
(703) 373-7185
(3) 8304 Orcutt Ave.
Hampton, VA 23605
(804) 827-1645
(4) 3474 Virginia Beach Blvd.
Norfolk, VA 23502
(804) 857-1227
(5) 11 Perry St.
Petersburg, VA 23803
(804) 748-7226
(6) 2113 North Hamilton St.
Richmond, VA 23230
(804) 353-7141; (804) 359-3275
(7) 441 South Lake Blvd.
Richmond, VA 23236
(804) 379-5200
(8) 926 Vernon St., S.E.
Roanoke, VA 24027
(703) 344-2083

Evans Electric Co.
451 Elm Ave.
Portsmouth, VA 23704
(804) 399-3044

Trible's, Inc. (2 locations)
(1) 8558-F Lee Highway
Merryfield, VA 22031
(703) 573-1000
(2) 6715A Backlick Rd.
Springfield, VA 22150
(703) 866-4600

**Wholesale Appliance Parts
Distributors, Inc.** (2 locations)
(1) 1141 Lance Rd.

Norfolk, VA 23502
(804) 461-3888
(2) 3100 West Cary St.
Richmond, VA 23221
(804) 353-7878

WASHINGTON

Appliance Parts Co. (6 locations)
(1) 12001 N.E. 12th
Suite 40
Bellevue, WA 98005
(206) 453-0406
(2) 400 9th Ave. North
Seattle, WA 98109
(206) 622-0152
(3) 917 West Mallon
Spokane, WA 99201
(509) 328-7062
(4) 3727 South "G"
Tacoma, WA 98408
(206) 473-1850
(5) 1009 Andover Park East
Tukwila, WA 98188
(206) 575-3244
(6) 14715 Aurora Ave. North
Seattle, WA 98133
(206) 365-6774

Pacific Appliance Parts Co.
(2 locations)
(1) 424 North Fruitland
Kennewick, WA 99336
(509) 582-2191; (800) 932-2455

(2) 607 West A St.
Yakima, WA 98902
(509) 248-2308

W.L. May Co.
9801 Aurora Ave. North
Seattle, WA 98103
(206) 525-4500; (800) 422-4062

WEST VIRGINIA

Dayton Appliance Parts Co.
116 Fifth Ave.
Huntington, WV 25701
(304) 523-1990

Mason Appliance Supply Co.
(3 locations)
(1) 312 21st St.
Charleston, WV 25312
(304) 344-3681
(2) 2033 Eighth Ave.
Huntington, WV 25703
(304) 522-8935
(3) 3303 Eoff St.
Wheeling, WV 26003
(304) 232-8940

Parts America (2 locations)
(1) 158 East Spring St.
Charleston, WV 25301
(304) 345-4400; (800) 362-2406
(2) 3330 Route 60 East

Huntington, WV 25705
(304) 529-4500

WISCONSIN

Dey Appliance Parts
1418 North Irwin Ave.
Green Bay, WI 54308
(414) 437-7022

Garrons Distributing Co.
333 South Hawley Rd.
Milwaukee, WI 53214
(414) 475-1070

Kenosha Appliance Parts
2601 Roosevelt Rd.
Kenosha, WI 53143
(414) 657-7329

Madison Appliance Parts, Inc.
1226 Williamson St.
Madison, WI 53703
(608) 257-2589

Power Equipment Co.
(2 locations)
(1) 2373 South Kinnickinnic Ave.
Milwaukee, WI 53207
(414) 744-3210; (800) 242-3939
(2) 9701 West Greenfield Ave.
West Allis, WI 53214
(414) 257-4220

Appendix C

Brand-Name Directory

CLOTHES WASHERS AND DRYERS

ADMIRAL
Admiral Home Appliances
740 King Edward
Cleveland, TN 37311
(615) 472-3371

AMANA
Amana Refrigeration, Inc.
Consumer Affairs Dept.
Amana, IA 52204
(800) 843-0304;
(800) 332-3039 in Iowa

FRIGIDAIRE
Frigidaire Co.
Dept. of Consumer Relations
P.O. Box 7181
Dublin, OH 43017
(800) 374-7714

GENERAL ELECTRIC
General Electric Co.
Appliance Park
Louisville, KY 40225
(800) 626-2000

GIBSON
See Frigidaire
(800) 374-7714

HOTPOINT
See General Electric
(800) 626-2000

KELVINATOR
See Frigidaire
(800) 374-7714

KITCHENAID
KitchenAid, Inc.
2303 Pipestone
Mail Drop Box 0100
Benton Harbor, MI 49022-2400
(800) 422-1230

MAYTAG
Maycore
240 Edwards, S.E.
Cleveland, TN 37311
(800) 688-9900;
(615) 472-3333 in Tennessee

MAGIC CHEF
Magic Chef Company
240 Edwards, S.E.
Cleveland, TN 37311
(615) 472-3500

MIELE
Miele Appliances, Inc.
22D World's Fair Dr.
Somerset, NJ 08873
(908) 560-0899

MONTGOMERY WARD
Montgomery Ward and Co., Inc.
535 West Chicago Ave.
Chicago, IL 60671
(312) 467-2000,
or check local directory

NORGE
See Admiral
(615) 472-3371

SANYO
Sanyo Fisher USA Corp.
200 Riser Road
Little Ferry, NJ 07643
(201) 641-2333

SEARS-KENMORE
Sears, Roebuck & Co.
Sears Tower
Chicago, IL 60684
(312) 875-2500,
or check local directory

SPEED QUEEN
Speed Queen Co.
Box 990
Shepard St.
Ripon, WI 54971-0990
(414) 748-3121

WHIRLPOOL
Whirlpool Corp.
Administrative Center
2000 M 63
Benton Harbor, MI 49022
(800) 253-1301;
(616) 926-5000 in Michigan

WHITE-WESTINGHOUSE
Frigidaire Co.
6000 Perimeter Dr.
Dublin, OH 43017
(614) 792-4100

DISHWASHERS

ADMIRAL
Admiral Home Appliances
Monmouth Blvd.
Galesburg, IL 61401
(309) 343-0181

AEG
Andi Appliance
65 Campus Plaza
Edison, NJ 08837
(908) 225-8837

AMANA
Amana Refrigeration, Inc.
Consumer Affairs Dept.
Amana, IA 52204
(319) 622-5511

BROWN
Brown Stove Works, Inc.
1422 Carolina Ave.
Cleveland, TN 37311
(615) 476-6544

CALORIC
Caloric Corp.
403 North Main St.
Topton, PA 19562-1499
(800) 272-3121

CROSLEY
Crosley Group, Inc.
Box 2111
Winston-Salem, NC 27102
(919) 761-1212

FRIGIDAIRE
Frigidaire Co.
Dept. of Consumer Relations
P.O. Box 7181
Dublin, OH 43017
(800) 451-7007

GAGGENAU
Gaggenau USA Corp.
425 University Ave.
Norwood, MA 02062
(617) 255-1766

GENERAL ELECTRIC
General Electric Co.
Appliance Park
Louisville, KY 40225
(800) 626-2000

GIBSON
See Frigidaire
(614) 792-4100

GLENWOOD
Glenwood Range Co.
435 Park Ave.
Delaware, OH 43015
(614) 363-1381

HOTPOINT
See General Electric
(800) 626-2000

IN-SINK-ERATOR
In-Sink-Erator Div.
Emerson Electric Co.
4700 21st St.
Racine, WI 53406
(800) 558-5700

JENN-AIR
Jenn-Air Co.
3035 Shadeland Ave.
Indianapolis, IN 46226
(317) 545-2271

KELVINATOR
See Frigidaire
(614) 792-4100

KITCHENAID
KitchenAid Inc.
2303 Pipestone
Mail Drop Box 0100
Benton Harbor, MI 49002-2400
(800) 422-1230

MAGIC CHEF
Magic Chef, Inc.
240 Edwards, S.E.
Cleveland, TN 37311
(615) 472-3371

MAYTAG
Maycore
240 Edwards, S.E.
Cleveland, TN 37311
(800) 688-9900;
(615) 472-3333 in Tennessee

MIELE
Miele Appliances, Inc.
22D World's Fair Dr.
Somerset, NJ 08873
(908) 560-0899

MODERN MAID
Caloric Corp.
Highway 220
Amana, IA 52204
(800) 272-3121

MONTGOMERY WARD
Montgomery Ward and Co.
535 West Chicago Ave.
Chicago, IL 60671
(312) 467-2000,
or check local directory

O'KEEFE & MERRIT
See Frigidaire
(614) 792-4100

PANASONIC
Panasonic Co.
50 Meadowland Pkwy.
Secaucus, NJ 07094
(201) 348-9090

PEERLESS-PREMIER
Peerless-Premier Appliance Co.
P.O. Box 387
Belleville, IL 62222
(618) 233-0475

ROPER
Whirlpool Corp.
Consumer Services
2303 Pipestone Rd.
Benton Harbor, MI 49022-2400
(800) 447-6737

SEARS
Sears, Roebuck & Co.
Sears Tower
Chicago, IL 60684
(312) 875-5188,
or check local directory

TAPPAN
See White-Westinghouse
(800) 537-5530

THERMADOR
Thermador/Waste King
5119 District Blvd.
Los Angeles, CA 90040
(213) 562-1133

WASTE KING
See Thermador
(213) 562-1133

WHIRLPOOL
Whirlpool Corp.
Administrative Center
2000 M 63
Benton Harbor, MI 49022
(800) 253-1301;
(800) 253-1121 in Arkansas

WHITE-WESTINGHOUSE
See Frigidaire
(800) 451-7007

ELECTRIC RANGES
(Including cooktops and wall ovens)

ADMIRAL
Admiral Home Appliances
246 King Edward Ave.
Cleveland, TN 37311
(615) 472-3371

AEG
Andi Appliances
65 Campus Plaza
Edison, NJ 08837
(908) 225-8837

AMANA
Amana Refrigeration, Inc.
Consumer Affairs Dept.
Amana, IA 52204
(800) 843-0304;
(800) 332-3039 in Iowa

BLANCO
Blanco
1001 Lowerlanding Road
Suite 607
Blackwood, NJ 08012
(609) 228-3500

BROWN
Brown Stove Works, Inc.
P.O. Box 2490
Cleveland, TN 37320
(615) 476-6544

CALORIC
Caloric Corp.
403 North Main St.
Topton, PA 19562-1499
(800) 272-3121

COUNTRY CHARM
The House of Webster
1013 North Second St.
Rogers, AR 72757
(602) 626-4640

CREDA
Creda, Inc.
5700 West Touhy
Niles, IL 60648
(708) 647-8024

DACOR
Dacor Distinctive Appliances
950 South Raymond Ave.
Pasadena, CA 91105
(800) 772-7778;
(213) 682-2803 in California

FRIGIDAIRE
Frigidaire Co.
Dept. of Consumer Relations
P.O. Box 7181
Dublin, OH 43017
(800) 451-7007

GAGGENAU
Gaggenau USA Corp.
425 University Ave.
Norwood, MA 02062
(717) 636-1000

GARLAND
Garland Commercial
185 East South St.
Freeland, PA 18224-1999
(717) 636-1000

GE MONOGRAM
See General Electric
(800) 626-2000

GENERAL ELECTRIC
General Electric Co.
Appliance Park
Louisville, KY 40225
(800) 626-2000

GIBSON
See White-Westinghouse
(800) 458-1445

HARDWICK
Hardwick Stove Co.
A Division of Maycore
240 Edwards St.
Cleveland, TN 37311
(800) 688-9900

HOTPOINT
See General Electric
(800) 626-2000

JENN-AIR
Jenn-Air Co.
3035 Shadeland Ave.
Indianapolis, IN 46226
(317) 545-2271

KELVINATOR
See Frigidaire
(800) 451-7007

KITCHENAID
KitchenAid, Inc.
2303 Pipestone
Benton Harbor, MI 49022
(800) 422-1230

MAGIC CHEF
Magic Chef, Inc.
740 King Edward Ave.
Cleveland, TN 37311
(615) 472-3371

MAYTAG
Maycore
240 Edwards, S.E.
Cleveland, TN 37311
(800) 688-9900;
(615) 472-3333 in Tennessee

MIELE
Miele Appliances, Inc.
22D World's Fair Dr.
Somerset, NJ 08873
(908) 560-0899

MODERN MAID
Caloric Corp.
Highway 220
Amana, IA 52204
(215) 682-4211

MONTGOMERY WARD
Montgomery Ward and Co.
535 West Chicago Ave.
Chicago, IL 60671
(312) 467-2000,
or check local directory

O'KEEFE & MERRITT
See Frigidaire
(614) 792-4100

PREMIER
Peerless Premier Appliance Co.
P.O. Box 387
Belleville, IL 62222
(618) 233-0475

RCA
RCA Appliances
Appliance Park
Louisville, KY 40225
(800) 626-2000,
or check local directory

ROPER
Whirlpool Corp.
Consumer Services
2303 Pipestone Rd.
Benton Harbor, MI 49022-2400
(800) 447-6737

SEARS
Sears, Roebuck & Co.
Sears Tower
Chicago, IL 60684
(312) 875-5188,
or check local directory

SUNRAY
Glenwood Range Co.
435 Park Ave.
Delaware, OH 43105
(614) 363-1381

TAPPAN
See Frigidaire
(800) 537-5530

THERMADOR
Thermador/Waste King
5119 District Blvd.
Los Angeles, CA 90040
(213) 562-1133

VULCAN
Vulcan-Hart Corp.
P.O. Box 696
Louisville, KY 40201-0696
(502) 778-2791

WELBILT
Welbilt Corp.
3333 New Hyde Park Rd.
New Hyde Park, NY 11042
(516) 365-5040

WHIRLPOOL
Whirlpool Corp.
Administrative Center
2000 M 63
Benton Harbor, MI 49022
(800) 253-1301;
(800) 253-1121 in Arkansas

WHITE-WESTINGHOUSE
See Frigidaire
(800) 537-5530

GAS RANGES
*(Including cooktops
and wall ovens)*

ADMIRAL
Admiral Home Appliances
246 King Edward Ave.
Cleveland, TN 37311
(615) 472-3371

AEG
Andi Appliances
65 Campus Plaza
Edison, NJ 08837
(908) 225-8837

AGA
Cooper and Turner, Inc.
17 Towne Farm Rd.
Stowe, VT 05672
(802) 253-9729

AMANA
Amana Refrigeration, Inc.
Consumer Affairs Dept.
Amana, IA 52204
(800) 843-0304;
(800) 332-3039 in Iowa

BROWN
Brown Stove Works, Inc.
P.O. Box 2490
Cleveland, TN 37320
(615) 476-6544

CALORIC
Caloric Corp.
403 North Main St.
Topton, PA 19562-1499
(800) 272-3121

CREDA
Creda, Inc.
5700 West Touhy
Niles, IL 60648
(708) 647-8024

DACOR
Dacor Distinctive Appliances
950 South Raymond Ave.
Pasadena, CA 91105
(800) 772-7778;
(213) 682-2802 in California

FRIGIDAIRE
Frigidaire Co.
Dept. of Consumer Relations
P.O. Box 7181
Dublin, OH 43017
(800) 451-7007

GAGGENAU
Gaggenau USA Corp.
425 University Ave.
Norwood, MA 02062
(617) 255-1766

GARLAND
Garland Commercial
  Industries, Inc.
185 East South St.
Freeland, PA 18224
(717) 636-1000

GENERAL ELECTRIC
General Electric Co.
Appliance Park
Louisville, KY 40225
(800) 626-2000

GIBSON
See Frigidaire
(800) 451-7007

HARDWICK
Hardwick Stove Co.
740 King Edward Ave., S.E.
Cleveland, TN 37311
(615) 479-4561

HOTPOINT
See General Electric
(800) 626-2000

JENN-AIR
Jenn-Air Co.
3035 Shadeland Ave.
Indianapolis, IN 46226
(317) 545-2271

KITCHENAID
KitchenAid, Inc.
2303 Pipestone
Mail Drop Box 0100
Benton Harbor, MI 49002-2400
(800) 422-1230

MAGIC CHEF
Magic Chef, Inc.
240 Edwards, S.E.
Cleveland, TN 37311
(615) 472-3371

MAYTAG
Maycore
240 Edwards, S.E.
Cleveland, TN 37311
(800) 688-9900;
(615) 472-3333 in Tennessee

MIELE
Miele Appliances, Inc.
22D World's Fair Dr.
Somerset, NJ 08873
(908) 560-0899

MODERN MAID
Caloric Corp.
Highway 220
Amana, IA 52204
(800) 272-3121

MONTGOMERY WARD
Montgomery Ward and Co.
535 West Chicago Ave.
Chicago, IL 60671
(312) 467-2000,
or check local directory

O'KEEFE & MERRITT
See Frigidaire
(800) 451-7007

PREMIER
Peerless Premier Appliance Co.
P.O. Box 387
Belleville, IL 62222
(618) 233-0475

ROPER
Whirlpool Corp.
Consumer Services
2303 Pipestone Rd.
Benton Harbor, MI 49022-2400
(800) 253-1302

SEARS
Sears, Roebuck & Co.
Sears Tower
Chicago, IL 60684
(312) 875-5188,
or check local directory

STERLING
New World Domestic
Appliance Ltd.
425 Rosarita Dr.
Fullerton, CA 92635
(714) 871-5244

SUNRAY
Glenwood Range Co.
435 Park Ave.
Delaware, OH 43015
(614) 363-1382

TAPPAN
See Frigidaire
(800) 451-7007

THERMADOR
Thermador/Waste King
5119 District Blvd.
Los Angeles, CA 90040
(213) 562-1133

VIKING
Viking Range Corp.
P.O. Box 8012
Greenwood, MS 38930
(601) 455-1200

VULCAN
Vulcan-Hart Corp.
P.O. Box 969
Louisville, KY 40201
(502) 778-2791

WELBILT
Welbilt Corp.
3333 New Hyde Park Rd.
New Hyde Park, NY 11042
(516) 747-9595

WHIRLPOOL
Whirlpool Corp.
Administrative Center
2000 M 63
Benton Harbor, MI 49022
(800) 253-1301;
(800) 253-1121 in Arkansas

WHITE-WESTINGHOUSE
See Frigidaire
(800) 451-7007

Microwave Ovens

ADMIRAL
Admiral Home Appliances
246 King Edwards Ave.
Cleveland, TN 37311
(615) 472-3371

AMANA
Amana Refrigeration
Consumer Affairs Dept.
Amana, IA 52204
(800) 843-0304;
(800) 332-3039 in Iowa

AVANTI
Avanti Products
8885 N.W. 23rd St.
Miami, FL 33172
(800) 323-5029;
(305) 592-7830 in Florida

BROTHER
Brother Intl. Corp.
Eight Corporate Pl.
Piscataway, NJ 08854
(901) 373-6256

CALORIC
Caloric Corp.
403 North Main St.
Topton, PA 19562-1499
(800) 688-9900

CONAIR
Conair Corp.
150 Milford Rd.
East Windsor, NJ 08520
(609) 426-1300

CROSLEY
Crosley Group, Inc.
P.O. Box 2111
Winston-Salem, NC 27102
(919) 761-1212

DAYTRON
Daewoo Intl. America Corp.
100 Daewoo Pl.
Carlstadt, NJ 07072
(201) 935-8700

EMERSON
Emerson Radio Corp.
One Emerson Lane
North Bergen, NJ 07047
(800) 922-0738

FRIGIDAIRE
Frigidaire Co.
Dept. of Consumer Relations
P.O. Box 7181
Dublin, OH 43017
(800) 451-7007

FUNAI
Funai Corp.
100 North St.
Teterboro, NJ 07608
(800) 966-3862

GENERAL ELECTRIC
General Electric Co.
Appliance Park
Louisville, KY 40225
(800) 626-2000

GERALD
Gerald Industries
16390 N.W. 52nd Ave.
Miami Lakes, FL 33014
(800) 327-3505;
(305) 625-5550 in Florida

HITACHI
Discontinued microwave ovens

HOTPOINT
See General Electric
(800) 626-2000

J.C. PENNEY
J.C. Penney Co.
5430 LBJ Freeway
Dallas, TX 75240
(214) 591-8500

JENN-AIR
Jenn-Air Co.
3035 Shadeland Ave.
Indianapolis, IN 46226
(317) 545-2271

KITCHENAID
KitchenAid, Inc.
2303 Pipestone
Mail Drop Box 0100
Benton Harbor, MI 49022-2400
(800) 422-1230

MAGIC CHEF
Magic Chef, Inc.
240 Edwards, S.E.
Cleveland, TN 37311
(615) 472-3371

MAYTAG
Maycore
240 Edwards, S.E.
Cleveland, TN 37311
(800) 688-9900;
(615) 472-3333 in Tennessee

MODERN MAID
Caloric Corp.
Highway 220
Amana, IA 52204
(800) 272-3121

MONTGOMERY WARD
Montgomery Ward and Co.
535 West Chicago Ave.
Chicago, IL 60671
(312) 467-2000,
or check local directory

PANASONIC
Panasonic Co.
Consumer Affairs Division
50 Meadowland Pkwy.
Secaucus, NJ 07094
(201) 348-9090

PORTLAND
See Daytron
(201) 935-8700

QUASAR
Quasar Electronics
1325 Pratt Blvd.
Elk Grove Village, IL 60007
(708) 228-6366

SAMSUNG
Samsung Electronics
America, Inc.
301 Mayhill St.
Saddle Brook, NJ 07662
(800) 524-1302

SANYO
Sanyo Fisher USA Corp.
200 Riser Road
Little Ferry, NJ 07643
(201) 641-2333

SEARS
Sears, Roebuck & Co.
Sears Tower
Chicago, IL 60684
(312) 875-2500,
or check local directory

SHARP
Sharp Electronics Corp.
Sharp Plaza
Mahwah, NJ 07430
(800) 526-0264

TAPPAN
See Frigidaire
(800) 451-7007

TATUNG
Tatung Co. of America, Inc.
2850 El Presidio St.
Long Beach, CA 90810
(213) 979-7055

THERMADOR
Thermador/Waste King
5119 District Blvd.
Los Angeles, CA 90040
(213) 562-1133

TOSHIBA
Toshiba America, Inc.
82 Totowa Rd.
Wayne, NJ 07470
(201) 628-8000

WELBILT
Welbilt Corp.
3333 New Hyde Park Rd.
New Hyde Park, NY 11042
(516) 747-9595

WHIRLPOOL
Whirlpool Corp.
Administrative Center
2000 M 63
Benton Harbor, MI 49022
(800) 253-1301;
(800) 253-1121 in Arkansas

WHITE-WESTINGHOUSE
See Frigidaire
(800) 451-7007

REFRIGERATORS

ADMIRAL
Admiral Home Appliances
246 King Edwards Ave.
Cleveland, TN 37311
(615) 472-3371

AMANA
Amana Refrigeration, Inc.
Consumer Affairs Dept.
Amana, IA 52204
(800) 843-0304;
(800) 332-3039 in Iowa

AVANTI
Avanti Products
8885 N.W. 23rd St.
Miami, FL 33712
(800) 323-5029;
(305) 592-7830 in Florida

CALORIC
Caloric Corp.
403 North Main St.
Topton, PA 19562-1499
(800) 272-3121

CROSLEY
Crosley Group, Inc.
P.O. Box 2111
Winston-Salem, NC 27102
(919) 761-1212

DEFIANCE
Northland Kitchen Appliances
701 Ranney Dr.
Greenville, MI 48838
(800) 223-3900

FRIGIDAIRE
Frigidaire Co.
Dept. of Consumer Relations
P.O. Box 7181
Dublin, OH 43017
(800) 451-7007

GENERAL ELECTRIC
General Electric Co.
Appliance Park
Louisville, KY 40225
(800) 626-2000

GIBSON
See Frigidaire
(800) 451-7007

JENN-AIR
Jenn-Air Co.
3035 Shadeland Ave.
Indianapolis, IN 46226
(317) 545-2271

KELVINATOR
See Frigidaire
(800) 323-7773

KITCHENAID
KitchenAid Inc.
2303 Pipestone
Mail Drop Box 0100
Benton Harbor, MI 49022-2400
(800) 422-1230

MAGIC CHEF
Magic Chef, Inc.
240 King Edwards Ave., S.E.
Cleveland, TN 37311
(615) 472-3371

MARVEL
Marvel Industries
P.O. Box 997
Richmond, IN 47375
(800) 428-6644

MODERN MAID
See Caloric
(800) 272-3121

MONTGOMERY WARD
Montgomery Ward and Co.
535 West Chicago Ave.
Chicago, IL 60671
(312) 467-2000,
or check local directory

NORGE
See Magic Chef
(800) 255-2370

QUASAR
Quasar Co.
1325 Pratt Blvd.
Elk Grove Village, IL 60007
(800) 447-4700;
(708) 228-6366 in Illinois

SANYO
Sanyo Fisher USA Corp.
200 Riser Rd.
Little Ferry, NJ 07643
(201) 641-2333

SEARS-KENMORE
Sears, Roebuck & Co.
Sears Tower
Chicago, IL 60684
(312) 875-5188,
or check local directory

SUB-ZERO
Sub-Zero Freezer Co., Inc.
Box 4130
Madison, WI 53744-4130
(800) 356-5826;
(608) 271-2233 in Wisconsin

TAPPAN
See Frigidaire
(800) 451-7007

TATUNG
Tatung Co. of America, Inc.
2850 El Prisidio St.
Long Beach, CA 90810-1178
(213) 979-7055

TRAULSEN
Traulsen & Co., Inc.
114-02 15th Ave.
College Point, NY 11356
(718) 463-9000

WARWICK
Maycore
240 Edwards, S.E.
Cleveland, TN 37311
(615) 472-3371

WHIRLPOOL
Whirlpool Corp.
2000 M 63
Benton Harbor, MI 49022
(800) 253-1301;
(616) 926-5000 in Michigan

WHITE-WESTINGHOUSE
See Frigidaire
(800) 451-7007

TELEPHONES / ANSWERING MACHINES

AMERTEL
Amertel Electronics Corp.
3653 San Gabriel River Pkwy.
Pico Rivera, CA 90660
(213) 692-0509

AT&T
AT&T
14250 Clayton Rd.
Ballwin, MO 63011
(800) 222-3111;
TDD* No. (800) 833-3232

*Telecommunications Device for the Deaf

BELLSOUTH
Bellsouth Advanced Products,
Inc.
1155 Peachtree St., N.E.
Atlanta, GA 30367
(800) 251-6118

BRONDI
European Telephone Co.
33 Emeline St.
Randolph, MA 02368
(617) 986-8650

CENTURION
Centurion Electronics
101 Chambers St.
St. Louis, MO 63102-1321
(800) 800-2368

COBRA
Cobra Corp.
6500 West Cortland
Chicago, IL 60635
(800) 262-7222

CODE-A-PHONE
Code-A-Phone Corp.
Box 5656
Portland, OR 97228
(503) 650-4357

CONAIRPHONE
Conair Corp.
150 Milford Rd.
East Windsor, NJ 08520
(800) 366-5391

COSMO
Cosmo Communications Corp.
16501 N.W. 16th Ct.
Miami, FL 33169
(305) 621-4227

ELECTRO
Electro Band, Inc.
5410 West Roosevelt Rd.
Chicago, IL 60650
(312) 261-5000

EMERSON
Emerson Radio Corp.
One Emerson Lane
North Bergen, NJ 07047
(800) 388-8333

FREEDOM PHONE
Southwestern Bell Telecom
7442 Shade Land Station Way
Indianapolis, IN 46256
(800) 255-8480;
(317) 841-8006 in Indiana

GENERAL ELECTRIC
Thompson Consumer
Electronics, Inc.
600 North Sherman Dr.
Box 1976
Indianapolis, IN 46206
(800) 447-1700

GOLDSTAR
Goldstar Products Co. Ltd.
P.O. Box 6166
Huntsville, AL 35824
(800) 222-6457

ITT/CORTELCO
ITT/CortelCo
Fulton Dr.
Corinth, MS 38834
(800) 288-3132

KRACO
Kraco Enterprises, Inc.
505 East Euclid Ave.
Compton, CA 90224
(800) 421-1910;
(213) 639-0666 in California

LAPHONE
Unical Enterprises Inc.
17101 Gale Ave.
City of Industry, CA 91745
(800) 423-4653;
(818) 965-5588 in California

LLOYDS
Lloyds Electronics Corp.
6450 West Cortland
Chicago, IL 60635
(708) 820-4800

LONESTAR
Lonestar Technologies
920 South Oyster Bay Rd.
Hicksville, NY 11801
(516) 939-6116

MAGNAVOX
Philips Consumer
P.O. Box 555
Jefferson City, TN 37877
(615) 475-0317

MCE
MCE Quality Electronic Products
120 Ansin Blvd.
Hallandale, FL 33009
(305) 458-1119

MESSAGE MINDER
IT Systems Corp.
7 Odell Plaza
Yonkers, NY 10701
(914) 968-2100

MURA
Mura Corp.
Division of Bartex
130 North 4th St.
Brooklyn, NY 11211
(718) 486-8400

NORTHWESTERN
BELL PHONES
Northwestern Bell Phones
Bell Service Center
9394 West Dodge Rd.
Omaha, NE 68114
(800) 822-1000

PACTEL
PacTel Corp.
2999 Oak Rd.
Walnut Creek, CA 94596
(510) 210-3900

PANASONIC
Panasonic Co.
Consumer Affairs Division
50 Meadowland Pkwy.
Secaucus, NJ 07094
(800) 447-4700;
(201) 348-9090 in New Jersey

PHONE-MATE
Phone-Mate, Inc.
20665 Manhattan Pl.
Torrance, CA 90501
(213) 618-9910

RADIO SHACK
Tandy Corp./Radio Shack
1600 One Tandy Center
Forth Worth, TX 76102
(817) 390-3011,
or check local directory

RANDIX
Randix Industries Ltd.
337 Turnpike
Southboro, MA 01772
(508) 460-1100

RECORD-A-CALL
Planned Technologies
92 South Oyster Bay Rd.
Hicksville, NY 11801
(516) 939-6116

SAMSUNG
Samsung Electronics
America, Inc.
301 Mayhill St.
Saddle Brook, NJ 07662
(800) 524-1302

SANYO
Sanyo Business Systems Corp.
51 Joseph St.
Moonachie, NJ 07074
(201) 440-9300

SHARP
Sharp Electronics Corp.
Sharp Plaza
Mahwah, NJ 07430
(800) 526-0264

SONY
Sony Corp. of America
386 Rte. 17 South
Mahwah, NJ 07656
(800) 222-7669;
(201) 529-1655 in New Jersey

SPECTRA-PHONE
Spectra Merchandising Intl., Inc.
3425 North Kimball Ave.
Chicago, IL 60618
(312) 463-1030

SOUTHWESTERN BELL
7442 Shadeland Station Way
Indianapolis, IN 46256
(800) 255-8480

TELKO
Telko, Inc.
26651 Cabot Rd.
Laguna Hills, CA 92653
(714) 367-1352

UNISONIC
Unisonic Products Corp.
1115 Broadway
New York, NY 10010
(212) 255-5400

TELEVISIONS

AMARK
See AOC
(816) 891-8066

AOC
AOC Intl.
10991 N.W. Airworld Dr.
Kansas City, MO 64153
(816) 891-8066

BARCO
Barco Electronics
1000 Cobb Pl., Suite 100
Kennesaw, GA 30144
(404) 590-7900

BROKSONIC
Hatzlachh Supply, Inc.
935 Broadway, 6th Fl.
New York, NY 10010
(212) 254-9012

CASIO
Casio, Inc.
570 Pleasant Ave.
Dover, NJ 07801
(201) 361-5400

CITIZEN
Citizen Watch of America
1200 Wall St. West
Lyndhurst, NJ 07071
(201) 438-8150, (800) 843-8270

CURTIS MATHES
Curtis Mathes Corp.
1450 Flatcreek Rd.
Athens, TX 75751
(214) 675-6886

DAYTRON
Daewoo Intl. America Corp.
100 Daewoo Pl.
Carlstadt, NJ 07072
(201) 935-8700

EMERSON
Emerson Radio Corp.
One Emerson Lane
North Bergen, NJ 07047
(800) 922-0738

FISHER
Sanyo Fisher USA Corp.
21350 Lassen St.
Chatsworth, CA 91311
(800) 421-5013

GENERAL ELECTRIC
Thompson Consumer
Electronics, Inc.
P.O. Box 1976
Indianapolis, IN 46206
(800) 447-1700

GOLDSTAR
Goldstar Electronics Intl.
P.O. Box 6166
Huntsville, AL 35824
(800) 222-6457

HEATHKIT
Heath Co.
Benton Harbor, MI 49022
(800) 253-0570;
(616) 982-3411 in Michigan

HITACHI
Hitachi Sales Corp.
3890 Steve Reynolds Blvd.
Norcross, GA 30093
(800) 241-6558

INFINITY
Infinity Systems, Inc.
9409 Owensmouth Ave.
Chatsworth, CA 91311
(818) 709-9400

J.C. PENNEY
J.C. Penney Co.
5430 LBJ Freeway
Dallas, TX 75240
(214) 591-8500,
or check local directory

JVC
JVC Co. of America
107 Little Falls Rd.
Fairfield, NJ 07006
(800) 526-5308, (201) 808-2100

KENWOOD
Kenwood USA Corp.
2201 East Dominguez St.
Long Beach, CA 90810
(213) 639-9000

LLOYDS
Lloyds Electronics Corp.
6450 West Cortland
Chicago, IL 60639
(312) 889-0319

MAGNAVOX
See Philips
(615) 521-4316

MGA
See Mitsubishi
(714) 220-1464

MITSUBISHI
Mitsubishi Electric Sales
of America, Inc.
5757 Plaza Dr.
Cypress, CA 90630-0007
(714) 220-1464

MONTGOMERY WARD
Montgomery Ward and Co.
535 West Chicago Ave.
Chicago, IL 60671
(312) 467-2000,
or check local directory

NAD
NAD USA, Inc.
633 Granite Ct.
Pickering, Ontario L1W 3K1
Canada
(800) 263-4641

NEC
NEC Home Electronics USA
1255 Michael Dr.
Wood Dale, IL 60191
(708) 860-9500

OPTONICA BY SHARP
See Sharp
(800) 526-0264

PANASONIC
Panasonic Co.
Consumer Affairs Division
50 Meadowland Pkwy.
Secaucus, NJ 07094
(800) 447-4700;
(201) 348-9090 in New Jersey

PHILCO
See Philips
(615) 521-4316

PHILIPS
Philips Consumer
P.O. Box 555
Jefferson City, TN 37877
(615) 521-4316

PIONEER
Pioneer Electronics
2265 East 220th St.
Box 1760
Long Beach, CA 90810
(800) 421-1404

PORTLAND
See Daytron
(201) 935-8700

PRISM BY PANASONIC
See Panasonic
(201) 348-9090

PROTON
Proton Corp.
5630 Cerritos Ave.
Cypress, CA 90630
(714) 952-6900

PULSAR
Pulsar Video Systems, Inc.
7670 Clairemont Mesa Blvd.
San Diego, CA 92111
(619) 278-4318

QUASAR
Quasar Co.
1325 Pratt Blvd.
Elk Grove Village, IL 60007
(800) 447-4700, (708) 228-6366

RADIO SHACK
Tandy Corp./Radio Shack
1600 One Tandy Center
Fort Worth, TX 76102
(817) 390-3700,
or check local directory

RCA
Thompson Consumer
Electronics, Inc.
600 North Sherman Dr.
Indianapolis, IN 46206
(800) 336-1900;
(317) 267-5000 in Indiana

SAMSUNG
Samsung Electronics
America, Inc.
301 Mayhill St.
Saddle Brook, NJ 07662
(800) 524-1302;
(201) 587-9600 in New Jersey

SANYO
Sanyo Fisher USA Corp.
21350 Lassen St.
Chatsworth, CA 91311
(800) 421-5013

SCOTT
H.H. Scott, Inc.
Highway 41 South
Princeton, IN 47670
(812) 386-3200

SEARS
Sears, Roebuck & Co.
Sears Tower
Chicago, IL 60684
(312) 875-5188,
or check local directory

SHARP
Sharp Electronics Corp.
Sharp Plaza
Mahwah, NJ 07430
(800) 526-0264

SONY
Sony Corp.
386 Rte. 17 South
Mahwah, NJ 07430
(800) 222-7669, (201) 529-1655

SSANGYONG
Ssangyong USA, Inc.
601 16th St.
Carlstadt, NJ 07072
(201) 939-4300

SYLVANIA
See Philips
(615) 521-4316

SYMPHONIC
Symphonic/Funai USA Corp.
100 North St.
Teterboro, NJ 07608
(800) 242-7158

TATUNG
Tatung Co. of America, Inc.
2850 El Presidio St.
Long Beach, CA 90810-1178
(213) 979-7055

TEKNIKA
Teknika Electronics Co.
353 Rte. 46 West
Fairfield, NJ 07004
(800) 835-6452;
(800) 962-1272 in New Jersey

TERA
Out of business

THOMPSON
National Viewtech Corp.
65 Orvile Dr.
Bohemia, NY 11716
(516) 589-6400

TOSHIBA
Toshiba America, Inc.
82 Totowa Rd.
Wayne, NJ 07470
(201) 628-8000

TOTE VISION
Tote Vision
969 Thomas St.
Seattle, WA 98109
(206) 682-4343

VECTOR RESEARCH
Vector Research
1230 Calle Suerte
Camarillo, CA 93012
(805) 987-1312

VIDIKRON
Vidikron USA, Inc.
150 Bay St.
Jersey City, NJ 07302
(201) 420-6666

YAMAHA
Yamaha Electronics Corp.
U.S.A.
P.O. Box 6660
6700 Orangethorpe Ave.
Buena Park, CA 90620
(800) 492-6242

ZENITH
Zenith Electronics Corp.
1000 Milwaukee Ave.
Glenview, IL 60025
(708) 391-7000

VIDEOCASSETTE RECORDERS

BROKSONIC
Hatzlachh Supply, Inc.
935 Broadway, 6th Floor
New York, NY 10010
(212) 254-9012

CANON
Canon USA, Inc.
Video Division
1 Jericho Plaza
Jericho, NY 11753
(800) 828-4040

CASIO
Casio, Inc.
570 Pleasant Ave.
Dover, NJ 07801
(201) 361-5400

CITIZEN
Citizen America Corp.
8506 Osage Ave.
Los Angeles, CA 90045
(800) 421-6516

CURTIS MATHES
Curtis Mathes Corp.
P.O. Box 2160
Athens, TX 75751
(903) 675-2292

DAYTRON
Daewoo Intl. America Corp.
100 Daewoo Pl.
Carlstadt, NJ 07072
(201) 935-8700

DENON
Denon America, Inc.
222 New Rd.
Parsippany, NJ 07054
(201) 575-7810

EMERSON
Emerson Radio Corp.
One Emerson Lane
North Bergen, NJ 07047
(800) 922-0738

FISHER
Sanyo Fisher USA Corp.
21314 Lassen St.
Chatsworth, CA 91311
(800) 421-5013

GENERAL ELECTRIC
Thompson Consumer
Electronics, Inc.
600 North Sherman Dr.
P.O. Box 1976
Indianapolis, IN 46206
(800) 447-1700

GOLDSTAR
Goldstar Electronics
P.O. Box 6166
Huntsville, AL 35824
(800) 222-6457

GO-VIDEO
Go-Video, Inc.
14455 North Haden Rd.
Scottsdale, AZ 85260-6949
(800) 279-1600;
(602) 998-3400 in Arizona

GRAN PRIX
Gran Prix Electronics
108 Madison St.
St. Louis, MO 63102
(314) 621-3314

GRUNDIG
Lextronix, Inc.
3520 Haven Ave., Unit L
Redwood City, CA 94063
(800) 872-2228;
(415) 361-1611 in California

HARMAN/KARDON
Harman America
240 Crossways Park West
Woodbury, NY 11797
(800) 645-7484;
(516) 496-3400 in New York

HITACHI
Hitachi Sales Corp.
3890 Steve Reynolds Blvd.
Norcross, GA 30093
(800) 241-6558

INSTANT REPLAY
Instant Replay Co.
2601 South Bayshore Dr.
Suite 1050
Miami, FL 33133
(305) 854-8777

J.C. PENNEY
J.C. Penney Co.
5430 LBJ Freeway
Dallas, TX 75265
(214) 591-8500,
or check local directory

JVC
JVC Co. of America
107 Little Falls Rd.
Fairfield, NJ 07006
(800) 526-5308, (201) 808-2100

KENWOOD
Kenwood U.S.A. Corp.
2201 East Dominguez St.
Long Beach, CA 90810
(213) 639-9000

LLOYDS
Lloyds Electronics Corp.
6450 West Cortland
Chicago, IL 60635
(708) 320-4800

MAGNAVOX
See Philips
(615) 521-4316

MEMOREX
Tandy Trading Intl.
A Division of Tandy Corp.
1600 One Tandy Center
Fort Worth, TX 76102
(817) 390-3011,
or check local directory

MINOLTA
Minolta Corp.
101 Williams Dr.
Ramsey, NJ 07446
(201) 825-4000

MITSUBISHI
Mitsubishi Electric Sales
of America, Inc.
5757 Plaza Dr.
Cypress, CA 90630-0007
(714) 220-1464

MONTGOMERY WARD
Montgomery Ward and Co.
535 West Chicago Ave.
Chicago, IL 60671
(312) 467-2000,
or check local directory

NEC
NEC Home Electronics
U.S.A., Inc.
1255 Michael Dr.
Wood Dale, IL 60191
(708) 860-9500

OPTONICA BY SHARP
See Sharp
(800) 526-0264

PANASONIC
Panasonic Co.
Consumer Affairs Division
50 Meadowland Pkwy.
Secaucus, NJ 07094
(800) 447-4700, (201) 348-9090

PHILCO
See Philips
(615) 521-4316

PHILIPS
Philips Consumer Electronics Co.
One Philips Dr.
P.O. Box 14810
Knoxville, TN 37914-1810
(615) 521-4316

PIONEER
Pioneer Electronics
P.O. Box 1720
Long Beach, CA 90810
(213) 835-6177

PORTLAND
See Daytron
(201) 935-8700

QUASAR
Quasar Co.
1325 Pratt Blvd.
Elk Grove Village, IL 60007
(800) 447-4700, (708) 228-6366

RADIO SHACK
Tandy Corp./Radio Shack
1600 One Tandy Center
Forth Worth, TX 76102
(817) 390-3011,
or check local directory

RCA
Thompson Consumer
Electronics, Inc.
600 North Sherman Dr.
Indianapolis, IN 46206
(800) 336-1900;
(317) 267-5000 in Indiana

SAMSUNG
Samsung Electronics
America, Inc.
301 Mayhill St.
Saddle Brook, NJ 07662
(800) 524-1302;
(201) 587-9600 in New Jersey

SANYO
Sanyo Fisher USA Corp.
21350 Lassen St.
Chatsworth, CA 91311
(800) 421-5013

SEARS
Sears, Roebuck & Co.
Sears Tower
Chicago, IL 60684
(312) 875-5188,
or check local directory

SHARP
Sharp Electronics Corp.
Sharp Plaza
Mahwah, NJ 07430
(800) 526-0264

SHINTOM
Shintom West Corp.
20435 South Western Ave.
Torrance, CA 90501
Information: (800) 333-1098;
Sales: (213) 328-7200;
Service: (714) 629-6508

SONY
Sony Corp. of America
386 Rte. 17 South
Mahwah, NJ 07430
(800) 222-7669, (201) 529-1655

SYLVANIA
See Philips
(615) 521-4316

SYMPHONIC
Symphonic/Funai Corp.
100 North St.
Teterboro, NJ 07608
(800) 242-7158, (201) 288-2606

Index